COLLECTION OF REPORTS,

(CONDENSED),

AND

OPINIONS OF CHEMISTS

IN REGARD TO THE USE OF

LEAD PIPE FOR SERVICE PIPE,

IN THE

DISTRIBUTION OF WATER

FOR THE

SUPPLY OF CITIES.

NEW YORK:

HOSFORD AND CO., STATIONERS AND PRINTERS,

Nos. 57 AND 59 WILLIAM STREET.

1859.

PREFACE.

Immediately before the introduction of the Cochituate water into Boston, considerable interest was manifested there, as regards the kind of service pipe to be used from the street mains to the dwelling houses, and for distribution within doors. Many persons entertained objections to the use of lead pipes for this purpose, although that description of pipe had been almost exclusively used for such service, for a long period of years.

When the Croton water was introduced into New York, there appeared, though less prominently, the same sensitiveness on the part of a portion of the community in regard to the employment of lead pipe, and the same desire to supply its place, if possible, by some other material less obnoxious to suspicion.

In other cities of the United States and of Europe the same feeling has at times more or less agitated the public mind, without leading however, thus far, to any serious modification of the long established practice, that I am aware of, except in Hartford, Conn., where iron pipes coated with zinc have been used, at the recommendation of the Water Commissioners there, almost exclusively, since the introduction of water into that city.

The chemical investigations instituted at different times by the authorities in charge of, or connected with the water supply of various large cities, have generally led these authorities to conclusions calculated to quiet the public mind upon the question of danger from the use of lead pipes, without entirely satisfying it.

Some of the citizens of Brooklyn have made inquiries about the kind of service pipe which it is best to use, and whether the Long Island water will be injuriously affected by being drawn from lead pipes.

Not being a chemist, I am not competent to offer any solution of this question, and judging from what has occurred elsewhere, no solution now, even coming from chemists, will carry either decided authority or general conviction with it, unless corroborated, for or against, by a clearness of medical testimony and statistics which has not hitherto been present. In order, however, that those persons desiring information on this subject may be able, if so minded, to examine the matter for themselves, I propose to place within their reach such information as I am in possession of, from which they can draw their own conclusions. When chemists of high standing differ so widely on the effects upon the human constitution of water which has been for more or less time in contact with lead, or whether such contact is productive of any objectionable effects, it does not become a non-professional observer to pronounce positively either way. It may be conceded from the testimony before us, that the *uninterrupted* flow of water through the lead pipes of a house, to immediate use, could nót affect it injuriously, whatever the character of the water. On the other hand, should the water stand long in the pipes without change, or should water be passed through lead pipes which have been some time empty, it may become sufficiently tainted to affect injuriously certain constitutions.

To avoid the risk of contamination from either of these two causes, it is customary with many persons to waste a portion of water at the faucets every morning, before allowing it to be used for culinary purposes or drinking. By emptying the service pipes in this way every morning or more frequently, where considerable intervals of non-use occur during the day, the risk of lead influence may be all but entirely avoided.

The Nassau water furnished to Brooklyn, by the works now in progress there, is what is termed a soft water, nearly resembling in this respect the Croton water, neither of these being so soft as the Loch Katrine water, which will be found referred to frequently in the reports which follow. Its chemical properties are stated below as given by Dr. Chilton; the similar characteristics of the Croton, Cochituate, Loch Katrine and Thames waters, are added for convenience of comparison.

TABLE.

Grains of in one gallon of Water	Nassau Water, Brooklyn	Croton		Cochituate, Boston	Loch Katrine, Glasgow	Thames, above London
		At its Source	N. Y. City from pipes			
Carbonate of Lime	1.092	1.42	1.52	....	....	13.13
Carbonate of Magnesia	0.408	0.70	0.84	....	0.216	....
Chloride of Sodium	0.244	....	....	....	....	1.56
Chloride of Magnesia	0.328	....	....	....	....	....
Chloride of Calcium	0.120	0.86	0.90	....	0.144	....
Alkaline Chlorides	....	....	....	....	0.433	....
Sulphate of Lime	0.120	....	0.44	....	0.381	2.73
Sulphate of Magnesia	0.288	....	....	....	....	....
Oxide of Iron	0.040	....	....	....	Trace	0.13
Silica	....	0.34	0.46	....	0.170	0.27
Residuary Carbon	....	....	....	....	....	0.11
Organic Matter	0.008	....	....	....	0.900	2.37
	2.648	3.32	4.16		2.244	20.30
Soap Test					0°.8	14°5

I will here give a summary of the opinions, the reasons for which will be found at large in the reports and extracts thrown together in this pamphlet. These reports merit a careful perusal, without which the value of the conclusions arrived at by their several authors can hardly be appreciated. They have been somewhat condensed to reduce this pamphlet to a reasonable size, but the omissions are not of a character to alter the general sense, or to convey a mistaken impression of the conclusions of their several writers.

Professor WILLIAM THOMAS BRANDE. *London.*

"Water by itself, without carbonic acid, will not hold in solution more than two grains of lime to a gallon; two grains of carbonate of lime and hardly that; the addition is held in solution by the carbonic acid."

"Many of these waters, (Farnham and Watford waters, soft), have a very considerable action upon lead, to an extent, I should think, to be very dangerous; much more so than either the Thames or the Lea water."

30*th July*, 1851. ALFRED S. TAYLOR, *Professor of Chemistry in Guy's Hospital.*

"The West Middlesex water (hard) is not liable to acquire any noxious impregnation from lead. When the saline substances which it contains, and which give to it its moderate degree of hardness, are separated from it by distillation, the water acquires a well marked impregnation from lead by a few minutes' contact with the metal. It is, therefore, evident that this saline matter confers on it the property of resisting this chemical action on lead. The statements which have been published respecting the action of some kinds of *hard* waters on lead, do not apply to West Middlesex water, either in a chemical or medical point of view." This water showed 14½ degrees of hardness by Dr. Clarke's test.

3d June, 1843. DR. THOMAS CLARKE, *Professor of Chemistry, Aberdeen University.*

"It is well known that distilled water acts very readily upon lead. The cause of this action I apprehend to be the remarkable power that distilled water, compared with ordinary water, has of dissolving free carbonic acid. In general an alkaline water will not act upon lead or upon iron. But, perhaps, I should not say, in general, for I have examined a sufficient number of cases to lay down a general rule. . . . . With respect to lead pipes, I should say, the less lead is used the better in all cases. . . . . It is desirable to use it [lead] as little as possible; not that it is in all cases objectionable, far from it."

28th March, 1844. JOSEPH QUICK, *Engineer of Southwark Water Company.*

"At Clapham Common the manor estate was supplied with water from a spring well in the center of the Common, through the lead pipes, and the inhabitants were attacked with severe illness, which was ascribed to the length of lead pipes through which the water passed. Lead was detected in the water upon analysis, and the lead pipes were taken up and iron pipes substituted."

ANGUS SMITH, M. D., *of Manchester.* 1850.

"It is acknowledged, that with soft water, lead is very dangerous, but I am disposed to think that it is dangerous even with hard, except when a crust forms upon it. It is time that the use of lead pipes and cisterns should be done away with, unless *they can* be protected."

JAMES WAYNE, M. D., *of Baltimore, U. S.*

"I have met with several cases of disease from lead amongst workmen engaged in its manufacture, since my residence here, but have never observed any lead disease which might be attributable to the use of hydrant water."

WILLIAM MELHUISCH, *Plumber*, *London.*

"Have you observed that all Thames water acts upon lead cisterns? Yes; but in some old cisterns of two hundred years of age, and which are made of very thick lead, the water has only eaten half through them, while in modern cisterns the water has eaten quite through the lead. . . . . Rain water never acts upon the lead; I never knew a rain water cistern that was destroyed."

WILLIAM HAWKINS, *Plumber*, *London.*

"Then, as the general result of your observation and experience, you would say that hard water acts upon lead in a greater degree than soft water? That is just what I have always observed."

DR. W. SPENCER, *of Liverpool*, *Chemist.*

"I have made a good deal of direct inquiry, and have had information from the best sources, but have not heard of any case even of suspected indisposition which has arisen from the use of lead pipes *kept always charged with water.*"

DR. SHIER, *Agricultural Chemist to the Colony of Demerara.*

"My attention was first called to the subject by Dr. Blair, our Colonial Surgeon General, in consequence of symptoms of lead poisoning occurring in his practice. On investigation I found lead in the suspected water, and in quantity too large to admit of a doubt of its being the cause of great and wide spread mischief."

HENRY M. WARD, *Lecturer on Chemistry in St. Guy's Hospital.*

"I am inclined to think that the action on lead depends greatly on the aeration of the water. In rainy weather, when the Dee water is colored and contains little air, the quantity of lead dissolved in any case appears to be less than when the water is clear and well aerated.

Chemical Report by THOS. GRAHAM, W. A. MILLER, *and* A. W. HOFMAN, *Chemists, on the London Water Supply.*

"We are disposed, therefore, to conclude that the danger from lead, in town supplies of water, has been overrated, and that with a supply from the water companies, not less frequent than daily, no danger is to be apprehended from the use of the present distributory apparatus, with any supply of moderately soft water which the metropolis is likely to obtain."

Professor CRACE CALVERT, *Chemist.*

"I cannot give a satisfactory explanation of the curious results which I have obtained, as they are in contradiction to facts which I and other chemists have published; for the two purest waters, (of those examined by us), act with extreme slowness on lead."

DR. W. A. MILLER, *of London, Professor of Chemistry.*

"It is a fact, but too well attested by experience, that numerous instances of poisoning have been traced to the employment of water which has become impregnated with lead from leaden service pipes or cisterns. There are two modes in which water may act on lead: 1st, It may corrode the metal and form a white deposit evident to the eye; 2d, It may dissolve the metal, in which case the employment of proper tests would be necessary to render the fact apparent."

"The proportion of lead required to produce serious ill effects in a case where Mr. Herapath analyzed the water, was found to be less than one-ninth (1-9) of a grain per gallon."

Dr. Geo. Wilson, *Lecturer on Chemistry, Edinburgh.*

LOCH KATRINE WATER.

"The entire amount of lead present in the water, (experimented on in lead pipes), both in the soluble and insoluble form, amounted to 1.58 grain in one case, and in another to 2 grains per gallon. The amount held in solution, after filtration through paper, averaged from 1-9th to 1-6th grain per gallon. A water which acts thus cannot possibly be conveyed through lead pipes with safety to the health of those doomed to drink it."

William Wallace, *Analytical Chemist, Glasgow.*

"It is my opinion that Loch Katrine water, (a very soft water), could not be introduced through lead pipes, or retained in lead cisterns, with safety to the inhabitants."

Dr. Penny, *Professor of Chemistry, Glasgow.*

"The water of Loch Katrine is the purest and softest water I have yet examined. It acts decidedly and strongly on lead cisterns and on lead piping, both old and new. There are many soft and excellent waters that do not possess the objectionable property of acting continuously on lead. It has been stated that 'one grain and a third ($1\frac{1}{3}$) of carbonate of lead,' (equal to about 1 grain of metallic lead), 'in an imperial gallon of water, is the smallest proportion which has been known to produce injury to health.' But we have on record a case by a distinguished chemist of Bristol, in which 1-9th of a grain of lead per gallon deranged the health of a whole community; and Dr. John Smith of Aberdeen concludes from his investigations, that the limit of manifestly deleterious action would seem to be somewhere between 1-10 and 1-20 of a grain. It would certainly be easy to adduce the evidence of many eminent practitioners who condemn the continued use of water having a much smaller degree of contamination than one grain of lead in a gallon of water."

DR. THOS. ANDERSON, *Professor of Chemistry; and* DUGALD CAMPBELL, *Analytical Chemist, London.*

Lock Katrine water (Glasgow) "contains in solution 7.25 cubic inches of air per gallon, 4.75 of which were nitrogen, and 2.50 oxygen, along with a trace of carbonic acid. Its hardness was 0.9. . . . We are of opinion that as it will be delivered in Glasgow, the Loch Katrine water may, with the utmost safety, be preserved in the pipes and cisterns now in use." (Lead). . . . "In all these towns, (Inverness, Whitehaven, Penrith, Sheffield, Haywood, Bury, Blackburn, Accrington, Rochdale, Shorley, Bolton), leaden service pipes are employed, and no bad effects have been observed. In every case we have tested the water drawn from the leaden service pipes, and have not found the slightest trace of lead."

DR. A. S. TAYLOR, *Professor of Chemistry, Guy's Hospital.*

"This water does not exert any noxious action on lead when the metal is in its ordinary dull state. This (Loch Katrine) water has no action on an alloy of lead and tin, in the proportion of five parts of tin to ninety-five parts of lead."

"Here then is a water (Inverness water, soft) acting powerfully on (specimens of bright) lead, and distributed through lead, yet it contains no lead; and it is and has been used for a long period by the population of Inverness without any injury to health. . . . The interior of the pipes and cisterns have no doubt been speedily coated with a deposit which has wholly prevented any injurious chemical action."

ROBT. DUNDAS THOMPSON, M.D., *Professor of Chemistry, London.*

"Although in the preceding report I have given it as my decided opinion that no more permanent danger is to be apprehended, in reference to health, from the transmission of Loch Katrine water through lead pipes and detention in lead cisterns, than there is in the case of other waters supplied to towns, I have always recommended the substitution of iron and other materials for water pipes, as much as possible, for lead, and also where lead is employed, that it should be alloyed with tin."

Professors GRAHAM *and* HOFFMAN, *of University College and Royal College of Chemistry, London.*

"The apprehension of danger, from the use of Loch Katrine water with leaden service pipes, is entirely speculative and cannot fail to be dissipated the moment that reference is made to the experience of other towns supplied with water of equal softness and purity."

WATER COMMISSIONERS OF BOSTON. 1849.

"We regard it as satisfactorily proved, that the water of Cochituate Lake, which is about to be introduced into the city, may be safely distributed to private dwellings by means of leaden pipes, without danger to the health of those who may freely use it with their food."

Professor HORSFORD, *of Cambridge University, Boston.*

"Cochituate water may be served from leaden pipes connected with iron mains without detriment to health."

Consulting Physicians, Boston: DRS. WARREN, SHATTUCK, BIGELOW, HAYWARD *and* WARE.

"Although leaden pipes, in certain waters and under certain circumstances, are known to communicate a highly deleterious quality to their contents, yet in the open waters, from which the large cities already named have been supplied through such pipes, no practical evil of a general nature is known to this Board to have resulted from their employment."

B. SILLIMAN, JR., *Analytical Chemist, New Haven.*

QUEBEC WATERS.

"We confidently state, therefore, the important fact, that the passage of water through iron pipes, prepares it for a more speedy and certain action on lead. . . . It must be admitted, however, that as far as our present knowledge of facts goes, the cases of poisoning with lead, in New York, have been rare exceptions, but the public attention has as yet not been fully awakened to the subject."

HORATIO ADAMS, M. D., *Waltham, Mass.*

"It is never safe to use water drawn through lead pipes, or stored in leaden cisterns for domestic purposes, and that any article of food or drink is dangerous to health, which, by any possibility, can be impregnated with saturnine matter."

Report of the General Board of Health, *on Supply of Water to the Metropolis, London. May,* 1850.

"The use of lead pipes should be discontinued as early as practicable. As a question of danger, however, a preponderance of testimony establishes the conclusion, that hard water, with an intermittent supply, is actually more dangerous than soft water with a constant supply."

Report of Croton Aqueduct Board. *December,* 1849.

"The Department is aware of but a single case in which any precautions can be necessary in the use of Croton water for drinking, and these only at elevations where the supply is not constant. In the upper stories of buildings, where the pipes are alternately wet and dry, caused by the daily variations of head, it is possible that the interior of the pipes, by the united action of air and water, may be so oxydized, as that particles of carbonate of lead might be carried off, held in suspension by the water, and received in the stomach by drinking it; it would be imprudent, therefore, habitually to drink water from taps so circumstanced."

Samuel L. Dana, M. D., *Chemist. Report on Lowell Water.*

"The fact so well known to our citizens that leaden pipes are corroded and destroyed by well water, would long ago have told them the effects of using such water, were it not that the disorders produced by it are of such slow and insidious character, that they have been attributed to other sources. That lead in continued small doses is a cause of disease and death, is the accumulated testimony of two thousand years."

First Annual Report of the WATER COMMISSIONERS OF THE CITY OF HARTFORD.

"The various kinds of service pipes have had the careful examination of the Board, and after deliberate consultation, and with the best advice they could procure, it has been decided to use the American galvanized iron pipe; this will deliver the water into the building as pure as it is received. The Commissioners recommend their fellow citizens to adopt it for the inside of dwellings and other places."

DR. C. J. JACKSON, *Assayer to the State of Massachusetts. June*, 1852.

"I have long since been convinced that it is unsafe to use lead for conducting water by aqueducts."

EDWARD TURNER, M. D. (*Turner's Chemistry*).

"Many kinds of spring water, owing to the salts which they contain, do not corrode lead; and hence though intended for drinking, it may be safely collected in leaden cisterns. Of this, the water of Edinburgh is a remarkable instance."

TANQUEREL DES PLANCHES *on Lead Diseases. Dana's Translation.*

"Dr. Wall has seen all the residents on a farm attacked with lead colic, from drinking water from a pump the cistern of which and the pipe were lined with lead. It is partly through pipes of lead that water is distributed in public and private establishments in Paris; and Tanquerel has never learned that water thus conveyed has caused lead colic there. The inhabitants of some cities, establishing fountains, have suffered with colic from using the water which first passed through the new pipes."

Appendix to same. S. L. DANA, M. D.

"My convictions are decidedly against the use of lead, pure or alloyed, or tin coated, for conduits of water to be employed for domestic purposes."

CHRISTISON'S *Treatise on Poisons.*

"Rain or snow water, for culinary use, should not be collected from leaden roofs, nor preserved, nor conveyed in lead; the same rule applies to spring waters of unusual purity, where, for example, the entire impregnation does not exceed a 15,000th of the water. Spring water which contains a 10,000th or 12,000th of salts may be safely conveyed in lead pipes, if the salts in the water be chiefly carbonates and sulphates. Lead pipes cannot be safely used, even where the water contains a 4,000th of saline matter, if this consist chiefly of muriates. Spring water, even though it contains a large proportion of salts, should not be kept for a long period in contact with lead; and cisterns should not be covered with lids of this metal."

Encyclopædia Britannica. Article "Lead."

"Bicarbonate of lime exerts a remarkable preservative influence, and as it is a very common impurity in water, few spring waters exert much action on lead. . . . . Water highly charged with carbonic acid may dissolve lead to a dangerous extent."

MURPRATT'S *Chemistry applied to the Arts: Lead.*

"The first stage of slow poisonings are very frequent, and well known to most of the general medical practitioners in every large town. The source is almost invariably found to be the water employed for domestic purposes. Several cases of this kind have come under the notice of the editor, wherein whole families were affected. Iron glazed pipes and pumps, with slate or cemented cisterns, were recommended for adoption, and with very marked effect, the health of the individuals being completely restored. So small a quantity as three or four grains of a sulphate or a phosphate in water prevents, after some time, the corrosion of the metal. It must, however, be remarked, that these salts do not protect the lead from the solvent action of waters which contain nitric or nitrous acids in solution. These two acids are products of the decomposition of animal matter, and any water containing them will infallibly act upon lead; and consequently it would be highly dangerous to pass such a water through leaden pipes or to store it in leaden cisterns."

I refer the reader again to the reports, etc., which follow, for further information.

JAMES P. KIRKWOOD.

BROOKLYN, 21*st February*, 1859.

NOTE.—The undersigned will feel much indebted to any gentleman who will communicate any specific information he may have on this subject, or direct him to any of the other reports or sources of information which must exist.

J. P. K.

REPORTS AND OPINIONS.

Report on the Water of the West Middlesex Water Works Company.

By Alfred S. Taylor, M. D., F. R. S., and Arthur Aikin, F. L. S.,
Professors of Chemistry in Guy's Hospital.

Having been requested by the Directors of the West Middlesex Company to make a complete analysis of their water, we here publish a summary of the results. It is proper to state that the Company left it entirely to ourselves to fix the time for taking the samples. The localities selected embraced various points, from the Thames inlet, to a private dwelling house in the Regent's Park, and therefore presented the water in all those conditions in which it was likely to undergo any change in quality. The samples were taken in our presence, and they were retained in our custody until the analysis was completed. The subjoined report contains the facts, and we here offer a few preliminary remarks for the information of those who are not accustomed to the perusal of scientific documents.

Water, to be *wholesome* and fit for dietetic use, should be free from color, taste and smell. It has also been considered indispensable that it should be free from vegetable, animal and mineral matter: but universal experience is adverse to this view. All terrestrial water, or that which has once reached the earth, dissolves some organic and mineral matter, but the properties of the water for dietetic use are not thereby injured, provided the quantity dissolved do not exceed a certain proportion, and the substances dissolved are not of a nature to render the water noxious or unwholesome. The special object of a chemical analysis is to determine these two points.

Water may be free from color, taste and smell, and yet contain so large a proportion of carbonate and sulphate of lime as to render it unsuitable for household purposes. The shallow well water of the chalk district is of this kind; it is in general much impregnated with carbonic acid, so that the calcareous salts are in a great measure concealed by its cool and fresh taste. The quantity of saline matter varies from fifty to one hundred grains in the imperial gallon; such a water is invariably hard, and causes a thick curd with soap; other kinds of water are found to contain so small a proportion of saline matter, that not more than four or five grains of solid residue are obtained by the evaporation of an imperial gallon.

This kind of water is preëminently soft, but as a general rule it cannot be safely transmitted through leaden pipes or stored in leaden cisterns. The water of the Bagshot sands is of this description; its great freedom from saline matter led to its becoming impregnated with lead, and caused the poisoning of the Queen's hounds, as well as an attack of painters' colic in one of the huntsmen. In another case, the same description of water led to the poisoning of thirteen out of thirty-eight persons in the establishment of the royal family of France at Claremont. Under the present mode of distribution and stowage, therefore, a water may be so pure as to endanger health and life by its action on lead. It is necessary that this fact should be fully impressed on the mind, or otherwise the excessive purity of water may become an unsuspected source of injury to health. Although all *soft* water does not necessarily act upon lead, the above facts, as well as the analysis of Messrs. Brande and Warington, prove that the Bagshot water is beyond doubt exposed to the risk of noxious impregnation by contact with this metal.

The West Middlesex Water occupies an intermediate position between very hard and very soft water. The saline contents do not exceed twenty grains in the imperial gallon, and the salts are not of a nature to affect health injuriously. They are in much smaller proportion than in a large number of potable waters, including all the varieties of well water. The water has also this property: when boiled it becomes as soft as the very soft kinds of spring water, and is then well fitted for washing, cooking, brewing, tea making and other household purposes, for which soft water is required. The statements to the contrary have been made by persons who have assumed that the *boiled* water retains all the hardness of the cold water, when our experiments, and those of other chemists, have clearly proved that it is reduced at least one half.

* * * * *

It will be seen from the Report, that the West Middlesex water is not liable to acquire any noxious impregnation from *lead*. When the saline substances which it contains and which give to it its moderate degree of hardness, are separated from it by distillation, the water acquires a well marked impregnation from lead by a few minutes contact with the metal. It is, therefore, evident, that this saline matter confers on it the property of resisting this chemical action on lead. We have further ascertained by diluting this water with variable proportions of absolutely pure or distilled water, that the action on lead became more and more apparent, until the water contained so little saline matter that the point of danger was reached. The inocuousness of this water supplied through lead, is inferred from direct experiment with the metal immersed in the water for long periods, under circumstances favorable to chemical action, as well as from the observation that no injurious effects have followed from the constant use of the cistern water (No. 7) during a period of seventeen years. The statements which have been published respecting the action of some kinds of *hard* waters on lead do not apply to the West Middlesex water, either in a chemical or medical point of view.

* * * * *

A qualitative analysis of the different specimens of the water showed that the principal ingredient in all was carbonate of lime held dissolved by carbonic acid. There were traces of carbonate of magnesia. The other chemical ingredients were sulphate of lime and common salt, but these were in comparatively small proportion. There was scarcely any perceptible difference in the action of the tests on the different samples.

An Imperial gallon of 70,000 grains contains, in grains:

Carbonate of lime	13.13
Sulphate of lime	2.73
Common Salt	1.56
Organic matter	2.37
Residuary Carbon	0.11
Silica	0.27
Oxide of Iron	0.13
Total grains in gallon	20.3

* * * * *

The average hardness of the water may be taken at 9° in considering distilled water as unity, i.e., it would require nine parts of soap to produce in a gallon of this water the effect produced by one part of soap in a gallon of distilled or absolutely pure water. Dr. Clark's test gives 14½° of hardness. The degrees on Dr. Clark's scale are arbitrary, and have no intelligible meaning. The degrees of hardness here refer to the water while *cold.* If the water be *boiled* for only *ten minutes*, so much carbonate of lime is precipitated, and so much of the hardness is thereby removed, that in an experiment with the reservoir water, the boiled water was found to have a hardness of 5°.3, or, on Dr. Clark's scale, of about 9°. Hence the effect of boiling, for a very short period, is to reduce the hardness of the water by nearly one half.

* * * * *

A most important question, regarding all kinds of water intended for dietetic use is, whether it is liable to acquire a noxious impregnation from lead by reason of its contact with this metal, either when collected in leaden cisterns, or distributed through leaden pipes. Bars of bright lead, exposing eight square inches of surface, were placed in contact with the twentieth part of a gallon of each sample, under the free access of air, for a period of *nineteen days.* The lead in each sample had become rather duller on the surface, and there were streaks of a brownish color, as if from the deposit of sedimentary matter adhering to the metal. There was no appearance on any part of the metallic surface, of white oxide or carbonate of lead. The water in each vessel was quite clear, there were no white particles of a salt of lead to be perceived in any sample, either as a sediment or otherwise.

Chemical tests were then applied to the various samples (seven) in which the bars of lead had been immersed, in order to determine whether any salt of lead had become *dissolved* in the water. In numbers 3, 4 and 5, there appeared to be a very minute trace of lead in a soluble form, but, according to a comparative estimate, the quantity thus dissolved could not have amounted to so much as the 1-280,000th part of the weight of the water. There are probably few waters which would not act on lead to this extent. We attribute this slight action on the metal to the accidental presence of some soluble nitrates. The proportion of lead present was wholly insufficient to render the water injurious in a dietetic point of view.

* * * * *

This water, unlike many waters which are called *pure*, may be safely stored in leaden cisterns, or distributed through leaden pipes.

Chemical Laboratory, Guy's Hospital,
April 19*th*, 1851.

On the Composition of certain Well Waters in the neighborhood of London, with some observations on the action on Lead.

By Henry M. Noad, Esq.,
Lecturer on Chemistry at St. George's Hospital.

The question whether water for drinking should or should not contain mineral matter, is still a vexed one, and as it is one of medicine rather than of chemistry, it need not be discussed here.

* * * * *

But whatever may be thought of the mineral constituents, there can be but one opinion as to the influence of those organic impregnations so constantly met with in the waters of large towns. These consist, for the most part, of bodies in a state of progressive change or decomposition, and chemistry teaches us that such substances, when brought into contact with other organic substances, have a remarkable disposition to communicate to them their own molecular disquietude.

* * * * *

Water containing organic matter is particularly objectionable on account of its liability to become contaminated with *lead* when kept in cisterns of that metal, and that earthy and alkaline sulphates and chlorides, even when present in considerable quantity, do not in such waters act as preservatives.

Among the constituents of the well waters of large towns, *nitric acid* has often been alluded to. . . . That it does occasionally exist in large quantities, is shown by the analysis by Mr. W. Fisher, of a well water from Highgate. . . . . Attention was directed to this water, *firstly*, in consequence of its powerful action on the leaden cistern in which it was retained, and *secondly*, on account of the unusual amount of saline matter which it contained. Its hardness has prevented its being much used for domestic purposes, which may probably be deemed a fortunate circumstance, as I have found the metal evidently acted upon after being immersed in a bottle of the water for a few days only. By the subjoined analysis, it will, I think, appear that the remarkable action of this water on lead is referable to the comparatively small quantities of sulphates and chlorides, and to the extraordinary amount of *nitrates* which it contains. The source of the latter is pretty clearly pointed out by the situation of the well, which is immediately contiguous to the old churchyard, on the very top of Highgate Hill, the loose and sandy soil of which must be teeming with organic substances in all stages of decay, and which, therefore, are constantly furnishing ammonia, from the oxidation of which the nitric acid is in all probability derived. The putrefaction of animal matters, in contact with calcareous soils, is well known to produce nitrate of lime, and it was long ago showed by Glauber, that a vault plastered over with a mixture of lime, wood-ashes, and cow dung, soon became covered with efflorescent nitre. In the water in question the nitric acid exists in combination with *lime* and *magnesia*, which earths would naturally have occurred in the form of carbonates held in solution by carbonic acid. Not a trace of carbonates now exists, neither does the water contain any appreciable quantity of organic matter, which has been destroyed by the powerful oxidizing operations which are constantly going on in the contiguous soil. * * * *

Now, though the presence of earthy nitrates does not perhaps communicate any injurious or unwholesome quality to a water, indeed from the entire absence of decomposing organic substances, it may be less objectionable as a beverage than the average waters of large cities, it is, nevertheless, important to bear in mind the powerful action of such waters on lead, and the possibility of its becoming the vehicle through which this subtle poison may be introduced into the system. The public, indeed, cannot be too emphatically warned against the too common practice of allowing *any* water intended for domestic use to remain stored up in leaden vessels; for, as I shall have to show presently, the existence in the water of considerable quantities of both sulphates and chlorides is not always a security against saturnine impregnation.

* * * * *

SALINE CONTENTS IN THE IMPERIAL PINT.

By direct estimation, 12.57 grains, consisting of:

Silica	0.1120	grains
Sulphate of Potash	2.1306	"
Sulphate of Soda	1.1894	"
Chloride of Sodium	1.2040	"
Chloride of Calcium	0.7390	"
Nitrate of Lime	5.0150	"
Nitrate of Magnesia	2.1330	"
	12.5230	grains

The next water to which I shall call the attention of the Society, is from a spring at Clapham, which was submitted to me for analysis in the summer of 1848, in consequence of its strong action on lead. I collected the water myself on the spot, and on the same occasion was shown the cistern, which was then nearly full of water, the surface of which was covered with a thick greasy scum, which proved on examination to consist almost entirely of oxide of lead. I expected to find this water unusually pure; to my surprise, however, it contained nearly 78 grains of solid matter per imperial gallon, the composition of which was:

Silica	0.24
Carbonate of Lime	15.09
Carbonate of Magnesia	13.97
Sulphate of Lime	15.32
Sulphate of Potassa	6.79
Sulphate of Soda	10.77
Chloride of Sodium	11.46
Organic r	4.10
	77.74

Here, then, we have an instance of a water containing an abundance of so-called "preservative salts," corroding lead with remarkable energy. I was shown, by the plumber, a piece of the bottom of the cistern, which, in the course of six months, had been eaten into holes.

The oxide of lead could be skimmed from the surface of the water in abundance, but on testing the water beneath, taking care to avoid filtering, by which a very considerable quantity of the metal, even when in solution, may be removed, no signs of lead could be detected. To what are we to ascribe this remarkable action? I believe to the presence in the water of an unusually large quantity of organic matter. It was during the summer months that the corrosion of the cistern took place so rapidly.

The organic matters would then be undergoing the most active decomposition, and carbonic acid being constantly evolved against the sides and bottom of the cistern, would enter into combination with the *surface* oxide, and so form carbonate of lead. This is by no means the only instance I have met with of water abounding in sulphates and chlorides acting strongly on lead, and in every case that I have yet examined, organic matter has been present in unusual quantity. It is worthy of remark that no lead could be found in solution, whenever this does occur, in any but pure or alkaline water; the metal is probably taken up in the form of oxichloride; carbonate of lead is wholly insoluble, even in water highly charged with carbonic acid. I mention this because an idea is very generally prevalent that carbonate of lead, like the carbonates of lime and magnesia, may be rendered soluble by taking up an extra atom of carbonic acid. I have made direct experiments which negative this assumption, and it has since been pointed out to me that the same had been previously done by Dr. Taylor. But water, though it cannot take up carbonate of lead in solution, may, by keeping it in mechanical suspension, be the means of introducing this dangerous form of saturnine poison into the system. The practice of filtering water preserved in leaden cisterns, and intended for domestic use, cannot therefore be too warmly recommended.

I wish, lastly, to say a few words on another class of waters which act strongly on lead, viz: *artesian well waters of the London basin.* These waters are, I believe, always alkaline; those which I have examined are remarkably free from organic matter, and as there is no deficiency of preservative salts, it is to their alkalinity that I am inclined to attribute the corrosive action which they exert on this metal. From several analyses of these waters which have lately been made in this laboratory, I select two; one from the premises of the Lord Chief Baron of Hatton, which was examined by Mr. Henry Pollock, in consequence of the rapidity with which it corroded the leaden cistern, and the other, from the lunatic asylum at Colney Hatch, which I analyzed at the request of Mr. Rotch, the chairman of the Board of Governors of that institution, with the view of ascertaining its general fitness for the purposes of the asylum, before fresh expenses were incurred for conveying it to different parts of the building. It is worthy of remark that Mr. Pollock was able to detect lead in the clear water of the cistern, which I had been unable to do in the case of the Clapham water.

The analysis of these two artesian waters gave the following results, per imperial gallon:

	Hatton.	Colney Hatch
Carbonate of lime	2.120	6.500
Carbonate of Magnesia	.880	1.320
Carbonate of Soda	15.196	7.100
Sulphate of Potash	traces	2.590
Sulphate of Soda	10.456	5.770
Sulphate of Lime	..	4.555
Chloride of Magnesium	..	4.260
Chloride of Sodium	9.288	..
Protocarbonate of Iron	.480	..
Soluble Organic Matter	..	.470
Phosphate of Lime	traces	traces
Silica	.050	.670
	38.470	33.235
Saline matter by direct estimation	38.6	32.97

Of the excellence of both these waters for domestic use the analyses bear ample testimony; but with the example of the Hatton water before me, I felt bound to warn the Governors of the Colney

Hatch Asylum, against the use of lead, either for storing the water, or for distributing it. I found, however, on visiting the institution, that my warning was not required, that metal being almost entirely banished from every part of the building.

On the Composition of the Waters of the Dee and Don at Aberdeen, with an Investigation into the Action of Dee Water on Lead Pipes and Cisterns.

By John Smith, M. D.,

Fordyce Lecturer on Agriculture and Assistant in the Laboratory of Marischal College.

The river banks are gravelly, and the alluvial deposits few, and of limited extent. The bounding ridges of the valley are mostly of granite and gneiss. The flow of the water is pretty rapid, the alteration of level between the Linn (16 or 17 miles below the source) and Aberdeen being nearly 1,200 feet.

* * * * *

The water for the supply of Aberdeen is taken from the Dee, about two miles from its mouth, and quite beyond the reach of the tide water. It percolates through the gravelly sides and bottom into drains, and is thence pumped up to the highest level of the town. It is distributed through iron mains, and taken into the houses by small lead pipes to which lead cisterns, generally of moderate dimensions, are commonly attached. The supply is constant, and amounts to about one million gallons per day.

* * * * *

COMPOSITION OF DEE WATER.

Lime	0.526	grains.
Magnesia	0.110	"
Potash and Soda	0.382	"
Carbonic Acid (in combined state)	0.374	"
Sulphuric Acid	0.275	"
Chlorine	0.338	"
Silica	0.140	"
Precipitate by Ammonia from acid solution	0.080	"
Organic matter and loss	1.775	"
Total	4.000	grains.

The acids and bases may be arranged thus:

Carbonate of lime	0.850
Sulphate of lime	0.121
" Magnesia	0.323
Chloride of Potassium and Sodium	0.670
Phosphate of lime and iron	0.080
Silica	0.140
Organic matter and loss	1.816
Total	4.000

ACTION OF CLARK'S SOAP TEST ON DEE WATER.

In many trials of Dee water, taken either directly from the river, or from the laboratory pipe, the hardness was found to vary between 1°. 1 or 1°. 2, and 1°. 75. But different trials of the same specimens have sometimes varied a little, such a variation as I have been accustomed to find in solutions of very low degrees of hardness, especially when this hardness is caused partly by magnesia.

* * * * *

ACTION OF DEE WATER ON LEAD.

Under this head I have recorded about forty trials, made at different times, and on water from houses in various parts of the town; besides upwards of a dozen experiments with lead bars in specimens of water not previously in contact with lead. In the sequel, I shall make such a selection from these trials as may serve to bring out the conclusions arrived at.

Mode of Operating.—The test used was sulphuretted hydrogen; the water being previously acidulated with hydrocloric acid, and the gas transmitted a sufficient length of time. In the earlier trials I used only one or two pints of each specimen, but it soon became apparent that much greater delicacy was attainable by employing a larger quantity. In proceeding with the experiments, therefore, I operated uniformly on a gallon, contained in a glass beaker, of such dimensions that the water had a depth of 10½ inches. By placing the beaker on a piece of white paper, and looking downwards, I was able to appreciate a very slight change in tint. Another similar vessel, with the same quantity of water, was always placed by the side of the first, for the sake of comparison.

In estimating the quantity of lead present in any case, I had recourse to a very simple expedient. A solution of lead was prepared of definite strength; chloride of lead was used at first, but afterwards pure nitrate, as more convenient. 1.6 grain of nitrate was dissolved in 1000 grains of distilled water, so that the solution contained 1 of metalic lead in 1000. From an accurately graduated measure, I dropped this solution into a gallon of water containing no lead, until, on transmission of sulphuretted hydrogen, the same depth of tint was developed as in the particular case on trial. Having come as near as possible to the right quantity in this way, I commonly then made a new mixture, adding at once the ascertained quantity of lead to a gallon of water, and transmitting the gas. If the two trials corresponded, the experiment was finished, but in case of any discrepancy, the trial was repeated. This method, I believe, will give very accurate results, until the quantity of lead exceeds ¼ grain per gallon, when the color gets so dark that slight differences cannot well be discriminated. I found that 1-100th of a grain of lead, added to a gallon of pure clear water, gave a tint quite perceptible, that is, 1 of metalic lead in 7 millions; and a less quantity could readily be distinguished by careful comparison. Even in specimens previously containing a considerable proportion of lead, the difference of 1-100th of a grain was plainly visible. Here is an instance: A gallon of Dee water, taken from a leaden pipe, having given a certain tint with sulphuretted hydrogen, a gallon of Dee water, not containing lead, was placed beside it, and 80 grains of the standard solution (containing 0.08 grain of lead) well mixed. By the action of sulphuretted hydrogen, the tint produced was a little lighter than in the other; 10 drops more made the tints equal; and again 10 drops rendered the last somewhat darker than the first. Now every 10 drops of solution contained 1-100th of a grain of metallic lead.

The preliminary acidulation with hydrochloric acid is very essential when the water under trial happens to contain any iron. In some spring waters that I examined, there was a blackening caused by sulphureted hydrogen, from the presence of iron in combination with organic matter. Acidulation with hydrochloric acid entirely prevents this blackening, or destroys it after it has been produced, leaving a milkiness in the water, from deposition of sulphur. To ascertain if the hydrosulphuric acid test would be affected by a minute quantity of iron, I dissolved 1 grain of the pharmaceutical ammonio-tartrate (which would contain about 1-7th of a grain of metallic iron, or 1-5th of a grain of red oxide) in a gallon of water. The solution had a greenish-yellow tint. On transmitting the gas, there was no change for some time, but ultimately an evident darkening, with deposition of sulphur.

SELECTION OF TRIALS OF WATER FROM HOUSE-PIPES (*lead*).

Specimens taken during the day, when the water would be in its usual condition, unless stated otherwise.

1. Pipe about 16 yards long, no cistern, no indication of lead.

2. Pipe 12 or 15 yards, no cistern, specimen drawn first in the morning showed a trace of lead (less than 1-100 of gr. per gallon), specimen drawn at mid-day, no lead.

3. Pipe about 36 yards, no cistern, about 1-30 of gr. metallic lead per gallon. On another occasion, this pipe gave rather more lead.

4. Pipe upwards of 100 yards, no cistern, tried on different days, the quantity of lead varied from 1-30 to 1-40 gr. per gallon.

5. Pipe 16 or 18 yards, small cistern, lead under 1-100 gr. per gallon.

6. Pipe about 24 yards, cistern, several families supplied, and much water used, no indication of lead.

7. Pipe about 15 yards, cistern, 1-50 gr. of lead per gallon.

8. Pipe about 30 yards, cistern, about 1-35 gr. of lead per gallon.

9. Pipe about 100 yards, leading into cistern with about two cubic feet of water, 1-20 gr. of lead per gallon. This being the largest quantity I have found in any water in ordinary domestic use, I made particular inquiries in regard to the health of the family. Nothing unusual had ever been noticed, except that, on coming into town for the winter (the family lived in the country during summer), the children speedily lost color. This, of course, is usually attributed to the *air* of the town, but it would be worth inquiring how much of the affect in such cases is due to the *water*. This case, however, shows that water containing 1-20th of a grain of metallic lead per gallon (equal to 1-15 gr. carbonate), may be used habitually without any notable injurious results. Mr. W. Herapath related a case in the "Times" (14th Sept. 1850), where 1-9th of a grain of lead per gallon deranged the health of a whole community. The limit of the deleterious action would seem thus to be somewhere between 1-10th and 1-20th of a grain.

* * * * *

SELECTION FROM EXPERIMENTS WITH LEAD BARS.

1. Bar of bright lead, immersed (to the extent of 23 square inches of surface) in two pints of Dee water, left 48 hours, water remained clear, no deposite, a thin whitish film had formed on lead. The water, after filtration through double filter, contained about 1-100 of a grain of lead per gallon.

2. Parallel experiment with distilled water; water speedily became milky, abundant white deposite. Passed several times through double filter, but milkiness not removed. After standing two days, the white matter subsided, and the water then filtered clear. No lead whatever in solution. (The oxide was probably entirely converted into insoluble carbonate by exposure.)

3. Bar No. 1 immersed, without cleaning, in two pints of Dee water, and left 48 hours, no deposite. Passed through double filters, the water contained about 1-20th of a grain of lead per gallon.

4. Bright bar, in 3 pints of Dee water, 32 square inches immersed, left 24 hours, filtered, contained trace of lead.

5. Same bar, without cleaning, in two pints, 26 inches immersed, left 48 hours, filtered, contained 1-20th of a grain of lead per gallon.

6. Lead bar tarnished in air, immersed (to 30 square inches) in 3 pints, left 48 hours, filtered, 1-20th of a grain of lead per gallon.

7. The bars used in experiments, 5 and 6, were placed, without cleaning, in similar quantities of water, and left 48 hours, not filtered. The water from bar 6 contained about 1-10th of a grain of lead per gallon. The water from bar 5 contained more.

8. The bar from experiments 5 and 7 being again immersed without cleaning, and left 48 hours, the water unfiltered, contained much more lead than in the last experiment, about 1-6th of a grain of lead per gallon.

9. Same bar, left 48 hours in two pints, water passed through double filter, contained about 1-10th of a grain (or rather more) of lead per gallon.

10. Bright bar of lead, immersed in two pints of Dee water for four days. The water had been kept for some time in a jar, in a warm room, so that a great part of the air had escaped from it. After filtration the water contained a mere trace of lead. Bar immersed again, without cleaning, in other two pints of same water, and left for two days. Water (filtered) contained more lead than in the last case, but still not much.

From these experiments, it appears that the Dee water acts more readily upon tarnished or crusted lead, than upon the bright metal; that the lead taken up by the water, is separated to a small extent by paper filters; and that when a crusted bar is immersed for a certain time in water, dried and immersed again for the same time, the action is greater the second time than the first; dried and immersed a third time, the action is still greater. (So that a lead cistern, alternately filled and emptied, is more unsafe than one kept constantly at the same level both being freely exposed to the air.)

From the foregoing observations I conclude that the action of Dee water on lead is comparatively feeble, but yet that by prolonged contact, more especially when there is free exposure to air, as in cisterns, a dangerous quantity of that metal may be taken up. With lead pipes of moderate length and no cisterns, no danger whatever is to be apprehended. With small cisterns, and a pretty constant use of the water, there is also no danger; but the risk increases with the length of the pipe, the size of the cistern, and the time the water lies unused. When large cisterns are required for general domestic use, I think it would be prudent to have them lined with gutta percha or some other innocuous material. With an uninterrupted supply, such as is enjoyed in Aberdeen, and with an improved form of tap, cisterns might probably to a great extent be dispensed with.

In some cases it has appeared to me that old pipes are more acted upon than new; the differences, however, may have arisen from impurities in the lead, or from other special causes not detected. I am also inclined to think that the action on lead depends greatly on the aeration of the water. In rainy weather, when the Dee water is colored and contains little air, the quantity of lead dissolved in any case appears to be less than when the water is clear and well aerated. This observation has been confirmed to some extent by the experiments with lead bars, but I am not prepared to state it unreservedly as a rule.

Chemical Report on the Supply of Water to the Metropolis,

By THOMAS GRAHAM, ESQ., F. R. S., W. A. MILLER, M. D., F. R. S., and A. W. HOFMANN, Ph. D. F. R.

THE existing Metropolitan Water Companies with their estimated delivery per day are as follows:

Water derived from the Thames 19,907,480 gallons,	Grand Junction Company,	3,541,717
	West Middlesex,	3,334,054
	Chelsea,	3,940,730
	Southwark and Vauxhall,	6,013,716
	Lambeth,	3,077,260
Water derived from other sources than the Thames 25,978,445 gallons,	New River,	15,435,617
	East London,	9,036,049
	Kent,	1,079,311
	Hampstead,	427,468
		45,885,925

It thus appears that of a daily supply of nearly 46 million gallons, 20 million gallons are taken from the Thames and 26 million gallons are obtained from other sources.

* * * * *

Specimens of the water of all the Companies were taken for analysis always from a main and generally at the nearest accessible point to the works of the Company or to a distributing reservoir. They were all drawn on the 29th, 30th and 31st of January last, after moderately rainy weather, with the river full but not flooded.

The specimens may be considered as representing the least favorable state of the water-supply to the metropolis during winter, but still such as it may continue for several months in a wet season like the last. The temperature of the river at the time was 44° Fahr.

The results are given in two forms, first the acids and bases separately, as actually found by analysis, and secondly the same acids and bases arranged in the form of salts, or chemically combined as they are believed to exist in the waters. The first group consists of waters not derived from the Thames.

ANALYSIS OF THE NEW RIVER, EAST LONDON, KENT AND HAMPSTEAD WATERS.

Grains in an imperial Gallon.

	New River Water Company	East London Water Company	Kent Water Company	Hampstead Water Company
Lime	5.7192	6.9034	7.82	2.9160
Magnesia	0.5280	0.7336	0.62	1.7098
Potassium	0.4972	0.5600	0.35	1.6471
Sodium	1.1634	0.9989	0.86	7.5761
Iron, Alumina and Phosphates	trace	0.4760	trace	trace
Sulphuric Acid (SO_3)	3.2550	2.5830	1.86	9.1702
Chlorine	1.0500	1.0682	1.52	4.1230
Carbonic Acid	11.1020	11.4527	11.56	10.9823
Silica	0.5005	0.6216	0.49	0.0728
Nitric Acid	0.0150	0.4800	......	0.050
Ammonia	trace	trace	trace	trace

ANALYSIS OF THE NEW RIVER, EAST LONDON, KENT AND HAMPSTEAD WATERS.

Grains in an imperial Gallon.

	New River Water Company	East London Water Works	Kent Water Company	Hampstead Water Company
Carbonate of Lime..........	7.82	10.16	11.64	4.95
Sulphate of Lime...........	3.23	2.33	3.16	....
Nitrate of Lime...	0.02	0.72	....	0.07
Carbonate of Magnesia......	1.09	1.51	1.28	3.53
Chloride of Sodium..........	1.73	1.76	2.24	6.79
Sulphate of Soda............	1.49	0.94	....	15.14
Chloride of Potassium.......	....	....	0.66	....
Sulphate of Potassa........	1.11	1.25	....	1.40
Carbonate of Potassa.......	....	....	....	1.80
Silica....................	0.50	0.62	0.49	0.07
Iron, Alumina and Phosphates	traces	0.47	traces	traces
Ammonia..................	traces	traces	traces	traces
Organic Matter............	2.79	4.12	2.61	1.84
Total..............	19.78	23.88	21.08	35.59
Solid residue obtained on evaporation................	19.58	23.51	29.71	35.41
Free Carbonic Acid in cubic inches at 44° F...........	14.49	12.38	10.15	13.30
Free Carbonic Acid grains in a gallon..................	7.24	6.19	5.07	6.67
Suspended Matter...........	1.49	1.07	....	0.52
Degree of hardness Clark's scale	14°.9	15°.0	16°.0	9°.8

The second group is composed of Thames waters.

ANALYSIS OF THAMES WATERS.

	Water taken at Thames Ditton	Grand Junction supplied at Kew	West Middlesex Company supplied at Barnes	Chelsea Company near Red House Battersea	Southwark and Vauxhall Company near Red House Battersea	Lambeth Company supplied at Lambeth
Lime	8.0046	7.4522	7.5390	7.5117	7.2751	6.7970
Magnesia	0.6070	0.5544	0.5628	0.5527	0.6020	0.7011
Potassium	0.4261	0.2769	0.2185	0.2821	0.6048	0.4291
Sodium	0.4330	0.6127	0.7387	0.5784	0.7861	0.7805
Iron, Alumina and Phosphates	0.0940	0.7630	0.7630	0.2910	0.3430	0.8505
Sulphuric Acid	1.8782	2.6460	3.0380	3.3005	2.4150	2.2015
Chlorine	0.9890	0.8512	1.1424	1.2229	1.1725	1.1746
Carbonic Acid	14.2170	11.9826	10.6260	10.6470	12.1100	12.8520
Silica	0.6290	0.4466	1.0013	0.7189	0.7679	1.0451
Nitric Acid	0.0180	trace	trace	trace	0.2360	trace
Ammonia	trace	trace	trace	trace	0.0309	trace
Carbonate of Lime	11.79	10.90	9.94	9.28	10.57	8.99
Sulphate of Lime	3.06	3.26	4.78	5.61	3.05	2.99
Nitrate of Lime	0.27	trace	trace	trace	0.35	trace
Carbonate of Magnesia	1.27	1.17	1.16	1.08	1.29	1.44
Chloride of Sodium	1.10	1.40	1.88	1.47	1.99	1.95
Sulphate of Soda	....	0.18	....	....	....	....
Chloride of Potassium	0.67	....	....	0.55	....	....
Sulphate of Potassa	0.17	0.61	0.48	....	1.34	0.95
Silica	0.62	0.44	1.00	0.71	0.76	1.04
Iron, Alumina and Phosphates	0.09	0.67	0.76	0.29	0.34	0.85
Ammonia	trace	trace	trace	trace	0.03	trace
Organic Matter	2.29	3.07	2.75	2.38	1.51	2.59
Total	21.33	21.70	22.75	21.37	21.23	20.80
Solid residue found on evaporation	20.78	21.72	22.67	21.28	21.08	20.40
Free Carbonic Acid in cubic inches at 44° F	16.89	13.46	11.56	12.30	13.57	16.64
Free Carbonic Acid gr's in gallon	8.25	6.73	5.78	6.15	6.78	8.32
Suspended Matter	....	0.01	0.02	....	1.92	1.15
Degree of hardness—Clark's scale	14.22	14.00	14.60	14.44	15.00	14.16

The soluble organic matter from two of the Thames waters was submitted to ultimate analysis, and found to give 0.105 grain of nitrogen in the Grand Junction water, and 0.031 grain of nitrogen in the Southwark and Vauxhall water. The existence of nitrogen is generally supposed to imply the animal origin of organic matter, and on such evidence, a minute and probably unimportant portion of animal organic matter would be admitted to be present.

* * * * *

It may be useful to distinguish the quality known as the "hardness" of water, according as it is of a *temporary* or *permanent* character. Perfectly pure or soft water, when exposed to contact with chalk (carbonate of lime) is capable of dissolving only a very minute quantity of that substance; one gallon of water, in weight equal to 70,000 grains, taking up no more than two grains of carbonate of lime.

This earthy impregnation is said to give the water two degrees of hardness. But waters are often found containing a much larger quantity of carbonate of lime, such as twelve, sixteen, or even twenty grains and upwards in the gallon. In such cases, the true solvent of the carbonate of lime, or at least of the excess above two grains, is carbonic acid gas, which is found to some extent in all natural waters. But this gas may be driven off by boiling the water, and the whole carbonate of lime then precipitates in consequence, or falls out of the water, with the exception of the two grains which are held in solution by the water itself. The gas dissolved carbonate of lime gives, therefore, *temporary* hardness, curable by boiling the water. An artificially prepared hard water, containing 13½ grains of carbonate of lime to the gallon, was observed to decrease from 13.5 to 11.2 degrees of hardness, merely by heating it in a kettle to the boiling point. Boiling for five minutes, reduced the hardness to 6.3 degrees; fifteen minutes, to 4.4 degrees; thirty minutes, to 2.6 degrees; and one hour, to 2.4 degrees. The softening effect of boiling does not, therefore, appear all at once, but the greatest proportional effect is certainly produced by the first five minutes' boiling.

The West Middlesex and New River waters were both found to soften by boiling, very much in the same manner as the preceding pure chalk water, except that the ultimate hardness of the two waters specified was somewhat higher. By an hour's boiling, the West Middlesex fell from 14.6 to 5.5 degrees, and the New River from 14.7 to 4.1 degrees.

* * * * *

The water at present supplied may be circulated through leaden pipes, or preserved in leaden cisterns, with an unusual degree of safety. The corrosion of water cisterns in London is generally occasioned by the mud which subsides to the bottom, particularly when the sediment includes organic matter, and the evil might be greatly diminished by more frequently cleaning out the cisterns. But it is to be particularly remarked, that this corrosion is not attended by any sensible solution of lead in the water, and that the water of the cistern is not poisoned in consequence. The London water may indeed be said to exert the least degree of solvent action upon lead. To the nature of the action of different waters on this metal, there will be occasion again to refer.

The circulating system of iron pipes, appears also to receive a certain amount of protection from the alkaline character of the present supply. The erosions and bulky deposits in cast iron pipes, which have given great trouble in the distribution of certain waters, are quite unknown in London.

Putrefactive decomposition appears also to occur less rapidly in hard than in soft water, and hard water seems to be more easily preserved in reservoirs or tanks, without deterioration, for a short time.

* * * * *

Caustic lime, when added to hard water in sufficient quantity to neutralize the carbonic acid, removes the solvent, and becoming at the same time carbonate of lime, must precipitate together with that originally in solution. The operation of this process was first witnessed by us at the Mayfield Print Works in Lancashire, where 300,000 gallons of water are submitted to it daily, at a trifling expense, and with little trouble, but more for the purpose of discoloration than softening. A careful series of experiments made in the Laboratory, left no doubt on our minds that the means of conducting this process are certain in their results, and sufficiently simple to be left to the execution of a workman of ordinary intelligence. The precipitation of the carbonate of lime was terminated within twenty-four hours, and the water, if free from turbidity before the lining, continued in that state, but if originally turbid it remained so, and required filtration, besides the lining, to make it clear. The New River and Thames waters were softened in this way to an average of about 3½ degrees of hardness, or to a lower point than by an hour's boiling.

* * * * *

The only precaution taken to insure the absence of any excess of caustic lime, consisted in testing the water in the settling reservoir by a drop of nitrate of silver, which shows if the quantity of lime required has been exceeded, by the brown color of the precipitate then formed. After subsiding generally for twenty-four hours or longer, the water was finally passed through the ordinary sand filters before being distributed. The degree of hardness before and after the softening process, (as tried at the Chelsea Water Works), in five experiments, was reported to us by Mr. Simpson, as follows:

THAMES WATER AT THE CHELSEA WATER WORKS.

1851	Degs. of Hardness		Remarks
	Before Lining	After Lining	
February 24....	14.0	4.5	The river was in good condition; the mixing was complete in 10 hours.
March 1.......	14.1	3.75	The river was in good condition; the mixing in 9¾ hours.
March 18......	10.5	5.	The river in flood; the flood tinge retained after liming.
March 22......	11.6	4.8	Recovering from flood; yellow flood tinge not removed.
April 17.......	15.5	3.6	Rises in an average condition.

* * * * *

Mr. Simpson believes that 20*s.* ($5), for one million gallons, would be a proper estimate of the cost of this process.

* * * * *

The influence which this addition to the cost might have upon the price of water, may be gathered from the following returns lately made to the General Board of Health, of the present cost to each water company, of one million gallons of water:

FIRST COST OF ONE MILLION GALLONS OF WATER.

	£	s.	d.
New River	9	17	4
East London	6	7	7½
Southwark	5	9	4
West Middlesex	16	9	7
Lambeth	15	0	6½
Chelsea	19	10	4½
Grand Junction	9	14	6¼
Kent	17	2	10¼
Hampstead	22	5	7¾
Average (about)	£10	10	9¾

The average charge of the companies is, by the same return about sixpence for one thousand gallons, or £25 for one million gallons. The softening process would, therefore, add about ten per cent. to the original cost of the water, or four per cent, to the price charged to the consumers.

* * * * *

But it is the solvent action of soft water on lead which is calculated to excite most alarm, with the general use of house cisterns, and the universal use of service pipes of that metal, under the present system of distribution.

Of the soft spring waters from Surrey, the corrosive action on lead is remarkably small, according to our own observations, which generally accord with the conclusions of Mr. Napier on that point, with the striking exception of the water from the Punch Bowl, Hindhead, of which the power to dissolve lead proved to be rather considerable. The inactivity of the other samples we would refer more to the smallness of the quantity of dissolved oxygen which they contain, than to the absence of carbonic acid, the cause suggested by Mr. Napier.

* * * * *

River water or spring water from the chalk strata, softened artificially to about three degrees of hardness, was proved by our own observation, to have no dangerous action upon lead.

The experimental results obtained in a long inquiry, undertaken to illustrate the action of water in various circumstances upon lead, are not adapted for statement in this Report. The subject is one of great difficulty, and is still far from being exhausted. The most important practical conclusions which we have arrived at are the following:

Certain salts, particularly sulphates, to which a protecting effect is usually ascribed, did not appear to exercise uniformly that useful property. Some salts, on the other hand, such as chlorides, and more particularly nitrates, may increase the solvent action of water. Of all protecting actions, that of carbonate of lime, dissolved in carbonic acid, appeared to be the most considerable and surest.

The most practical, perhaps, of our observations, is the extraordinary influence remarked of the small quantity of carbonic acid, which water usually contains upon the results. This effect is fortunately to neutralize, to an extraordinary degree, the usual solvent action on lead which water exercises through the agency of the oxygen dissolved in it. The soluble oxide of lead is converted into the carbonate, which although not absolutely insoluble, appears to be the least soluble of all the salts of lead.

Pure water did not dissolve a quantity of carbonate of lead greater than one sixtieth of a grain to the gallon, or one part of lead in four millions of water; while water, on the other hand, which contained already so much as six grains of oxide of lead dissolved in it to the gallon, had the quantity of metal reduced to one fifty-seventh of a grain, by free exposure to the atmosphere for twenty-four hours; the lead being deposited as carbonate of lead in consequence of the absorption of carbonic acid gas. So minute a trace of lead remaining in the water could have no possible influence on health.

The quantities just stated also represent, pretty closely, the proportion of lead which was dissolved by water left in contact with the metal in a divided state, during a period of not more than twenty-four hours in two experiments; the water being simply distilled water in one experiment, and distilled water containing three per cent. of its volume of carbonic acid gas in the other. The pure water became highly poisonous, but that containing carbonic acid remained safe. The lead was in the form of lead pyrophorus, prepared from the tartrate of lead, in which the metal is in an extreme state of division, and therefore exposes an enormous surface to the water.

Carbonic acid is usually present in well, river and lake waters, in the quantity sufficient for protection; and the immunity of such waters from lead impregnation, we would ascribe often more to their carbonic acid than to the salts which they may also contain; for lead placed in distilled water which has been boiled to expel its carbonic acid, is no longer sufficiently protected by the addition of the same salts.

It is true, however, that a certain excess of carbonic acid in waters, such, however, as is very unusual, may give solubility to the carbonate of lead; but this solubility is not to be compared to that of the carbonate of lime, the carbonate of lead requiring for solution a proportionally much larger qnantity of gas.

Organic matter in a soft water, is doubly dangerous, as the rapid corrosion which it occasions may be followed by solution of the lead salt formed, when the carbonic acid is either deficient, as in rain water generally, or present above the safe proportion.

The properties of water which enable it to act at times with unusual vigor upon lead, are little understood, and seem often to arise from the accidental action of local and very limited causes, such as the presence of decaying leaves and impurities, which may only affect a small volume of water. These causes are of a kind most to be dreaded in the supply of a single residence, in which the whole volume of water might at a time assume the same dangerous composition. But such causes probably often counteract each other, when large volumes of water are mixed together, as in the supply for a town.

It is at least difficult to account otherwise for the fact, that no recent and authenticated case can be cited of the health of any of the numerous towns lately supplied with soft water being affected by the use of leaden distributory tubes, although apprehensions were often entertained from the introduction of soft water, as at Boston, in the United States, where the subject has excited much attention; and at New York since the introduction of the Croton River.

From Whitehaven, where water of extreme softness has been in use for the last six months, we learn that no case of lead poisoning had been seen or heard of by the medical practitioners of the town which could be attributed to the use of the water. No cisterns however are used there, nor in any other towns where soft water has lately been introduced, as they may be dispensed with on the system of constant supply, which appears always to have been adopted with the soft water.

We are disposed, therefore, to conclude that the danger from lead in town supplies of water has been over rated; and that with a supply from the Water Companies, not less frequent than daily, no danger is to be apprehended from the use of the present distributory apparatus, with any supply of moderately soft water, which the metropolis is likely to obtain.

* * * * *

On the Examination of Water for Towns, for its Hardness, and for the Incrustation it deposits on Boiling.

By Professor Clark.

At various times during the last few years, I have been applied to for information respecting methods I had adopted for examining waters for towns.

* * * * *

The processes alluded to for the examination of waters are two: one for ascertaining the hardness of water, one for ascertaining the alkalinity.

Each of these processes is fully described in the specification of a patent printed in the Number of the "Repertory of Patent Inventions" for October, 1841.

PROCESS FOR ASCERTAINING THE HARDNESS OF WATER.

In June, 1843, having occasionally before met with some few specimens of waters, and more especially soft waters from springs, where the indications of the soap-test, which in general are remarkably distinct, were obscure, I discovered the cause of this obscurity to be an excess of carbonic acid, that is, an excess over and above what is necessary to form alkaline or earthly bicarbonates. This excess has the property of slowly decomposing a lather once formed.

For the purpose of guarding against an excess of carbonic acid in all cases, I recommend that, before you measure out the water for trial, you shake it briskly in a stoppered glass bottle half-filled with it, sucking out the air from the bottle at intervals by means of a glass tube, so as to change the atmosphere in the bottle.

In all trials of waters above 16 degrees hardness, not only should such waters, and the distilled water to be used along with them in the trials, be treated in this manner, previous to their being measured out and mixed, but the measured mixtures themselves should be treated in like manner, before any soap-test is added to them. The soap-test itself should be occasionally so treated before it is measured out.

To obtain uniform results with the soap-test, I recommend that as soon as you observe that a lather is formed, such as will remain all over the surface of the water for five minutes, you take a note, but only an *interim* one, of the quantity of the soap-test that has been added. In about half an hour you should shake the bottle again, to see whether the lather will still remain for five minutes. If the water under trial do not exceed 4 or 5 degrees of hardness, it is likely to require a little more soap-test upon this renewed shaking; but in every case where more soap-test is required, let more be added to the water. This latter quantity and the former will together make up the whole soap-test that is to determine the hardness of the water under trial. For hours afterwards, unless perhaps the water does not exceed 1 or 2 degrees of hardness, a lather lasting for five minutes may be restored by your shaking the phial. This mode of procedure, by producing a lather whose permanence we may repeatedly verify, will conduce much to the uniformity and accuracy of our trials.

TABLE FOR CONVERTING SOAP-TEST MEASURES INTO DEGREES OF HARDNESS.

Degree of Hardness.	Soap-test Measures.	Differences for the next 1st deg. of Hardness.
0 (distilled water)	1.4	1.8
1	3.2	2.2
2	5.4	2.2
3	7.6	2.0
4	9.6	2.0
5	11.6	2.0
6	13.6	2.0
7	15.6	1.9
8	17.5	1.9
9	19.4	1.9
10	21.3	1.8
11	23.1	1.8
12	24.9	1.8
13	26.7	1.8
14	28.5	1.8
15	30.3	1.7
16	32.0	

When the measures of soap-test necessary to form a lather, with 100 test-measures of a water, exactly correspond with a standard solution, then the degree of hardness will be the corresponding integral number found in the first column. Thus 24.9 of soap-test will indicate 12 degrees of hardness; 26.7 of soap-test will indicate 13 degrees of hardness.

But if the measures of soap-test do not exactly correspond with a number in the first column, the hardness will be expressed partly by an integer and partly by a fraction.

The *integer* will be the hardness corresponding to the next lower number in the soap-test column.

The *numerator* of the fraction will be the excess of the soap-test measures in question above this number. The *denominator* of the fraction will be the corresponding difference which follows the soap-test in the next column.

Example.—Let 25.8 be the measures of soap-test required by 100 test-measures of a given water.

24.9 is the next lower number in the soap-test column. Therefore 12 degrees of hardness, the corresponding degree, is *the integral part* of the required hardness.

The numerator of the fraction is 25.8—24.9 = 0.9. The denominator is the corresponding difference = 1.8. *The fraction* itself is

$$\frac{0.9}{1.8} = 0.5.$$

The whole hardness therefore is 12.5 degrees.

PROCESS FOR ASCERTAINING THE ALKALINITY OF A WATER.

The tests employed are two,—test-paper and the acid test. Respecting these I have little to add to what is given in the specification.

Test-paper.—The color should be first separated from the solid matter of the litmus by boiling, subsidence, filtration, &c. The colored solution thus obtained being too weak for use, will require to be concentrated by evaporation. The color will then have to be brought to a proper tint by means of dilute nitric acid, and afterwards applied to the paper by a flat camel-hair brush. The only paper that I have found to be sufficiently free from acid or alkaline impurities to be unexceptionable for test-paper, is the drawing-paper stamped with the name of Harding.

Acid test.—In purifying oxalic acid, it is desirable to reject a very small crop, consisting of such of the crystals as fall first. These, I find, contain quadroxalate of potash. I find a little of this salt, even when the acid has been made by means of pure (?) nitric acid and specimens of the best refined sugar of commerce—a circumstance well worthy of the attention of chemists engaged in the study vegetation.

DEGREES OF HARDNESS AND DEGREES OF ALKALINITY EXPLAINED.

Degrees of Hardness.—Each degree of hardness indicates as much hardness as would be produced by 1 gr. of chalk per gallon, held in solution in the form of bicarbonate of lime, free from any excess of carbonic acid. The degree of hardness caused by a lime salt depends not on the state of combination of the calcium it contains, but on the quantity of the calcium. If, instead of being in the form of bicarbonate of lime, the calcium this compound contains were in the form of chloride of calcium, or of nitrate of lime, or of sulphate of lime, or even of lime-water, the soap-test destroyed by it, and consequently the degree of hardness indicated, would be precisely the same.

A quantity of a soluble magnesian salt equivalent to 1 grain of chalk, destroys a like quantity of soap-test, and consequently indicates one degree of hardness. The same is the case with salts of iron and salts of alumina. Salts of the alkalies do not produce hardness.

Degrees of Alkalinity.—For each degree of alkalinity that a water possesses, a gallon of it will require as much acid to neutralize it as 1 grain of chalk would require. Hence a solution of lime-water, or of bicarbonate of lime, in distilled water should be of the same degree of hardness as of alkalinity. The most usual cause of alkalinity in water is bicarbonate of lime; but bicarbonate of magnesia, which causes hardness, likewise causes alkalinity; and bicarbonate either of soda or of potash, which does not cause hardness, causes alkalinity.*

TO INFER THE DEGREES OF HARDNESS AND THE DEGREES OF ALKALINITY FROM AN ORDINARY ANALYSIS.

For Hardness.—Compute the grains of lime, magnesia, oxides of iron and alumina, in a gallon of the water, each into its equivalent of chalk. The sum of those equivalents will be the hardness of the water.

For Alkalinity.—Compute in like manner the grains of bicarbonates of lime, magnesia, soda and potash, in a gallon of the water, each into its equivalent of chalk. The sum of those equivalents will be the alkalinity of the water. But the results thus obtained have much less chance to be accurate than the hardness and the alkalinity ascertained directly by means of the soap-test and the acid-test.

* When a phosphate of lime is present, as happens rarely and in small quantities, it is probable that for every two degrees of hardness the phosphate occasions it will produce only one degree of alkalinity; that is, all the lime in the phosphate will cause hardness; but one half of it will be neutralized, and only the remaining half alkaline.

DELICACY OF THE TESTS.

For Hardness.—Suppose the Thames water to yield a mean of 14 degrees of hardness. Carefully conducted experiments should then range between 14.1 and 13.9 degrees of hardness. That is to say, the mean result of more experiments than one should be within 0.1 degrees of the extremes; and it is to be remembered that the hardness of a water may be ascertained repeatedly within an hour. But 0.1 degrees of hardness is equivalent to one-tenth of a grain of chalk per gallon; that is, 1 of chalk in 700,000 times its weight of water. But as the operation is performed on only the 70th of a gallon, (1000 grains), the whole weight of hardening matter that we actually operate upon in this experiment is a 70th of 14 grains, that is, one-fifth of a grain; and the smallest weight to which we actually measure is the 70th of the 10th of a grain, that is, the 700th of a grain. I do not remember any process of equal quantitative delicacy in the whole range of chemical analysis; and this one is the more remarkable as it is performed with soap-test, previously known as almost the rudest and least determinate of chemical reägents.

For Alkalinity.—If the Thames be at 14 degrees of hardness, it would probably yield 13.1 degrees of alkalinity. Such a water, if tried according to the directions of the specification, should give 13.1 degrees of alkalinity each time. The difference between the experiments, if carefully performed, should appear not on the first, but only on the second place of decimals. Now since 1 degree of alkalinity corresponds to 1 grain of chalk per gallon, and since the acid test indicates less than 0.1 degrees of alkalinity, or 1 of chalk in 700,000 of water, we may safely infer that the acid test will measure 1 of chalk in 1,000,000 of water. Thus we obtain for record even more accurate results by the acid test than we do by the soap test. Nevertheless the soap test is, in the abstract, the most delicate, for although we use nearly the same quantity of each test, yet in the case of the acid test we act on the 8th of a gallon, whereas in the case of the soap-test we act on only the 70th of a gallon.

HOW TO MAKE THE FOREGOING PROCESSES AVAILABLE FOR ASCERTAINING THE QUANTITY OF INCRUSTATION THE WATER DEPOSITS ON BOILING.

For this purpose the points to be ascertained are:

1. The hardness and the alkalinity of a given water, unboiled.
2. The like particulars of the same water, after being boiled without loss of steam, for at least $2\frac{1}{2}$ hours, and then cooled, and (if necessary) filtered.

From these indications, the weight per gallon of earthy deposit formed by boiling, if there be any, is deduced as follows:

Let $\begin{cases} h = \text{hardness of unboiled.} \\ h' = \text{hardness of boiled.} \\ h - h' = H, \end{cases}$ that is, degrees of hardness lost by boiling, occasioned by the precipitation of earthy salts, which may be either alkaline or neutral, or partly both.

Let $\begin{cases} a = \text{alkalinity of unboiled.} \\ a' = \text{alkalinity of boiled.} \\ a - a' = A, \end{cases}$ that is, degrees of alkalinity lost by boiling, occasioned by the precipitation of alkaline earthy salts.

NOTE.—Observe that H is equal to A only in the case where ***all*** the precipitate is chalk and carbonate of magnesia, which is but seldom the case.

$H - A$ = so much of the hardness lost by boiling as is produced by the precipitation of neutral earthy salts.

$(H - A) \times 1.36 = B$, that is, the above neutral earthy salts, calculated as dried sulphate of lime, in grains per gallon.

Collected and represented in a report thus:

Hardness of the water	Unboiled	
	Boiled	
Deposit by boiling, in grains, per gallon:		
Alkaline earthy salts, calculated as chalk............		A
Neutral earthy salts, calculated as dried sulphate of lime		B
	Total.............	$A+B$
Alkalinity of the water	Unboiled	
	Boiled	

When the alkalinity is only 1 or 2 degrees, it is not worth while boiling the water, as hardly any precipitation will take place.

If you cannot conveniently arrange so as to boil the water without loss of steam, I recommend that you boil it with as little loss as possible, and, when the water has cooled, that you make up the loss in weight of the vessel and its contents by adding distilled water. Mere boiling causes one change in the saline contents of the water. Boiling with evaporation causes an additional change.

I recommend that the alkalinity of a water be always stated by itself in a report, that is, not mixed up with the hardness; perhaps, indeed, it should be given in the Appendix to the Report, for persons not familiar with chemistry are apt to be puzzled about the alkalinity, whereas the degree of hardness and weight of deposit per gallon scarcely ever give them any difficulty. But the alkalinity should not be altogether omitted from the Report, as the statement of it is necessary for a comparison of the results obtained by different chemists.

It will be for others to decide whether the ascertaining of the quantity of the deposit that a water forms on boiling should or should not form a part of the chemical analysis serving to specify "its adaptation for domestic and manufacturing purposes," as required by the Commissioners of Woods and Forests. T. C.

Report on the Water Supply of the Town of Preston.

By Professor Crace Calvert.

To the Local Board of Health, Preston: Gentlemen—After several months of most careful and minute analysis, I have the honor to lay before you a report containing the results I have arrived at.

ANALYSIS

	Cowley Brook.	Loud scales.	North side of Longridge Hill.	Dutton Brook.	Service Reservoir.
Lime	0.473	4.446	1.534	0.952	3.251
Magnesia	0.186	0.561	0.195	0.286	0.730
Per oxide of iron	0.150	0.200	0.053	0.257	0.104
Sodium	0.627	0.554	0.419	0.530	0.595
Potassium	0.048	0.076	0.048	0.096	0.418
Sulphuric acid	0.300	0.798	0.601	0.587	2.055
Chlorine	0.721	0.642	0.556	0.706	1.222
Silica	0.850	0.400	0.426	0.481	1.200
Combined carbonic acid	0.514	3.942	1.190	0.913	1.648
Free carbonic acid	a trace	5.556	1.274	v.sm.quan	3.300
Nitric acid	none	none	none	none	0.329
Phosphates	......	......	......	......	} 0.200
Alumina	a trace	traces	......	none	

From the above results the following saline compounds are supposed to exist in the waters:

	Cowley Brook.	Loud-scales.	North side of Longridge Hill.	Dutton Brook.	Service Reservoir.
Sulphate of lime	0.210	0.385	0.374	0.126	3.520
Carbonate of lime	0.690	7.352	2.350	1.610	2.203
Chloride of calcium	none	0.380	0.128	none	0.501
Sulphate of magnesia	......	......	0.215	0.472	none
Carbonate of do	0.285	1.158	0.249	0.260	1.209
Chloride of magnesium	0.109	none	none	none	none
Sulphate of soda	none	0.887	0.339	0.205	......
Silicate of do	0.417	none	none	none	......
Chloride of sodium	1.125	0.660	0.781	1.163	1.500
Sulphate of potassa	0.344	0.159	0.105	0.190	none
Silicate of do	0.112	none	none	none	1.000
Carbonate of protoxide of iron	0.176	0.290	0.075	0.182	0.150
Creanate of do	none	none	none	0.743	none
Silica	0.510	0.400	0.426	0.481	0.170
Crenic acid	none	......	......	......	......
Silicate of lime	......	......	......	......	0.302
Nitrate of do	......	......	......	......	0.500
Silicate of magnesia	......	......	......	......	0.500
Phosphates and alumina	......	......	......	......	0.200
	3.987	11.761	5.042	5.432	11.755

	Cowley Brook.	Loud-scales.	North side of Longridge Hill.	Dutton Brook.	Service Resoir-voir.
Crenic acid substance......				.634	
Total fixed residue per gal.				4.798	
obtained by evaporation.	4.200	11.200	4.900	4.970	12.012
Organic matter per gallon.	1.400	1.400	1.400	0.941	4.550
Free carbonic acid in grains	trace	5.556	1.274	small qr	3.300

The water taken from *Cowley brook*, near the bridge, is the *purest* of the five that I have analysed: it has a beautiful appearance and an agreeable taste. It is one of the purest spring waters that has ever been analysed either in England or abroad, for (as you may observe) it contains only four grains of fixed saline matter per gallon. You will be more able to appreciate its high degree of purity when you are informed that chemists consider a water which contains from seven to nine grains per gallon of saline matter to be very good for domestic purposes. The water of the Thames contains twenty-one grains per gallon of fixed saline matter, and, that of the Seine 9.6 grains per gallon.

* * * * *

The five waters were submitted to Clark's process for appreciating their relative degrees of hardness, and the following results were obtained:

	Natural degrees per gallon.	*Boiled.*
Cowley Brook................	1.25	.........1.25
North side of Longridge Hill....	2.00	.........1.75
Dutton Brook................	1.50	.........1.25
Loudscales.................	12.00	.........2.00
Service-reservoir	4.40	.........4.15

ACTION OF THE WATERS ON LEAD.

The action of the five waters on lead piping has also drawn my attention. I cannot give a satisfactory explanation of the curious results I have obtained, as they are in contradiction to facts which I and other chemists have published; for the two purest waters, Cowley Brook and north side of Longridge Hill, act with extreme slowness on lead. In fact, samples of these waters, after having been left two months in contact with perfectly cleansed lead piping, contained only a very small amount of lead; whilst Dutton Brook, a water nearly as pure as the two above mentioned, contained a much larger amount. It is known that lead is rapidly attacked by pure waters, as rain or distilled waters, even when the latter has been boiled to expel any trace of air or carbonic acid it may contain. The action of the waters from Cowley Brook and Longridge Hill on lead piping cannot be ascribed to the presence of carbonic acid, as they only contain a usual proportion of that gas.

To settle this question, lead was put in contact with distilled water partly charged with carbonic acid; but although the lead was much less acted on than by another portion of the same water not containing this gas, still it contained more lead than samples of the waters from Cowley Brook and north side of Longridge Hill. Although the action of water on lead has drawn the attention of the most learned chemists, viz: Chevreul, Christason, Graham, &c., the subject is far from being exhausted. Dutton Brook, Service-reservoir water, and Loudscales water, have nearly the same action on lead; but although they act slowly, still they are much more active than the two first waters examined.

The following are the results I have obtained:—

1.—After twenty-four hours contact, none of the waters contained an appreciable quantity of lead.

2.—After three days' contact,

Cowley Brook, North side of Longridge Fell,	Traces.
Dutton Brook, Loudscales, Service-Reservoir,	Sufficient quantity of lead to assume a brown tinge with sulphuretted hydrogen.

3.—After two months contact,

Cowley Brook, North side of Longridge Fell,	Assume a brown color, with sulphuretted hydrogen.
Dutton Brook, Loudscales, Service-Reservoir,	Become quite brown and turbid from sulphuret of lead.

Report of the Consulting Physicians of the City of Boston in relation to the Action of Cochituate Water upon Mineral Substances.— With Documents Accompanying.

THE Board of Consulting Physicians of the City of Boston, having been desired to give an opinion as to the material of which pipes for conveying water from the mains into private houses should be composed, so far as the same may affect the purity of the water and the health of the citizens; have had the subject under careful consideration, and submit the following Report.

It is desirable that the materials of which the pipes of aqueducts are made, should be cheap, of competent strength and durability, easy of application, and free from the liability to communicate any noxious property to the water contained in them. It is to the last of these considerations that the Board of Physicians have devoted their attention, as falling within their particular province.

Of the various *organic* products which have been employed to convey water, *Wood* is the primitive material resorted to in most countries, until seperseded by more appropriate substances. *Leather* made into hollow trunks, or *hose*, is used on ship board, and in connection with fire engines. *India rubber* applied in the form of varnish to tubes made of fibrous textures, is employed in certain hydraulic machines. *Gutta percha*, a newly imported substance, has qualities which seem to render it suitable for the conveyance of water. The three first mentioned substances are considered unexceptionable on the score of safety, and to the last, no objection on the same ground is known to the undersigned.

Of brittle and inflexible mineral substances, *soap-stone* and *marble*, also *glass* and *burnt clay* glazed with siliceous earth, are not injurious to health.

Iron. Pipes and trunks made of cast iron are the most common material used for the conveyance of large bodies of water, and constitute the mains of the Cochituate aqueduct. Smaller pipes, both of cast and wrought iron, have been used for distribution in the interior of houses. The advantage of this metal over others, consists in its entire safety as far as health is concerned. Its disadvantages are, that it is somewhat difficult to adjust, and still more so to repair when broken or separated; also, that it is easy of oxidation, impairs the purity of the water, and in small pipes is liable to obstruction from the accumulation of its oxide. Nevertheless, in some situations, wrought iron pipes have been found to answer well for periods of five years and upwards.

It is proposed by Mr. Dexter to line the inside of iron pipes with charred wood, soap-stone, or other safe material, which may diminish or prevent the action of water upon the metal of the pipes. (See Appendix.)

A siliceous glazing, of a well-known appearance, has been for many years applied to the inside of culinary vessels of cast iron, to protect them from the action of water, and other chemical agents. These vessels are now manufactured by Messrs. Savery & Co., of Philadelphia. Experiments appear to be wanting to decide the fitness of this material.

Tin. Tubes made of pure tin are found to be acted on by water. A portion of Cochituate water which had stood two months in pipes made of block tin, exhibited abundant proofs of the presence of that metal. Tin appears to be less noxious than copper or lead, and the common use of vessels made of tinned iron, for various economical purposes, seems to afford evidence of its general safety. Tin pipes are flexible, fuseble, and easy of adjustment and repair.

Copper, in the form of some of its salts, is an active poison. In its metallic state, it is not very ready of solution in water, yet, according to Professor Horsford's experiments, it sensibly affects that of Cochituate Lake. Copper, exposed to the action of air and water, becomes coated with a carbonate, or oxide, which, in a great degree, protects it from farther action. Copper coins and bronze figures, which have been exposed to these agents for two thousand years, are found in good preservation. Copper pipes, thoroughly coated with tin, in the manner suggested by Mr. Hayes in his report, are considered by that gentleman as one of the most eligible materials, both as to durability and safety. From Professor Horsford's observations, it seems probable that the action of water, both upon copper and tin, diminishes gradually during use.

Lead pipes have been in use for the conveyance of water, from the time of the ancients to the present day. The cheapness of this metal, its ductility, flexibility, and the ease with which it is wrought, have caused it to be employed for service pipes more than all the other materials together. Leaden pipes are liable to be corroded by the water of certain wells and springs, and probably also by rain water. But in the water of open lakes and streams, which are comparatively free from saline ingredients, and which contain portions of organic matter, these pipes are durable for a long period. Lead, in aqueducts, has often been suspected of insalubrity, abandoned, re-placed with other materials, and again restored.

The Committee have devoted their especial attention to the subject of this metal, by examining the published authorities, by making extensive inquiries among practical men, and by engaging the attention of learned and able chemists in fresh investigations bearing on the particular case in question. Certain general facts, in regard to lead, seem at present to be admitted, by the common experience of the world. 1. That lead, received into the body, in certain quantities and for a certain time, is liable to produce some alarming complaints, among which are a species of colic, and a species of paralysis. 2. That most of the natural waters, which are introduced through pipes into the cities of this country, and probably of Europe, are capable, under certain circumstances, of dissolving lead. 3. That notwithstanding these general facts, a large portion of the population of Boston, Philadelphia, New York and London, have for years consumed the water introduced from various sources through leaden pipes, with apparent impunity.

In the hope of obtaining light on these seemingly discrepant facts, the undersigned have caused to be procured specimens of water from the respective aqueducts of the Schuylkill and Croton Rivers, and of Jamaica Pond and Cochituate Lake, which they have submitted to Augustus A. Hayes, Esq., of Lowell, and to Professor Horsford, of Harvard University, with a request that they would put to a suitable test the action of each of these waters upon metallic lead. From the reports of these gentlemen, which are subjoined in the Appendix to this document, it appears that each of these waters dissolves speedily a portion of the lead with which it is in contact. The partial exception of the Fairmount or Schuylkill water seems to be explained by the attendant circumstances.

But an interesting result deducible from Professor Horsford's experiments, is, that the solvent action of these natural waters upon a given surface of lead, diminishes from day to day, and at length wholly disappears. So that it is not improbable that a coating of an insoluble compound, perhaps arising from the action of organic matter upon oxide of lead, is gradually formed, which protects the metallic lead from the farther action of the water. These experiments may explain the cause why so many persons drink the water from leaden pipes without detriment, and why the waters from Jamaica Pond and other aqueducts have so often failed to furnish evidence of the presence of lead, when submitted to the test of chemical experiment.

In connection with the above explanation, it is proper to state, that the undersigned have procured numerous specimens of Jamaica Pond water, drawn from leaden pipes in various parts of the city, in many of which it had stood over night, and in one instance in a pipe one hundred feet long, for more than twenty-four hours. These specimens were submitted to the chemical examination of Professor Horsford, who reports that he finds no lead present in any of them, Dr. C. T. Jackson reports, "I have never found lead in the water of Jamaica Pond, which was drawn through lead pipe, though nearly all the well waters of this city, drawn through such pipes, are charged with lead." Other chemists have arrived at the same result, in regard to the water of Jamaica aqueduct.

In furtherance of their investigation, the undersigned have caused inquiries to be made in more than a hundred families, residing in Washington, Tremont, Pleasant, Warren, Essex, Harrison, Kneeland, Edingburg, Oxford, Beech, Tyler, Hudson, South, Sea, Purchase, Summer, Atkinson, Charles, Cambridge, North Russell, Lowell, and other streeets, who have used the water of Jamaica Pond drawn from leaden pipes, as common drink, for periods of from two to twenty years; and in no instance has any of the specific diseases attributable to lead, been remembered to have existed in these families.

It is by no means certain that minute quantities of lead, even when received into the human body, do occasion the injurious effects which result from larger quantities. In the ordinary conditions of civilized life, very few persons can hope to escape so receiving them. Lead is present in the paint of houses, and in that of buckets and other receptacles of water. It is contained in the solder of tin plate vessels, and in that of water pipes of various metals.

It is used to make tight the joints of iron mains in large aqueducts. It helps to form the cheap pewter of which spoons, plates, and other culinary vessels are made. It is present in the glazing of the coarsest pottery, and in the finest flint glass. It affords the lining of tea chests, and often the coloring material of wafers and other common substances. It is carried through life in the bodies of wounded soldiers, and is applied in various forms by surgeons and physicians, to recent wounds and absorbing surfaces. It is also administered internally as a medicine. The continual liability to mechanical attrition or chemical solution which exists in these cases, while it goes far to establish the inactivity of lead in certain minute quantities, should nevertheless put the community on their guard against the reception of larger quantities, through carelessness, of this and of other metals deleterious to health.

In conclusion, the Board of Consulting Physicians beg leave to express, as the opinion derived from the present state of their knowledge on the subject,

1. That pipes, made of cast or wrought iron, may be safely used for the transmission of water, as far as health is concerned.

2. That copper pipes, effectually tinned throughout by reliable workmen, are a safe material for the contemplated transmission of water to dwelling houses in Boston, so long as the internal coating keeps in repair.

3. That although leaden pipes, in certain waters, and under certain circumstances, are known to communicate a highly deleterious quality to their contents, yet in the open waters, from which the large cities, already named, have been supplied through such pipes, no practical evil of a general nature is known to this Board to have resulted from their employment.

4. That when individuals may prefer not to employ, for purposes of food, water which has passed through leaden pipes, they may introduce it into a lower reservoir through pipes of iron, or other safe material, and conduct it from thence for other purposes to different parts of the house, through lead tubes properly guarded by stopcocks, valves, or other mechanism.

The Board of Consulting Physicians feel furthermore bound to state, that an imperfection necessarily exists in the experience hitherto had upon this important subject, owing to the difference in samples of metal upon which observations have been obtained, and possibly from the different quality of the same waters in different seasons of the year.

Their investigations, also, have brought them to the belief, that notwithstanding the attention which has been paid to the action of water upon certain metals, in different parts of the world, yet the subject is by no means satisfactorily understood. And they trust that more light may be shed upon it, after the conclusion of a course of observations and experiments now in process of being made by Professor Horsford, of the University.

JOHN C. WARREN,
GEO. C. SHATTUCK,
JACOB BIGELOW,
GEO. HAYWARD,
JOHN WARE.

Boston, April 3d, 1848.

APPENDIX.

No. I.—Mr. DEXTER'S LETTER.

Boston, Nov. 12, 1847.

Dear Sir :—In reply to your request, that I would give my opinion as to the best material for conducting water into dwelling-houses, I say that I know of nothing so good as Iron.

It is wholesome, strong, easily obtained, and readily adapted to the purpose. It is however practically inconvenient for service pipes. The action of the water causes rust, and a deposit is formed on the iron which gradually closes the pipe, particularly in service pipes, where the water remains for a length of time undisturbed.

To prevent this inconvenience of rust and foreign deposit, a thin lining or coating of charred wood can be introduced into the pipe, and these secured by hydraulic cement, poured, when liquid, between the iron and wood. The cement indurates, and prevents any action of the water on the iron. The charring of the wood prevents any taste being communicated to the water, and also decay is prevented.

* * * * *

I remain, respectfully and truly yours,

G. M. DEXTER.

No. III.—Dr. A. E. HOSACK'S LETTER.

—

New York, Nov. 16th, 1847.

My Dear Sir:—Since the receipt of your favor of the 11th inst., requesting information respecting the use of lead pipe to convey the Croton water into dwelling-houses in our city, I have made particular inquiry of several of our leading practitioners of medicine, as well as of the agents at the Croton water office, and principal plumbers connected with the same, and also of Dr. Chilton, for instances of the poisonous effects of lead from using the Croton water drawn from leaden tubes. They all, with the exception of Dr. Chilton, assert that they had never heard of any complaints, nor have they ever heard of a single instance of the effects of lead from the use of the Croton water. Dr. Chilton informs me, however, that he had been called upon to analyze water taken from leaden pipes in a house in New York, (which had been closed for some time previous), where several persons had been made seriously ill from drinking the same water, and that he had detected the presence of lead in it. He also states that it is his opinion that the effect of lead from drinking of Croton water under such circumstances, is of frequent occurrence, but not recognized as such by the physicians, or rather not attributed by them to the true cause. Dr. Chilton, is, as you are doubtless aware, one of our best chemists, and in whom the public have the most unbounded confidence. I enclose you a circular of Mr. Ewbank. upon which, (as it speaks for itself,) I will not trouble you with any comments further than to say that lead pipes are generally in use throughout the city; while those lined and coated with tin are but seldom employed. If you wish any further particulars or certificates from Plumbers, or the head of the Croton water department, I will be most happy to obtain them for you.

Your friend,

ALEX. E. HOSACK.

No. IV.—Dr. GRISCOM'S LETTER.

—

New York, Dec. 14, 1847.

Prof. Webster; Dear Friend :

* * * * *

My own opinion is very decided as to the non-injuriousness of lead pipe as a means of conveying water. I was an attentive listener to the testimony given on this subject some years ago, at a trial in this city, in reference to a patent for tinning pipe ; and as far as my recollection serves me, nothing was elicited on that occasion at all convincing that any injurious effects had ever been observed from drinking water that had passed through tubes of pure lead. And it is fair to presume that on such an occasion, when the *utility* of the patent was one of the points in dispute, if any thing could be adduced to prove its necessity, it would have had all possible weight given it. But nothing satisfactory, so far as *facts* went, was discovered.

* * * * *

To render assurance doubly sure, with regard to the medical experience of this city, I last week laid the subject of your letter before the academy of medicine, the largest professional body we have. At the meeting were several of our oldest and best practitioners. I requested if any gentleman had ever known or heard of any evil results from the use of lead pipe, he would oblige both you and me by communicating the facts. No intimation of such results was offered, as would have been, had any ever been noticed. A negative has been the invariable answer also, from several of our acutest practitioners with whom I have personally conferred.

I have also made inquiries at two of our largest plumbing establishments, as to the popular sentiment on the subject, and the relative amount of tinned and untinned lead pipe called for in their orders. The answer is the same from both ; no tin pipe at all is used. In one establishment the opinion was given that the tinning was detrimental to the strength of the lead ; that under undue pressure, the pure lead tube will yield a little, but the tin lining, under the same circumstances, will crack and cause the lead to split also, without the expansion. I am unable to say what value there may be in this idea.

From its less flexible character, block tin, which was for a while employed to a small extent as a material for water pipe, has been, I believe, wholly discarded.

Nothing but lead pipe is now used in this city "for the conveyance of water into and within the residences of the citizens."

With great respect, I am very truly,

JNO. H. GRISCOM.

P. S. There has been frequently observed in pipe which has been removed after use, an internal coating of brown color, which is doubtless the vegetable matter suspended in the Croton, and which is deposited when the water is at rest, and forms a slightly adherent layer. This interposed between the water and lead would prevent any action of the two upon each other; but before it could occur, the deleterious effects of the leaded water ought, if ever, to be exhibited.

No. V.—Dr. WEBSTER'S LETTER.

Laboratory of the Massachusetts Medical College,
Boston, December 15th, 1847.

George C. Shattuck, M.D.—Dear Sir.—I have now the honor fo communicating to you the results of the examination of the water received from you, contained in a stone ware flask and marked "Cochituate water." The water was quite free from any turbid appearance, and agreeable to the taste.

As you requested me to direct my attention particularly to its action, if any, upon lead, my experiments have been confined to that point.

A piece of new lead pipe was procured, such as is usually employed for the conveyance of water, and such as will be most probably used should the water be distributed in pipes of that material. Should such pipe be used, it will be in contact with solder and the alloy of which the cocks for delivering water are usually made; I therefore deemed it important, to place the water in contact with those materials. Eighteen inches of lead pipe were therefore soldered to one of the common brass cocks (so called). This was filled with the water, and placed in a situation, and under the same exposure to light and air, as a pipe of this kind would be ordinarily. After the lapse of eight days the water was taken from the pipe and tested for lead by hydrosulphuric acid. The change of color indicated the presence of that metal.

* * * * *

Another portion of the lead pipe was placed in a large jar of the water, covered slightly with a paper, so that the air could have free admission. At the line where the air and water meet, there has been formed a continuous ring of carbonate of protoxide of lead.

From these results, although the quantity of lead which would be taken up by the water with its present constitution, is quite small, I should consider the constant daily use of it if drawn from leaden pipes dangerous. The water is remarkably pure, and, if we are to rely upon high chemical authorities, this increases the probability of its becoming the more impregnated with lead when in contact with extensive surfaces of that metal.

Attempts have been made to protect lead from the action of water by tinning, but I am inclined to think the process has not as yet been brought to that state of perfection which will insure a perfect and continuous coating of tin on the inner surface of lead pipe.

The objections to copper pipes I need not mention. In my opinion iron pipes, and if practicable even tinned, especially in the inside, are to be preferred. They would be still better if glazed on the inside like the iron culinary vessels now so much employed. This glazing resists even strong acids.

A certain degree of flexibility is desirable in the material; if with this we can have resistance to the action of the water and such a state of adhesion of the particles as will not be injuriously affected by heat and cold, we shall have the best material for interior water pipes.

A material with these good qualities, I am encouraged to think, from experiments in which I am engaged, will be found.

With great respect, I am, my dear sir, yours truly,

J. W. WEBSTER.

No. VI.—Dr. HAYES' LETTER.

—

Lowell, Jan. 6th, 1848.

John C. Warren, M. D.,
Chairman of Board of Consulting Physicians, &c.

Dear Sir: Your note, asking the expression of an opinion, "as to the best material for conducting water into private houses, with a view to its effects on the purity of the water," is received, and it is with pleasure that I reply.

* * * * *

It has been supposed, from imperfect experiments, that waters containing certain small portions of salts, do not act on lead. Some years have passed since the opinion, favoring such a conclusion, was published. The lapse of that time has permitted the accumulation of facts and observations, which, placing the fallacy of such an opinion beyond doubt, have established the conclusion, that, *all natural waters act on lead chemically, under the varying states of atmospheric changes.* Lead, as a material for pipes, cannot be safely used for conducting water, which is to be used for domestic purposes. The water, from the source of supply, for the city of Boston, has, in a high degree, the power of destroying lead pipes; and even salts, in a crystalized form, have been observed to result from this action.

* * * * *

The daily use of water from such pipes for ten years, in addition to observations made in the laboratory, lead me to prefer pipes made by combining pure tin with the surface of copper, for all situations where small pipes are required. They are, even when quite thin, strong enough to resist ordinary pressure; are easily bent and united together. The cost of such pipes, for the volume of water delivered, is less than the cost of lead pipes—their durability much greater.

In expressing an opinion on a subject of so great importance, I have thought proper to briefly allude to the points which have led to the conclusions formed, making a lengthy reply, without entering into details.

With high respect,

A. A. HAYES.

No. VII.—Dr. HAYES' REPORT.

Observations on the action of some Lake and River Waters on Leaden Pipes, containing them.

The samples of water, four in number, were marked Jamaica Pond, Cochituate Lake, Croton River and Fairmount. Excepting the last, they were clear, without being perfectly transparent; slightly tinted by a yellowish brown color. At the temperature of 42 degrees F., they were destitute of odor.

By preserving the samples at from .36 to 40 degrees, F., any tendency to decomposition was prevented during the time of the observations.

Two kinds of lead pipes are found in commerce; the one made by the "patent" process, in which heated lead is forced through dies, has its surfaces imperfectly coated with tin. The other, cold drawn from thick tube, in general chemical use, better resists corrosion.

* * * * *

(A) Twelve tubes, after being carefully cleaned, were filled with water from Cochituate Lake, and exposed to the temperature of 45 degrees Fahrenheit. Twelve hours after, portions three inches from the surface were withdrawn and tested. In all of the samples lead was found. Portions from nine inches below, gave nearly the same indications. Twenty-four hours after, the quantity of lead dissolved was increased, and a sediment was found in each tube, composed in part of oxide of lead.

(B) The tubes had been carefully washed and filled with water from Croton river; a repetition of the observations gave nearly the same indications as were obtained with the Cochituate water.

(C) Returning to the water of Cochituate Lake, the same general indications were found. There were some slight differences observed between the samples of leaden pipes and the time; for the same amount of action varied among them, and was not constant for any one sample. An elevation of temperature accelerated the solution of the lead.

(D) On substituting Croton river water, the first observations gave only slight indications of lead, but after the lapse of twenty-four hours, all the tubes contained solutions of lead.

(E) Jamaica pond water was next used in the clean tubes; the indications corresponded with those of the Croton river; a repetition confirmed them.

(F) The Fairmount water exhibited in the trials no considerable action on the pipes after some days. Pipes which had contained it, unless carefully cleansed, were not readily acted on by the other waters following. A slight inspection was sufficient to show that the sample was not in its natural state. Besides the organic matter having taken the form of flocks and filaments, there was a perceptible odor resembling that of alcohol.

(G) Observations with the pipes closed, gave positive evidence of the rapid solution of the lead, and there was always an absorption of the air over the water, to the extent of one-fourth, or one-fifth of its bulk. The experiments on the water at different levels, did not show any special disposition to corrode in distinct portions of the column, and there were just such indications as would result from testing any solution in the act of taking metal. After the lapse of a certain time, in all cases, a cessation of action took place, matter was deposited which contained lead, and a saturnine solution in clear water remained.

The *quantity* of metal dissolved and suspended was several times obtained. Metallic lead, in a globule as lârge as an ordinary pinhead, was obtained from one quart of Cochituate water, after twenty-four hours' exposure, as a mean result.

(I) The observations with clean, tinned copper pipes, gave only negative results. By every mode of aiding action which suggested itself, these tubes were exposed, and neither the odor, taste, nor composition of the water was affected. I have observed the same resistance to the agency of various waters, for the lapse of ten years, and consider the last observations, like the first, as a demonstration, that natural waters do not act on, or corrode, the compound metal forming the surface of such pipes.

The general results obtained, show that the corrosive action of the waters of Cochituate Lake, Jamaica Pond, and Croton River, is not prevented by the low temperature of 45 degrees F., or the temperature of ordinary wells. At the higher temperature of 75 degrees F., the action is more rapidly produced, and the water contains both soluble and slightly soluble compounds of lead.

Presence of air has also a marked influence: the air being excluded until a portion of water had become contaminated with lead salts, its admission caused a rapid increase in the quantity of slightly soluble lead salts.

* * * * *

In acting on leaden surfaces, the dissolved oxygen in the water assists in preparing the metal for solution. Air, if present, is absorbed; the continued corrosion of the metal goes on until the solvent power of the water is exhausted. Some of the compounds are deposited, others remain disssolved.

In the actual state of a system of leaden pipes for distribution, the longest time we can assume, is that which would apply to the portions of pipe connected with the mains, and any pipe thus situated would poison the water flowing. If other pipes were used for delivering the water into cisterns placed within dwellings, the farther distribution for all, excepting culinary purposes, might be effected by leaden pipes.

* * * * *

With the highest respect,

AUGUSTUS A. HAYES, M. D.,

State Assayer.

No. XI.—MR. JERVIS'S LETTER.

New York, April 22, 1848.

To the Board of Water Commissioners of the City of Boston.

Gentlemen: I called on Mr. Chilton, (Chemist,) who early enlisted as the advocate of *tinned* lead pipe, regarding the pure lead as dangerous to health. I inquired if he knew of any cases, in this city, of lead poisoning? He replied that persons had complained to him of being affected by the use of watar in lead pipe in this city; or rather, he had attributed to the use of water from lead pipe the effect complained of. On more close inquiry, he said he could not say that such complaints were produced by the use of water from lead pipes, but that they were similar to what would be produced by such cause. He uses the water from an iron pipe. He further stated, there was no doubt that lead was taken up by pure water, and that cases had occurred, where the use of water drawn through lead pipes had been very injurious to health. At the same time, he did not think any perceptible injury would be experienced from the use in passing the short pipe required to lead the water from the street into the dwellings, or such detention as would be likely to occur during the day, in the use by ordinary families using the water from pressure, taking the precaution to let the water run from the pipes after standing over night, or any considerable time.

A trial in the U. S. Courts, as to patent of tinning lead pipe, in this city, was had. On this trial, Prof. Renwick was called as a witness, and testified decidedly as to the injury of unprotected lead on water, and the necessity of protecting by tinning the lead; that he would not, on any account, use lead pipe without tinning. On cross-examination: Do you use Croton water? Yes. Ever experience any injury? None whatever. What pipe is used? I presume tinned lead. The plumber who put in the pipe was then called, and testified that the pipe laid was all common lead pipe.

On the same trial, Doctor Lee was called, who testified strongly as to the deleterious effect of lead pipe, that he would not have the water brought into his house, because his landlord refused to put in tinned pipe, and he therefore got his water in the street, from a free hydrant, where he said no lead was used. On cross-examination: Have you experienced any ill effect from using the Croton water from the street hydrant? No. The plumber who put in this hydrant was called, and testified that the pipe used for the hydrant was *pure lead.*

Thus much for learned opinions. I called on Mr. Coffin, who for about five years has been President of the Water Board, and who has been in constant intercourse with water takers. By the mode of doing this business, the application for tapping the pipe is required to be accompanied by the name of the plumber who is to do the work; and this brings the plumbers in frequent contact with the President of the Board. At his office much discussion takes place as to all matters relating to water, and the manner of introducing it into houses; and any complaint as to the injury of lead, would most probably be known to him. Mr. Coffin says he does not recollect to have heard of any complaint that lead pipe had injured any person; and expresses, in most unqualified terms, his belief, that not one well-attested case of injury has occurred in this city from the use of lead pipe.

I have observed, with much care, the effect of lead pipe in use in my own family; and more especially, as I had from experience known the ill effect of lead on water drawn from a well, some 200 feet; and was much in favor of tinned pipe. From experience I was able to detect the taste of lead, where the water was used some three years, without any apparent injury to the family, who used the precaution of drawing off when it had been allowed to stand any considerable time in the pipe. My observation has led to the conclusion, that with the precaution of running off the water that has stood through the night, or for any considerable time in the pipe, no practical effect, of an injurious nature, will be experienced from the use of lead.

The assertion, "that numerous cases of lead poisoning had occurred" in this city, is believed to be without any well-attested facts to sustain it. Some one must have made a large draft on fancy, to give color to it. One thing is obvious, that in this city, where there was at one time an active discussion on the injurious effects of lead pipe, the subject has become entirely quiet, and the question seems not the least agitated.

Respectfully, your obedient servant,

JOHN B. JERVIS,

Consulting Engineer Boston Water Works

Service Pipes for Water: an Investigation made at the suggestion of the Board of Consulting Physicians of Boston.

By E. N. Horsford,

Rumford Professor in the University at Cambridge.

As pipes of lead have been long in use, and possess in an eminent degree most of the properties required for aqueduct service, and as the following research has been more especially directed to ascertain the true value of leaden pipes for the distribution of water, a brief historical sketch of the opinions that have been entertained with regard to the safety of employing them may not be without interest.

The period of the first employment of lead for transmitting water is unknown; but the circumstance that it was condemned by Vitruvius, a Roman architect believed to have lived about nineteen hundred years ago, is evidence of its having at that time been long enough in use to furnish experience as the basis of its rejection as a material for aqueducts. Galen, a physician of Amsterdam, who wrote in the seventeenth century, coincided with Vitruvius. Both had observed the formation of white lead in water-pipes, and attributed to it the illness which was known to affect those who drank certain waters served through leaden pipes. Notwithstanding these strongly expressed opinions and occasional fatal consequences from drinking water containing lead in solution, public sentiment continued strongly in favor of this kind of pipes, and until about the commencement of the present century no experimental examination of the subject had been undertaken. Dr. Lamb of England, and later Guyton Morveau of France, devoted their attention for a time to this inquiry. Their opinions are evidence of what must attend the earlier labors in every field of investigation. The one believed that most, if not all, spring waters possess the property of acting upon lead to such an extent as to render their conveyance through leaden tubes unsafe, and this *because of the salts in solution*; the other, that many natural waters scarcely act on lead at all, and *because of the salts in solution*. The former believed that rain or snow water (eminently pure) does not corrode lead; the latter, that distilled water, the purest of all waters, acts rapidly on it. Dr. Thompson, of Glasgow, subsequently gave some consideration to the subject, and came to the conclusion that, though Dr. Lamb's general proposition was true, the lead was not *dissolved*, but *suspended merely*.

Such was the doubt upon this point, the insolubility of oxide of lead, that a scientific association in Germany made it a prize problem. The honor of deciding the question was accredited to Brendecke, whose views were coincided in by his unsuccessful competitor, Siebold, and also by Herberger, who prepared his oxide of lead in a different manner, and reported his results at a later period. They decided that *oxide of lead is insoluble* in water.

The imperfection of the investigation and the injustice of this award have since been established by the labors of Yorke and Bonsdorff, who have found that aerated, distilled water, deprived of carbonic acid, oxidates metallic lead and dissolves the oxide in the proportion of from 1-7000th to 1-12000th. Even the acute Scheele had remarked the same fact in the last century. Philips denied the accuracy of the conclusions of both Yorke and Bonsdorff, and maintained, with Thompson, that the oxide of lead was not soluble, but was only in suspension. His view was supported by the fact, that filtration seemed to separate the lead from the water that originally contained it. In 1846 Yorke* reviewed the investigation of Philips, and showed that, in the process of filtration, the oxide of lead enters into combination with the woody fiber of the filtering paper. By filtering for some time through the same paper it became saturated, and the lead in solution passed without detention.

Christison, to whom we are indebted for a careful record of the principal conflicting opinions upon this subject, repeated and extended the experiments of Guyton Morveau, to ascertain the effect of solutions of certain salts in water. He came to the conclusion that arseniates, phosphates, sulphates, tartrates, and even chlorides, acetates and nitrates, possess the power of protecting lead from the action of the water. Of the nature of this protecting power he acknowledges that he has no clear conception. He assured himself that it does not in all cases arise from the formation of an insoluble coat consisting of the acid of the employed salt united to the oxide of lead, by finding that the coat, which for the most part, in his experiments, consisted of carbonate of lead, readily dissolved in acetic acid. This author has suggested that leaden pipes, before being laid down for service, should be exposed a length of time to solutions of some of the salts, denominated *protecting*, since he had observed that leaden pipes, which poisoned certain waters when first served, after a time became coated, and passed the same waters without injury to the health of those who drank them.

The city of London has long been supplied with water distributed through lead, and though occasional excitements upon this subject have sprung up in Great Britain from individual cases of poisoning,

* *Phil. Mag.*, xxviii., pp. 17–20.

the prevailing public sentiment is in favor of lead. Professor Graham states that in London lead only is used for service pipes.

The exemption of Paris from illness derived from this cause is asserted by Tanquerel. This is believed to be true of all the larger European towns whose inhabitants are supplied with water from public reservoirs. On the other hand, the inhabitants of Amsterdam were poisoned by drinking rain water that had fallen on leaden roofs. Upon replacing the lead with tiles, the maladies ascribed to the former disappeared.

We find ourselves at the conclusion of the literature of the Old World upon this subject with these impressions:

1st. That some natural waters may be served from leaden pipes without detriment to health.

2d. That others may not; and

3d. That we have no method of determining beforehand whether a given water may or may not be transmitted safely through lead.

Professor Silliman, Jr., in his able report on the various waters submitted to him by the Water Commissioners, in 1845, has given the results of some experiments upon the action of several waters on lead, which conducted him to the general conclusions above expressed. Among those who have taken strong ground against leaden service pipes for the transmission of water may be mentioned Drs. Chilton and Lee, of New York, and Drs. Dana and Hayes, of Lowell.

The inquiry that early presented itself to the Board of Consulting Physicians was the following:—*Will there be greater liability to lead disease from drinking Cochituate water served through iron mains and leaden pipes, than there is now from drinking Fairmount or Croton waters similarly served, or Jamaica water possibly less favorably served than Cochituate water will be?*

To answer this question, Croton, Fairmount, Jamaica and Cochituate waters were provided with care, and the proposition made, that lead should be presented to them all under similar circumstances.

* * * * *

Such experiments have been made with all the waters above mentioned, and at the same time, in many cases, parallel suites with Albany and Troy reservoir waters, Cambridge well water, and distilled water, contemplating all the conditions that could be expected to occur.

* * * * *

With the exception of Cochituate water, which possessed a yellowish brown tint, the samples were colorless.

A determination of their general relations to each other was made.

* * * * *

The results may be expressed in tabular form as follows:

TABLE I.

	Residue	Loss upon being Ignited	Inorganic Matter	Insoluble after Ignition
	gr.	gr.	gr.	gr.
Distilled water	0.0000	0.0000	0.0000	0.0000
Albany "	0.0924	0.0198	0.0726	....
Cambridge "	0.3918	0.0990	0.2928	0.0676
Cambridge water that acts on lead	0.1380	0.0540	0.0840	....
Cochituate water....	0.0267	0.0122	0.0145	0.0050
" "	0.0267	....	....	....
Croton "	0.2175	0.1496	0.0679	....
Fairmount "	0.3007	0.1032	0.1975	0.0239
Jamaica "	0.0268	0.0115	0.0153	0.0070
Troy "	0.0593	0.0181	0.0412	0.0278

The following tables of results will sufficiently explain themselves. They exhibit quantities of lead which, for practical purposes, have little more than relative value in the columns in which they occur.

The experiments were made with bars of lead cast in a common mould, of uniform diameter and length. The quantities of water were constant, or as nearly so as might be, in the same series of experiments. The bars were covered, in test tubes of a given diameter, with fifteen cubic centimetres.

After exposure out of direct sunlight, except where otherwise stated, a length of time indicated in the column of days at the left, a suite of similar tubes was filled to the requisite depth with corresponding waters, and the bars transferred with the least delay.

The waters were then acidulated with acetic acid, received each a drop of acetate of potassa, which Fresenius has observed decomposes all lead salts not decomposed by hydrosulphuric acid, and exposed to a stream of washed hydrosulphuric acid till the liquid became clear, if it had been at first discolored by the precipitate of lead.

If concentration occurred, it is so stated. The quantities were estimated by a method to be described farther on.

Table II.

EXPERIMENTS WITH LEAD TO ASCERTAIN THE ACTION OF WATER ON SUCCESSIVE DAYS.

One bar resting on the bottom of each test tube. Waters replaced at the date of each result.

Days	Cochituate	Croton	Fairmount	Jamaica
1	5.000	2.000	7.000	10.000
3	0.500	0.500	0.000	10.000
4	1.000	0.500	2.000	0.000
5	10.000	2.000	5.000	1.000
6	0.100	0.100	0.100	0.500
7	0.100	0.100	0.100	0.100
8	0.200	0.200	0.200	3.000
11	0.100	0.100	0.100	1.000
12	0.100	0.100	0.200	0.500
13	0.000	0.000	0.100	0.500

The first modification of the experiment was in the extent of surface of lead.

Table III.

EXPERIMENTS WITH TWO BARS OF LEAD.

In all other respects the conditions were the same as in the foregoing experiments.

Days	Cochituate	Croton	Fairmount	Jamaica
1	5.000	5.000	1.000	10.000
3	3.000	2.000	1.000	2.000
4	0.500	0.500	1.000	0.000
5	0.100	0.100	0.100	0.100
6	0.100	0.100	0.100	0.010
7	0 100	0.100	0.010	0.200
8	0.100	0.100	0.010	3.000
11	0.100	0.100	0.100	1.000
12	0.100	0.200	0.100	5.000
13	0.100	0.200	0.200	5.000

TABLE IV.

EXPERIMENTS WITH THREE BARS.

Other conditions same as before

Days	Cochituate	Croton	Fairmount	Jamaica
1	1.000	0.500	0.500	10.000
3	10.000	2.000	1.000	4.000
4	5.000	0.500	3.000	40.000
5	0.000	0.500	1.000	15.000
6	1.000	0.200	0.100	10.000
7	0.500	0.100	0.100	8.000
8	0.100	0.100	0.100	4.000
11	0.100	0.200	0.200	2.000
12	0.100	0.100	0.100	5.000
13	0.100	0.200	0.100	3.000

From the foregoing experiments it was deducible,—

1st. That the action upon lead was most energetic during the first few days of exposure.

2d. That the differences between the action on one, two, and three bars, the volume of water remaining the same, being inconsiderable, the action could not be dependant upon the *surface* of lead exposed, but upon some other constant condition.

The observation, that, where the bar touched the containing tube, the action seemed most vigorous, suggested an explanation of the want of uniformity in results. It further suggested experiments with *suspended bars*, the results of which are detailed in the following table.

Table V.

EXPERIMENTS WITH BARS SUSPENDED OUT OF CONTACT WITH THE CONTAINING VESSEL.

Waters not exposed to sunlight. Average results of four series of experiments. One bar to each tube. No concentration.

Days	Cochituate	Croton	Fairmount	Jamaica
1	15.500	1.500	0.280	80.000
2	0.012	0.012	0.012	2.750
3	0.012	0.001	0.000	0.027
4	0.000	0.000	0.000	0.000

These experiments and the foregoing seemed to show that, without contact of the solid metal with the containing vessel, the influence of the "constant condition" was so far enfeebled, after the first few days, as not to have its effects recognized by the ordinary reagents, without concentration, after a period of twenty-four hours' exposure. The following table of results confirms this deduction.

Table VI.

EXPERIMENTS WITH WATER SEVERAL WEEKS EXPOSED TO LIGHT AND THE WARMTH OF THE APARTMENT IN WHICH THE EXPERIMENTS WERE MADE, BY WHICH MUCH OF THE CONTAINED AIR HAD BEEN EXPELLED.

Bars suspended out of contact with the tube. Volume as in the preceding experiments.

Days	Cochituate	Croton	Fairmount	Jamaica	Distilled Water
1	1.000	0.500	0.000	0.050	25.000
3	0.050	0.010	0.000	2.000	15.000
5	0.010	0.000	0.000	0.050	15.000
7	0.000	0.000	0.000	0.000	15.000
9	0.000	0.000	0.000	0.000	15.000
12	0.000	0.000	0.000	0.000	15.000
17	0.020	0.010	0.000	0.000	30.000
24	0.050	0.000	0.000	0.000	0.500
39	0.500	0.000	0.100	0.100	3.000

As the street mains are of iron, it was desirable to know if the contact of lead with iron could be more injurious to Cochituate than to Croton, Fairmount, or Jamaica water. Experiments were also made with Albany and Troy reservoir waters, and the Cambridge well-water first in the order of succession in Table I.

Table VII.

EXPERIMENTS WITH LEAD AND IRON.

Iron uppermost. Lead solder. Volume of water the same as in previous experiments.

Days	Distilled Water	Albany	Cambridge	Cochituate	Croton	Fairmount	Jamaica	Troy
3	8.000	1.000	2.000	1.000	1.000	10.000	10.000	25.000
7	10.000	0.010	0.010	0.010	0.010	0.010	0.500	0.000
9	2.000	0.000	0.000	0.000	0.000	0.000	0.000	0.000
11	0.000	0.000	0.000	0.000	0.000	0.000	0.000	0.000
20	0.000	0.100	0.000	0.100	0.000	0.000	0.100	0.000
30	1.000	0.400	0.500	0.800	0.500	0.500	0.500	0.100
48	0.100	0.005	0.100	0.010	0.050	0.000	0.010	Lost.

Discoloration of the bars of lead was least in this order: Albany, Cambridge, Croton, Fairmount, Distilled Water, Jamaica, Cochituate. That is, Cochituate, apparently, most promptly and completely coats the lead.

Table VIII.

EXPERIMENTS WITH LEAD AND IRON.

Lead uppermost. Lead solder. Volume of water same as in previous experiment.

Days	Distilled Water	Albany	Cambridge	Cochituate	Croton	Fairm'nt	Jamaica	Troy
2	0.500	0.500	0.500	0.500	0.500	0.500	0.500	0.500
3	0.000	0.000	0.000	0.000	0.000	0.000	0.000	0.000
7	0.000	0.000	0.000	0.000	0.000	0.000	0.000	0.000
16	0.010	0.010	0.100	0.010	0.010	0.010	0.010	0.010
26	0.500	0.100	0.010	0.010	0.010	0.010	0.010	0.010
44	3.000	0.050	0.100	0.100	0.100	0.100	0.100	Lost

Sections of each bar at first less coated near the iron. Larger measure of protoxide of iron in Cochituate and Croton waters than in the others, as indicated by ferrocyanide of potassium. Discoloration of the bars least in this order: Fairmount, Distilled Water, Albany, Troy, Croton, Jamaica, Cochituate.

Table IX.

EXPERIMENTS WITH LEAD AND IRON.

Soft solder. Volume and other conditions as in previous experiments.

Days	Distilled Water	Albany	Cambridge	Cochituate	Croton	Fairm'nt	Jamaica	Troy
3	10.000	6.000	6.000	6.000	1.000	10.000	7.000	7.000
12	....	1.000	Lost	1.000	1.000	1.000	1.000	2.000
17	30.000	0.000	0.050	0.010	0.500	0.000	0.500	0.000

As the stopcocks will, many of them, be of brass, it was important to ascertain the influence of this connection.

TABLE X.

EXPERIMENTS WITH LEAD AND BRASS.

Surfaces of lead and brass nearly equal. Volume of water as before mentioned.

Days	Distilled Water	Albany	Cambridge	Cochituate	Croton	Fairm'nt	Jamaica	Troy
1	5.000	2.000	0.500	0.800	25.000	0.100	1.000	5.000
3	8.000	2.000	1.500	1.500	2.000	1.500	1.500	8.000
7	20.000	0.800	10.000	10.000	2.000	1.500	20.000	7.000
33	10.000	0.100	7.000	0.200	0.100	0.100	4.000	7.000
37	20.000	0.800	10.000	2.000	10.000	1.000	8.000	5.000
38	12.000	—	—	0.800	0.800	—	0.400	—
39	2.000	—	—	0.800	0.300	—	0.400	—
40	1.250	—	—	0.400	0.600	—	0.800	—
41	1.500	—	—	—	0.250	—	0.800	—
43	2.000	—	—	1.200	0.500	—	0.800	—

As some stopcocks may be of copper, a suite of experiments was made to ascertain the effect of this union.

TABLE XI.

EXPERIMENTS WITH LEAD AND COPPER.

A bar of lead and copper nail three fourths of an inch long. Lead solder.

Days	Distilled Water	Cochituate	Croton	Fairmount
1	5.000	0.500	0.500	0.100
3	1.500	8.000	0.150	0.500
7	20.000	2.500	1.000	1.000
14	25.000	7.000	1.000	1.000
39	10.000	1.000	1.000	1.000
40	1.500	1.000	1.000	0.250
44	1.200	0.500	0.500	1.500
45	2.000	0.200	0.300	2.000
46	5.000	0.800	0.800	3.000
47	3.000	0.050	0.020	1.500
49	2.300	0.010	0.800	2.000

The effect of the contact of lead with tin, all the external circumstances being the same, is exhibited in the following table.

Table XII.

EXPERIMENTS WITH LEAD AND TIN.

A half-bar of each soldered without alloy. Volume of water as before mentioned.

Days	Distilled Water	Albany	Cambridge	Cochituate	Croton	Fairmount	Jamaica	Troy
1	40.000	0.500	0.500	0.500	0.500	0.500	0.500	0.500
8	60.000	0.100	0.100	0.100	0.200	0.500	0.800	0.500
32	50.000	1.500	4.000	0.500	0.100	1.500	2.000	—
36	12.000	—	—	0.050	0.050	—	1.500	—
38	1.500	—	—	0.500	1.500	—	3.000	—
39	2.000	—	—	0.500	0.300	—	0.400	—
40	0.500	—	—	0.500	0.500	—	0.700	—
41	2.000	—	—	0.010	0.010	—	0.010	—
43	3.000	—	—	0.010	0.020	—	0.700	—

Variations in some of the properties of the Cochituate water might be expected to take place. First, *in the percentage of organic matter*. Second, *in temperature*. Third, *in percentage of salts*.

The effect of increasing the percentage of organic matter is exhibited in the following table.

Table XIII.

EXPERIMENTS WITH LEAD IN GRADUATED SOLUTIONS OF ORGANIC MATTER (TANNIN) IN COCHITUATE WATER.

Days	Cochituate	Cochituate and 1–100 of Tannin	Coch'tuate and 1–1000 of Tannin	Cochituate and 1–10000 of Tannin	Cochituate and 1–100000 of Tannin	Distilled Water
3	1.000	0.800	0.400	0.600	0.600	5.000
5	0.000	20.000*	0.500	0.250	0.250	20.000
6	0.500	2.000	0.500	0.100	0.100	4.000
7	0.000	2.000	0.200	0.000	0.000	3.000
8	0.050	0.500	0.100	0.000	0.000	2.500
10	0.000	0.500	0.000	0.000	0.100	3.000
11	0.000	0.000	0.000	0.000	0.000	2.000
12	0.100	0.000	0.000	0.000	0.000	3.000
13	0.050	0.000	0.000	0.000	0.000	2.000

The bars of the third and fourth columns became more or less coated with a loose reddish-brown coat of organic matter and lead.

The influence of increased organic matter of this form (which is as nearly allied to the vegetable matters that might be expected to occur in lake water as could be readily found) was to lessen the action on lead. The organic matters of lake and river waters consist of living and deceased organisms, animal and vegetable, and of soluble substances derived from decaying vegetation. When exposed a sufficient length of time, these matters become thoroughly inorganic. The carbon becomes carbonic acid, and the hydrogen becomes water, by the consumption of oxygen in solution in the water.

My experiments have shown, that, if the quantity of organic matter, such as the extract of bark, be more than 1–10000 of the weight of the water, precipitates of the organic matter in combination with oxide of lead, if any is in solution, will take place. This is one of the methods frequently resorted to for separating organic bodies from solutions.

The effect of temperature was sought in a variety of ways. The following experiments are recorded

* A kind of fungous or flocculent mass fell with the lead, augmenting the volume of the precipitate.

Table XIV.

EXPERIMENTS WITH BARS PREVIOUSLY COATED, EXPOSED TO DIRECT SUNLIGHT FROM THE 21st TO THE 26TH OF JUNE.

Bars resting on the bottom of the tubes.

Days	Cochituate	Croton	Jamaica	Distilled Water
1	0.100	0.200	3.000	3.000
2	0.250	1.500	2.000	2.000
3	0.100	0.400	2.000	1.000
4	0.050	1.000	1.500	2.000

The influence of extreme temperature and exposure to air and moisture, under the most favorable circumstances, was ascertained by transmitting steam mixed with air through a leaden pipe thirty-six feet long, coiled like a still-worm, and placed in cold water to produce condensation.

One hundred and ten cubic centimetres of the condensed water, after acidulation with acetic acid, were treated with a stream of hydrosulphuric acid. The precipitate was collected on a filter, previously dried at 100° C., and gave 0.0225 gr. of sulphide of lead, equal to 0.0196 gr. of lead, which is equivalent to 0.8095 gr. of lead in a gallon.

Whatever influence might result from such changes, it must be remembered that pipes under ground will preserve a tolerably even temperature; and be the effect of increased heat what it may, it has been *more* energetic in Philadelphia than it ever can be in Boston.

The effect of increasing the percentage of common salt is exhibited in the following table.

Table XV.

EXPERIMENTS WITH COCHITUATE WATER AND GRADUATED SOLUTIONS OF COMMON SALT.

Bars and volumes as in the foregoing experiments. No concentration. Bars resting on the bottom of the tubes.

Days	Pure Cochituate	Cochituate and 1-100 of Chloride of Sodium	Cochituate and 1-1000 of Chloride of Sodium	Cochituate and 1-10000 of Chloride of Sodium	Cochituate and 1-100000 of Chloride of Sodium
1	2.00	.20	.30	1.60	2.00
2	1.80	.10	.15	.60	1.20
3	.20	.10	.08	.08	.30
8	.30	2.50	1.20	.30	.50

These results show:

1st. The immediate effect of the salt in preventing the action on lead by lessening the solvent power for air; and

2d. The influence of salt in dissolving the coat formed, by double decomposition, or by the formation of the double salt of the oxide and chloride; as shown in the last suite of results.

The preceding experiments, as a whole, go to *show that Cochituate water may be distributed through iron mains and leaden service pipes with as little danger as Schuylkill, Croton, or Jamaica water.*

The consideration that was to give value to these determinations was that of the health of the citizens of Philadelphia, New York and Boston, so far as it might be influenced by the waters served through lead in the respective cities. This was to be decided, as already intimated, by an appeal to the most enlightened testimony that could be furnished: that of eminent physicians of extensive practice in the localities where lead pipe is employed.

The following summary of opinions is chiefly compiled from the letters addressed to me, and published in the Appendix to the Water Commissioners' Report of August 14th, 1848. They refer not only to the waters above mentioned, but to several other similar waters, and to some spring waters.

"In regard to the New York water works, which have for several years supplied many thousands of families, Dr. Griscom, in a letter to Dr. Webster, dated Dec. 14, 1847, and appended to the Report of the Consulting Physicians, says: '*Nothing but lead pipe is now used in this city for the conveyance of water into, and within, the residences of the citizens.*'

"He states also, that, during the period of five or six years in which the Croton water has been used by a population of nearly 400,000 persons, he has had no knowledge of any evil consequences which could be attributed to the use of the lead pipe. He states, in addition, that he laid Dr. Webster's inquiry before 'the Academy of Medicine, the largest professional body' in the city, and requested that, 'if any gentleman had ever known or heard of any evil results from the use of lead pipes,' he would communicate the facts. 'No intimation of such results was offered,' and a negative answer had been also given by several of the practitioners in the city, with whom the writer had personally conferred. . . . .

"The water works of the city of Philadelphia have been in successful operation for more than twenty-five years, and they have afforded a wide field of experience, which has been of great value to the directors of other similar works. . . . . . B. H. Coates, M. D., physician to the Pennsylvania Hospital, Philadadelphia, after remarking that, in twelve years' service in the Hospital, he had not known any case of disease from the poison of lead, not distinctly traceable to some other source than the use of water drawn from leaden pipes, adds: 'We certainly feel ourselves quite safe in the employment of the water from Fairmount, and no case of lead disease from this cause is ever heard of.'

"Professor Dunglison, of Jefferson Medical College, Pennsylvania, says: 'I have never witnessed the slightest effect from the use of the waters of the Schuylkill, conveyed in leaden service pipes, which could lead me to suppose that there was any injurious impregnation.' He quotes the remark of Professor Hare, that he had used the Schuylkill water conveyed in leaden pipes, in his laboratory in the University, for more than twenty-five years, and had never perceived the slightest indication of the presence of the metal in it. Professor Dunglison adds: 'The results of all my observations in Philadelphia and elsewhere would lead me to express very confidently the belief, that leaden service pipes, constantly filled, as they necessarily are, are entirely innocuous.'"

In furtherance of this investigation, "the Board of Consulting Physicians caused inquiries to be made in more than a hundred families, residing in Washington, Tremont, Pleasant, Warren, Essex, Harrison, Kneeland, Edinburg, Oxford, Beach, Tyler, Hudson, South, Sea, Purchase, Summer, Atkinson, Charles, Cambridge, North Russell, Lowell, and other streets, who have used the water of Jamaica Pond drawn from leaden pipes, as common drink, for periods of from two to twenty years; and in no instance has any of the specific diseases attributable to lead been remembered to have existed in these families."

"In Baltimore, the distribution of water through leaden pipes is not found to be injurious to health. Dr. Aiken says,—'No case of lead poisoning has come to my knowledge, during a residence of thirteen years in Baltimore, arising from the use of our hydrant water. The lead pipes seem to answer the purpose very perfectly and very safely.'

"Dr. McNaughton, of Albany, where leaden pipes are partially used for the distribution of water, states that his own family have, for a period of sixteen years, freely used, for all purposes, water introduced to his house, a distance of at least one hundred and seventy-five feet, through a leaden pipe, and they have never had, in that time, a case of lead or other colic. He has known no case of lead poisoning from the use of the Albany water-works, and he has been informed, on inquiry of some of the oldest physicians of the city, that they know of no such case.

"Dr. Brinsmade, of Troy, N. Y., where nearly all the pipes for the distribution of the water supplied by the city water-works about the yards and buildings are of lead, states that the water is used by nearly all the inhabitants for culinary purposes and for drink; and that in a large practice in the city, for the last fifteen years, he has never seen a case in which he suspected poisoning from lead, caused by the use of water passing through leaden pipes. A similar statement was made to Dr. Brinsmade by several of the most intelligent and experienced physicians of the city, and by the Superintendent of the Water-Works.

"Professor Hubbard, of Dartmouth College, where the inhabitants of the village have been supplied, for a period of twenty-six years, with water conveyed nearly two miles through a leaden pipe, and distributed through pipes of the same material, states, as the result of his own observation, and that of Professor Crosby for ten years, Professor Muzzy for sixteen years, and Professor Peaslee for eight years, that they have had no knowledge of lead poisoning, or disease of any sort, from the use of the water, and they speak highly of the healthfulness of the village. . . . . .

"In the village of New Boston, in the town of Lancaster, about two hundred inhabitants are supplied with water, conveyed through leaden pipes extending one and a half miles. Dr. Lincoln, who has been engaged in medical practice there more than twelve years, has known no disease which can be ascribed to the use of the water. No action of the water is perceptible upon the internal surface of the pipe, but the pipe is in many places much corroded externally, where laid down near stables and other buildings.

"The water of the London water-works is distributed from the houses in leaden pipes, and is usually preserved for use in tanks lined with lead, and without complaint of any injurious effects from the metal. On this subject, Professor Graham, of University College, London, in reply to an inquiry, says,—'The point has been settled here by long experience. *Lead alone is used to conduct the water from the street main into the houses*, or for service-pipes. No evil is experienced in London, either from these pipes, or the leaden cisterns. Yet, as the latter are filled in general only twice a week, the water must remain in them for several days.' . . . . .

"Leaden pipes are extensively used in Paris for the distribution of the water of the Seine and the Ourq to the places of delivery for the supply of families, without injury to health. M. Tanquerel, in his elaborate treatise on lead diseases, lately republished in this country by Dr. Dana, discovered no indications of those diseases among the citizens of Paris, from drinking water supplied through leaden pipes."

The decision of this question does not depend upon the presence or absence of a minute quantity of lead in water that has been standing a given length of time in leaden pipes, or upon the *absolute* freedom from corrosion of pipes long in use. For if a certain quantity, more or less, has found its way into the human system in the everyday regular use of Croton and Schuylkill waters, then must the human system be capable of sustaining without injury this quantity; and the possibility of receiving an equal quantity hereafter by those who drink Cochituate water may be contemplated without solicitude, since the experiment has been made. Nevertheless, examinations for lead have been made in many well-waters, and in Croton, Jamaica, Schuylkill, and Troy waters, and Dedham spring water. The results follow.

Table XVI.

DETERMINATIONS OF LEAD IN WELL-WATERS SERVED THROUGH LEADEN PIPES IN CAMBRIDGE.

	Volume	Hours Exposed	Reduced Volume	Sulphide of Lead
				gr.
a	100cc.	36	10cc.	0.000
"	200	36	10	0.000
"	300	36	10	0.000
b	500	12	16	0.000
c	100	12	10	Precipitate
"	50	12	10	"
"	40	12	10	"
"	30	12	10	0.000
	gallon	12	10	0.100
d	500cc.	12	5	0.000
e	100	12	5	Precipitate
	gallon	12		0.080
f	300cc.	12	5	Precipitate
	gallon	12		0.0004
g	500cc.	12	20	0.000
h	200	36	5	0.00005
	gallon			0.00113
i	300cc.	12	10	0.0009
	gallon			0.0136

Well in Boston.—200cc., first drawn in the morning, gave, when concentrated to 5cc., 0.00003 gr. = 0.00068 gr. in a gallon. Dr. Charles T. Jackson has detected lead in a well-water in Waltham.

Well in Dedham.—100cc. water standing over night in the pipe serving from the reservoir supplied by a forcing pump, concentrated to 5cc., gave a trace of lead.

Water supplied from the spring in Dedham, which is known to have corroded leaden pipes, and poisoned at least one individual. 100cc., at rest twelve hours in leaden pipe several years in use, gave 0.00003 gr. = 0.0013 gr. in a gallon. Several years since, my friend, Dr. Webster, examined some of this water from the pipes of the gentleman who was made ill, and detected lead, without concentration, by treatment with sulphide of ammonium. This branch pipe was

150 feet in length. The main pipe, two inches in diameter, is about three quarters of a mile long. This pipe must be capable of holding a gallon in a little more than seven and one third feet, or 540 gallons in its whole length. Thus, the entire morning draught of *spring water* of each family had ordinarily been at rest twelve hours in the main and lateral pipes. In some instances it had doubtless been longer at rest ; and yet, so far as I have been informed, but one well established case of lead disease is known to have occurred from the use of this water.

TABLE XVII.

DETERMINATIONS OF LEAD IN THE CROTON WATER OF NEW YORK.

Drawn, after thirty-six hours' exposure, from leaden pipes, at seven different localities in the neighborhood of John Street.

Bottles.	Volume.		Volume.				
1.	500cc.	reduced	to 10cc.	gave,	of Sulphide	of Lead,	00
2.	"	"	"	"	"	"	00
3.	"	"	"	"	"	"	00
4.	"	"	"	"	"	"	00
5.	"	"	"	"	"	"	00
6.	"	"	"	"	"	"	00
7.	"	"	"	"	"	"	trace.

1000cc. derived from bottles 1, 2, and 3, concentrated to 10cc. gave, with hydrosulphuric acid, a precipitate which, ignited with saltpetre and redissolved, gave, with bichromate of potassa and hydrosulphuric acid, distinct precipitates of lead. The whole quantity equalled about 0.0001 gr., or for a gallon 0.00045 gr.

DETERMINATION OF LEAD IN THE SCHUYLKILL WATER OF PHILADELPHIA.

According to Professor Booth, 100 apothecaries' ounces, after exposure 36 hours in leaden pipe, a year and a half in use, concentrated to the bulk of half an ounce, gave not the slightest discoloration after transmitting hydrosulphuric acid through it for an hour.

TROY RESERVOIR WATER.

2000cc., 24 hours at rest in leaden pipes several years in use, gave, when concentrated to one hundreth of its volume, no trace of lead.

Table XVIII.

DETERMINATIONS OF LEAD IN JAMAICA WATER SERVED THROUGH LEADEN PIPES IN THE CITY OF BOSTON.

April 13th.		Exposed to the Lead.			Gave of Sulphide of Lead.
No. 6 Hudson Street,	200cc.,	12 hours,	reduced	to 20cc.	00
No. 10 " "	"	"	"	"	00
No. 98 " "	"	"	"	"	00
No. 800 Washington Street,	"	"	"	"	00
No. 10 Tyler Street,	"	"	"	"	00

April 13th. Worcester Rail Road Depot, 1000cc., exposed to the lead 36 hours, reduced to 20cc. gave, of sulphide of lead, 00 gr.

June 19th. Worcester Rail Road Depot, 500cc., exposed to the lead 36 hours, reduced to 5cc. gave, of sulphide of lead, 0.00002 gr. = 0.00018 gr. in a gallon.

The magnitude of this quantity, and the influence its known presence in a water should have, may be over-estimated.

500 cubic centimetres contain 0.00002 gr.
1000 " " " 0.00004 gr.

Wiesbaden water contains of arsenious acid, in 1000cc., 0.00045 gr.—a quantity more than ten times as great as the lead in Jamaica water,—and yet this water is renowned for its medicinal virtues. It may be said, that the arsenic is in combination with oxide of iron. Chevalier and Gobley have come to the conclusion, that its occurrence in springs is not dependant upon the presence of iron. It is found in water whose character is determined by the presence of carbonic acid or sulphates. This body occurs in *solution* in waters from nine mineral springs in France. Its occurrence in Germany has been recognized among others, by Will. Tripier found it in Algiers.

The appearance of leaden pipes taken up after several years' use, in New York, is what might have been expected. I have examined twelve pieces from as many different localities. Most of the specimens that had been in use for only one and two years were covered with a bluish-gray coat, and some of them could scarcely be distinguished from ordinary pipe for sale in the shops. A specimen in use five years is coated with a transparent, exceedingly thin, reddish-brown film, apparently composed of organic matter, oxide of lead, and oxide of iron. The crystaline laminæ upon the inner surface, characteristic of new pipe, are to be seen with the utmost distinctness, and present, with the exception of the coating, no appearance distinguishing it from new pipe.

Jamaica pipe, in use from fifteen to twenty years, is coated with a thick, reddish coat, which, when dry, may be readily disengaged, and in one specimen examined shows traces of slight corrosion beneath. The corrosion from without was such as to have nearly eaten through in some places. The lead of this pipe contained great proportions of antimony where corrosion occurred, but no sulphide of lead, which I am informed, occurs in much lead pipe.

Pipe employed to conduct Dedham spring water is internally corroded, and presents at intervals deep depressions, the result of more extreme local action. Pipe of one well in Cambridge is appreciably corroded. Pipe of wells in Boston is frequently consumed in periods of from six to eighteen months.

The above results and observations show, that,—

1st. Many well-waters, in a space of time comparatively short, act on lead. This has been fully established by the researches of Dr. Dana in this country, and by observations in England.

2d. That, except after longer exposure than will ordinarily occur in actual use, the amount of lead coming into solution in Croton, Schuylkill, or Jamaica waters is too small to occasion any solicitude.

Hence it may be inferred from the above, and from the great similarity of Cochituate to Jamaica, Croton, and Schuykill waters, in its relations to lead, that *the quantity of lead that will be dissolved in Cochituate water in actual service will, for all practical purposes, be of no moment.*

INFLUENCE OF NITRATES.

Although medical testimony and public sentiment were conclusive upon the subject of the health of our larger cities, so far as it might be influenced by the lead contained in the reservoir-waters used for culinary and general purposes, it was equally certain that individuals had been poisoned from drinking the waters of wells, and in one case, at least, from drinking water from a spring.

It was obvious, therefore, that between these two classes, river, lake, pond, and open reservoir waters on the one hand, and well and some spring waters on the other, there must be differences in their relations to lead.

Experiments were made with well-water, and at the same time with the river and lake waters in my possession. The following result shows with what success.

TABLE XIX.

Days	Well-water	Cochituate	Fairmount
3	1.00	1.00	.15
5	.20	.00	.60
6	.30	.50	.00
7	.10	.00	.00
8	.00	.05	.00
10	.50	.00	.00
11	.00	.00	.00

The bars rested on the bottoms of the tubes, and the waters had been some time standing in sunlight. These experiments threw little light upon the subject. The differences in favor of the Cochituate and Fairmount, as compared with a well-water known to act vigorously on lead pipe, were too inconsiderable to be worthy of notice. These waters contained in 500cc.

	Of Solid Residue.	Of Organic Matter.	Of Inorganic Matter.
Well-water	...0.1380 gr.	0.0540 gr.	0.0840 gr.
Cochituate	....0.0267	0.0122	0.0145
Fairmount	.... 0.3007	0.1032	0.1975

On comparing these, it will be seen that the water which contained the most solid residue acted least on lead, and that the action of that which contained least solid residue was next in order.

The comparison of the analyses of waters made by different individuals led to no satisfactory results. Ingredients that might have been presumed to be in all had in some cases not been recognized. The only large suite of analyses made by a single individual first fell under my eye in the early part of June of 1848. In the following table are compared the average total amounts of inorganic matters, and also the relative amounts of the more prominent salts, in three wells, six springs and six rivers, as determined by Deville.

	Total	Nitrates	Chlorides	Sulphates	Carbonates
Wells....	6455	1701	650	1394	2291
Springs...	3344	86	77	365	2336
Rivers ...	1949	65	38	157	1185

The compounds of sulphuric and carbonic acids with oxide of lead are eminently insoluble. The chlorides are less insoluble, and the nitrates are highly soluble. The contrast between the quantities of nitrates in well and river waters suggested the experiment with lead and graduated solutions of saltpetre. The results follow.

TABLE XX.

Days	Pure Cochituate	Cochituate and 1-1000 of Saltpetre	Cochituate and 1-10000 of Saltpetre	Cochituate and 1-100000 of Saltpetre	Cochituate and 1-1000000 of Saltpetre
1	1.00	1.00	2.25	0.75	0.50
2	..	..	..	..	..
3	0.00	2.00	1.00	0.50	0.10
4	0.50	2.00	0.25	0.10	0.10
5	0.00	2.50	1.00	0.30	0.20
6	0.05	2.50	0.50	0.30	0.00
7	..	..	..	..	..
8	0.00	2.00	0.80	0.05	0.00
9	0.00	1.80	0.70	0.00	0.00

TABLE XXI.

Days	Pure Fairmount	Fairmount and 1-1000 of Saltpetre	Fairmount and 1-10000 of Saltpetre	Fairmount and 1-100000 of Saltpetre	Fairmount and 1-1000000 of Saltpetre
1	0.15	1.00	0.80	0.80	0.80
2	..	..	..	..	..
3	0.60	3.00	1.25	0.25	0.20
4	0.00	1.80	0.50	0.00	0.00
5	0.00	2.25	1.50	0.40	0.10
6	0.00	1.80	0.80	0.05	0.00
7	..	..	..	..	..
8	0.00	2.50	0.80	0.20	0.05
9	0.00	1.80	0.80	0.20	0.00
10	0.00	1.80	0.80	0.20	0.10
11	0.00	1.20	0.80	0.00	0.00

The mode of action of the saltpetre has been the subject of experiment. I had previously exposed bright bars of lead to natural waters containing traces of nitrates, which were deprived of air and sealed in glass flasks. Months had produced no action upon the lead, and had conducted to the opinion, that lead was not acted upon by nitrates in natural waters.

As the reaction of the Cochituate or Fairmount water was perfectly neutral, the decomposition of the saltpetre by free acid, which should expose the lead to uncombined nitric acid, was not possible.

Fresenius had observed that the carbonate of lead was less soluble in water containing nitrate of ammonia and ammonia than in pure water. I was aware that alkaline chlorides promoted the solution of certain lead compounds, and it occurred to me that they might be more soluble in waters from the presence of nitrate of potassa, soda, or lime.

In changing the waters from day to day, exposure to the air would furnish the oxygen and carbonic acid more directly than the absorption from the surface, for the formation of the hydrated oxide and carbonate, and these might to a slight extent, it seemed possible, experience decomposition with the saltpetre.

The decision of this point rested upon the following experiments.

1. A solution of saltpetre, the usual laboratory reägent, was poured upon a quantity of common white lead, and after repeated agitation and alternate rest, filtered off and tested with hydrosulphuric acid for lead. There followed an instantaneous, distinct, though not large, precipitate of sulphide of lead.

There was an objection to the experiment. White lead prepared from the acetate might not be altogether free from acetate of lead. This, if present, might be brought into solution by the nitrate of potassa.

2. To settle this point, a portion was carefully ignited upon platinum. Had there been appreciable acetic acid, the mass would have more or less blackened, or would have revealed to the sense of smell some evidence of its presence. It gave no indication whatever.

3. A quantity of the white lead was then treated with sulphuric acid and alcohol in a test-tube, in the usual manner for detecting acetic acid by the formation of acetic ether. This failed to give a trace of acetic acid. The quantity of white lead was small.

4. Four ounces of white lead were then boiled three hours with a large measure of diluted soda, filtered, concentrated, and treated with sulphuric acid and afcohol as before. It yielded no distinct trace of acetic acid.

5. To meet the question fully, and give to the experiment the advantage of the nacent state which in actual practice must occur, and to give to the view an entirely unobjectionable foundation, I added to a solution of nitrate of lead, first, potassa, which threw down a hydrate of lead, until the solution yielded an alkaline reaction. There were then hydrate and carbonate of lead in the precipitate, and nitrate of potassa, carbonate of potassa, and if any lead, a nitrate of lead in solution. The liquor was filtered, and upon adding hydrosulphuric acid to the filtrate, I obtained a precipitate of the black sulphide, more voluminous than in the first experiment with white lead and a solution of saltpetre,

6. Soda and carbonate of soda gave the same reaction.

7. Nitrate of lime in solution gave the same reaction as nitrate of potassa.

My attention has been drawn by a friend to the following sentence in Berzelius:—"When nitrate of lime is boiled with carbonate of lead, the oxide of lead is dissolved, while the carbonate of lime is deposited."

If with the aid of heat such decomposition results, it might be conceived that, favored by the nascent condition, quantity, and time, there might be to some small extent a corresponding decomposition.

The first was the principal experiment bearing on this point made at the date of my last letter to the Water Commissioners, and upon this experiment, and the known solubility of the nitrate, I ascribed the increased action of water consequent upon the addition of nitrates to a slight double decomposition. It has been ascribed by Dr. Dana to the conversion of the protoxide of iron, in solution as protosulphate, into the peroxide, by which he conceived there would be free sulphuric acid, and therefore free nitric acid, in water containing protosulphate of iron nitrates.

This explanation would not apply to the action of neutral waters, or of those containing no protosalts of iron, though nitrates were present.

The whole subject has undergone a more thorough examination. The conclusion that nitrates are not reduced by lead I have found to be erroneous; for experiment has shown that upon boiling a strong solution of nitrate of potash to expel the air, and introducing a bar of bright lead, it became immediately coated with suboxide of lead, and this without the evolution of gas. There had been a partial reduction of the nitric acid. Upon testing the solution with hydrosulphuric acid, it gave, after long digestion, but a faint discoloration. Upon pouring off the liquor, and adding to it oxide of lead, and continuing the digestion, a large quantity of lead was dissolved, which in 66cc. gave of sulphide of lead 0.0106 gr.=0.7296 gr. in a gallon. The solution reacted strongly alkaline.

As the only known inorganic salts of nitrous acid are its compounds with lead, it was probable that, upon the reduction of the nitric acid to nitrous acid, it had abandoned the potash to unite with the oxide of lead, or a baser soluble salt had been formed, in which potash was present.

Upon examining the nitrate of potash employed as a reägent in the first experiment, and which had been purchased for this purpose because it was labelled *pure*, it was found to contain alkaline chlorides,—a circumstance to which the lead in the first experiment might in part be ascribed. A repetition of it with pure nitrate of potash and the hydrate and carbonate of lead, prepared by exposing lead to distilled water in an open vessel, gave but a faint discoloration with hydrosulphuric acid. I am inclined to ascribe to the reduction of the nitric acid much the greater part in the action of nitrates upon lead.

ACTION OF AIR.

The importance of air in order to the action of a water upon lead has been intimated in the results already recorded. The following experiments confirm the observations of Yorke, Bonsdoff, and others, and, more recently of Dr. Hayes, as expressed in his Report to the Consulting Physicians.

1*st experiment.*—June 17th. An apparatus consisting of a half-gill flask, containing lead scrapings and Cochituate water, filled to half its depth, the lead all below the surface of the water, was connected by a tube, bent twice at right angles, with a vessel of mercury. The cork uniting the tube and the flask was carefully covered with sealing wax. If, now, in the oxidation of the lead, oxygen should be withdrawn from the space above the water, mercury would rise to occupy its place. The mercury had risen June 19th, three fourths of an inch; July 1st, four inches; July 22d, six inches; and in August, the mercury passed over into the flask.

Another similar apparatus prepared on the 16th of May showed, on the 10th of August, mercury at a height of 6½ inches.

2*d experiment.*—A flask of a half gill capacity was filled to two thirds its depth with distilled water, and boiled five minutes. While hot, and without delay, bars of bright lead were added, and the flask filled from another flask containing distilled water, that had been boiled an equal length of time. In this condition a nicely-fitting cork was adjusted to the neck, and expeditiously sealed, so as to prevent the admission of air.

Another flask was filled in the same manner with Cochituate water, and sealed. Both are in possession still. The bar in distilled water is quite as bright as when immersed, except around the end in contact with the glass, which has become a little coated. The bar in Cochituate water was bright for some months, but has at length become slightly dimmed in small patches, which may be attributed to the less complete expulsion of the air by boiling, or the less accurate stopping of the flask, though at the time the experiment was made both were regarded as unobjectionable.

The following experiment shows how much is due to a change of water. The bars in the Cochituate remained quite bright, and those in the other waters were but slightly coated.

Two bars in 15cc. for thirteen consecutive days, without changing the water, gave, in Cochituate, 0.500 gr.; Croton, 0.500 gr.; Fairmount, 0.500 gr.; Jamaica, 1.000 gr.

These experiments seemed to show that, without a renewal of the air, the action nearly or quite ceases after a short time.

Professor Silliman, Jr., made a similar observation in his experiments with the various waters submitted to him for analysis by the Water Commissioners in 1845. He used a large volume of water, and yet the bar remained quite bright. There was no *alternate exposure to water and air.*

Christison remarks, that, while certain waters might doubtless be kept with safety in leaden cisterns, the covers of the cisterns should not be of lead, but of wood, since the moisture condensing on them, furnishing, as he observes, *pure* water, would act on the lead, and the product falling would poison the water. The joint action of air and water is here presented under exceedingly favorable circumstances. The corrosion of cisterns along the line where air and water meet might be expected.

It will be readily seen, from considering the important part air plays, how rain-water must act with great vigor upon lead. It contains air, and is surrounded by air, and, aside from temperature, could not be more favorably constituted for acting upon lead.

The well known prevalence of lead maladies in Amsterdam, while leaden roofs were in use, and the restoration of health on their replacement with tile, find here a ready explanation.

Dr. Dana has recorded an experiment with rain water, which furnishes a valuable confirmation of what is stated above.

In a series of experiments with lead pipe of considerable length, if an interval of half a minute, or even less, occurred between the emptying of the pipe and refilling, there was invariably found lead in the water. This has been observed on a large scale in the practical service of lead pipe. Where from any cause the pipes have been empty for a length of time and then filled, the first water drawn contains a very considerable quantity of lead.

In the experiments of the preceding tables, the tubes intended to receive the bars were previously filled, and thus the transfer of the bar from one tube to another occupied scarcely a second of time. Even this short period was doubtless adequate to provide for some of the oxidation which the bar experienced.

Important as the office of air is, it is not adequate of itself to oxidate lead. A bar of lead scraped bright and placed in a desiccator over sulphuric acid remained undimmed for weeks, during the whole time of the experiment.

* * * * *

Of the various popular reasons why lead should not be employed for distributing water, the following have been found not to be sustained by experiment or authority.

1. THE GALVANIC ACTION OF IRON AND LEAD.

The effect of contact with iron, in most of its points of view, has been investigated. In diluted acids, *bright* lead in contact with iron is positive; *coated* lead, *negative.* YORKE — Diluted acid facilitates the solution of iron in contact with lead. RUNGE — In strong nitric acid, iron, in connection with lead, is *positive.* DELARIVE — In potash solution or lime-water, bright lead is positive to iron, but *oxidated* or *coated* lead is *negative.* This is also true of these metals in a solution of saltpetre. YORKE — It is also true in a solution of salammoniac. WETZLAR.

Thus in *acid*, *alkaline*, and *saline* solutions, all the conditions in which Cochituate water can occur, iron, if not at first, will, after a short interval, be the metal at whose expense the galvanic action will be sustained.

* * * * *

It is scarcely necessary to state that the iron rust, in actual service, does not come in contact with *lead*, but with the suboxide or other coat.

3. THE SOLUBILITY OF THE SUBOXIDE OF LEAD.

I have been unable to procure the slightest trace of lead in water deprived of its air, after long contact with the suboxide of lead.

4. THE ACTION OF ALKALINE CHLORIDES UPON LEAD, IN THE ABSENCE OF OXYGEN OR ATMOSPHERIC AIR.

The following experiment was made and several times repeated by me with graduated solutions of common salt.

A flask of one gill capacity, containing a quantity of lead shavings, presenting an extent of surface comparatively great, was one third filled with a solution of common salt. This flask was connected by a tube, bent twice at right angles, with a cup of mercury. The cork, tube, and neck, at the connections, were carefully covered with sealing-wax, that the flask might be air-tight. So arranged, the flask was slightly warmed; the air thereby driven out was of course replaced with quicksilver, the upper surface of which, after the original temperature had been reëstablished, was marked. Now, if any decomposition of common salt occurred by the agency of lead, the chlorine would be freed from the sodium, the sodium would decompose the water, hydrogen would be set free, and the column of mercury depressed. Instead of any such result, the column of mercury regularly rose in every instance. An apparatus of this description, several months in action, is still preserved in my laboratory.

It might still have been said, that, had the flask been deprived of air, the lead would have been acted on by the simple chloride.

The experiment of lead and sea-water, in a flask deprived of air, has been made. The flask was sealed on the 25th of May last. The bar for a long time retained its perfect brightness, and is but very faintly dimmed at this late day, February 1st, 1849.

5. ACTION OF ORGANIC MATTER.

It has been conceived that organic matter might exert a deleterious influence. Experiments, already recorded, show that the presence of organic matter increases the protecting power of water which is to be transmitted through lead. If the quantity exceed one ten-thousanth of the weight of the water, precipitates of oxide of lead, united to organic matter take place. Orfila has remarked the precipitation of the coloring matter from Burgundy by neutralizing it with litharge.

Its influence in withdrawing the oxygen from solution has also been alluded to. In the important researches of Dr. Smith upon the air and water of towns, it is mentioned that the presence of nitrates in the London water prevents the formation of organic matter, and that organic matter, in filtering through soils, becomes rapidly oxidated. Additional experiments bearing upon this point are recorded farther on.

INFLUENCE OF IMPURITIES IN WATER.

It is a prevailing conviction, that the more impure a water is, or, in general terms, the more salts it contains in solution, the less will be its action on lead.

The influence of sulphate of magnesia (epsom salts) and chloride of sodium (common salt) in distilled water was the subject of experiment. The action, it will be seen, was more vigorous in distilled than in the impure waters.

TABLE XXII.

EXPERIMENTS WITH LEAD AND GRADUATED SOLUTIONS OF SULPHATE OF MAGNESIA (EPSOM SALTS).

Days	Distilled Water	Distilled Water and 1-10000 of Epsom Salt	Distilled Water and 1-100000 of Epsom Salt	Distilled Water and 1-1000000 of Epsom Salt
1	——	——	——	——
3	5.000	2.500	2.000	1.750
5	20.000	1.500	2.000	1.800
6	4.000	2.500	2.000	1.800
7	3.000	1.800	2.000	1.500
8	2.500	2.500	2.000	0.800
10	3.000	1.800	3.000	1.800
11	2.000	1.500	1.800	1.500
12	3.000	1.200	2.000	0.800
13	2.000	1.200	1.200	0.800

Table XXIII.

EXPERIMENTS WITH LEAD AND GRADUATED SOLUTIONS OF CHLORIDE OF SODIUM.

Days	Distilled Water	Distilled Water and 1-10000 of Salt	Distilled Water and 1-100000 of Salt	Distilled Water and 1-1000000 of Salt
1	——	——	——	——
3	5.000	2.500	2.000	1.500
5	20.000	1.800	2.500	2.000
6	4.000	1.800	1.800	2.000
7	3.000	1.800	2.000	2.000
8	2.500	2.000	2.000	1.800
10	3.000	2.500	2.250	2.500
11	2.000	1.800	1.800	1.500
12	3.000	1.200	1.200	1.200
13	2.000	1.000	1.200	1.200

COATS THAT FORM ON LEAD.

In seeking to ascertain the nature of the protecting coat which forms in all the waters hitherto experimented with, the influence of organic matter was first considered.

500cc. of each of several waters were evaporated to dryness over a water-bath, ignited, and redissolved in an equal measure of distilled water. There remained a small insoluble residue, which readily dissolved, with effervescence, in hydrochloric or acetic acid, indicating carbonate of lime. Bars of lead were exposed to these prepared solutions. A bluish-white coat formed upon the lead in each.

Table XXIV.

EXPERIMENTS WITH THE SEVERAL WATERS DEPRIVED OF THEIR ORGANIC MATTER AND CARBONATE OF LIME.

Days	Distilled Water	Albany	Cambridge	Cochituate	Croton	Fairmount	Jamaica	Troy
1	3.000	0.000	0.500	5.000	6.000	15.000	5.000	4.000
4	1.000	0.000	0.500	0.500	2.500	2.000	12.000	2.000
5	1.500	0.010	0.010	0.020	8.000	1.000	15.000	0.500
8	2.000	0.010	0.500	0.800	10.000	2.000	3.000	1.000
9	0.500	0.050	0.050	0.100	4.000	4.000	1.500	1.500
11	0.500	0.100	0.100	0.100	0.800	0.100	0.100	0.100
18	0.500	0.800	0.800	0.800	20.000	30.000	0.800	0.500
37	1.500	1.000	2.000	1.250	12.000	3.000	0.700	1.500
42	1.250	1.000	1.000	2.000	2.000	20.000	8.000	0.100
44	15.000	1.500	1.000	0.800	0.200	0.100	0.100	0.100
47	15.000	0.500	0.100	1.500	0.500	0.100	0.100	0.100
48	0.200	0.100	0.300	0.100	1.000	0.200	0.100	0.300
49	0.400	0.400	0.500	0.300	2.000	0.500	0.400	0.400
50	0.500	0.200	0.900	1.000	2.000	2.500	1.000	0.100
52	1.750	0.010	1.800	1.800	1.000	3.000	0.100	0.100

It will be seen, on comparing the results of their actions with those of the natural waters, that they are more protracted and vigorous, that they approach more nearly the action of distilled water, and that no protecting coat can be said to have formed.

Three kinds of coating upon lead have fallen under my notice: a bluish gray one, which, according to Winkelbleck, Mitscherlich, and others, is a simple suboxide; a reddish one, which formed in Croton, Schuylkill and Jamaica waters; and a white one.

The coat of *suboxide* is insoluble in water. When the quantity of oxygen in solution in a given water is small, this coat will be first formed. It is the only one I have seen in Croton pipes less than two years in use. The addition to this coat of slimy organic matter, oxide of iron, and, to some extent, carbonate of lead, forms the *reddish* coat, the impermeable character of which, for all practical purposes, is illustrated in the appearance of Croton pipe five years in use, and already referred to. The *white* coat, it has been observed, consists chiefly of carbonates and sulphates.

SOLUBILITY OF OXIDE OF LEAD.

I have already noticed the contrariety of opinion upon the solubility of the oxide of lead. I have repeated the experiments of Yorke, and confirmed his results, and am, moreover, satisfied that had Thompson and Philips concentrated the filtrates which they supposed to contain no lead, they would have detected it without difficulty.

A flask containing distilled water and lead shavings was corked and placed aside for a few days. A deposit of carbonate and hydrate of lead formed around and upon the lead shavings. The contents of the flask were carefully poured upon a double filter of Swedish paper, and the filtrate concentrated. It gave a distinct precipitate with hydrosulphuric acid.

TEA AND COFFEE GROUNDS UNITE WITH LEAD IN SOLUTION.

It has been an occasion of surprise, that numerous families have for a long period employed well-water that corroded leaden pipe so rapidly as to require replacement in from six to eighteen months, and yet, so far as they or their physicians know, have suffered no illness attributable to the water. This fact suggested two considerations:

1st. Are all lead compounds equally poiosnous?

2d. If so, is the quantity which finds its way into the organism sufficient to produce the maladies attributed to lead?

It may be assumed that water flowing directly through a leaden pipe of an inch bore and not more than thirty feet in length will ordinarily be identical in constitution with that in the source from which it is drawn. That only which has been some time at rest would be expected to contain lead. Accordingly, there is more care that the water first drawn be thrown away. The first morning draught is usually in the form of tea or coffee.

The following experiments throw light upon this point.

To boiling water containing lead in solution tea was added, in the quantity usually taken in the preparation of the beverage (a gramme to 50cc.), the temperature maintained three minutes just below the boiling point, and the decoction filtered off.

The filtrate was evaporated to dryness, ignited, re-dissolved, and the precipitate with hydrosulphuric acid made and estimated as already described.

I. 50cc. of lead solution, containing one thousandth of its weight of lead, with 1 gr. of black tea, lost ninety-nine hundredths of its lead.

Originally present,	0.05 gr. of lead.
After separation from the grounds,	0.0005 "

II. 55cc. of solution containing one tenth as much lead as the above, with the above quantity of tea, lost more than eleven twelfths of its lead.

Originally present in solution,	0.005 gr. of lead.
After separation from the grounds,	0.0004 "

The experiments with coffee yielded the following results:—

I. 50cc. of lead solution, containing one thousandth of its weight of lead, with 10cc. of coffee-grounds, were boiled three minutes, and the decoction poured off. The residue was drained through Swedish filtering-paper, the filtrate added to the liquor poured off, and evaporated to dryness, ignited, redissolved, treated with hydrosulphuric acid, and the precipitate estimated as before.

It had lost more than forty-nine fiftieths of the lead.

Originally in solution,	0.05 gr. of lead.
After separation from the grounds,	0.0009 "

II. 50cc. of solution, containing one tenth as much lead as that in the last experiment, were boiled with 5cc. of coffee-grounds, and treated as above. It had lost more than eleven twelfths of its lead.

Originally in solution,	0.005 gr. of lead.
After separation from the grounds,	0.0005 "

These results contribute to account for the circumstance mentioned above.

* * * * *

SUMMARY OF CONCLUSIONS RELATING TO THE DIFFERENT KINDS OF WATER AND LEADEN SERVICE-PIPE.

The waters used by man, in the various forms of beverage and for culinary purposes, are of two classes, viz:—

1. *Open waters, derived from rain-falls and surface drainage, like ponds, lakes, rivers, and some springs; and*
2. *Waters concealed from sunlight, and supplied by lixiviation through soils of rock, or both, of greater or less depth, such as wells and certain springs.*

They differ, (*a.*) in temperature; well-water, through a large part of the year, is colder than lake, pond, or river water;—(*b.*) in the percentage of gases in solution; recently drawn well-water, in summer particularly, parts with a quantity of air upon exposure to the surface temperature. In winter these relationships must to some extent be inverted, in high latitudes for a longer, and in lower latitudes for a shorter period.

(*c.*) They differ in the percentage of inorganic matter in solution; well-waters contain more;—(*d.*) in the relative proportions of salts in solution; well-waters contain more nitrates and chlorides;—and (*e.*) in the percentage of organic matter; well-waters contain less.

RELATIONS OF LEAD TO AIR AND WATER.

(*a.*) Lead is not oxidated in dry air, or (*b.*) in pure water deprived of air. (*c.*) It is oxidated in water, other things being equal, in general proportion to the amount of uncombined oxygen in solution. (*d.*) When present in sufficient quantity, nitrates in neutral waters are, to some extent, reduced by lead. (*e.*) Both nitrates and chlorides promote the solution of some coats formed on lead.

(*f.*) Organic matter influences the action of water upon lead. If insoluble, it impairs the action by facilitating the escape of air; if soluble, by consuming the oxygen in solution, and by reducing the nitrates when present. The green plants, so called, and animalculæ which evolve oxygen, are abundant in open waters in warm weather only, and of course when the capacity of water to retain air in solution is lowest; so that, although oxygen is produced in open waters by these microscopic organisms, it does not increase the vigor of their action upon lead.

(*g.*) Hydrated peroxide of iron (iron-rust) in water is not reduced by lead. Hence may be inferred the freedom from corrosion of leaden pipes connected with iron mains, so far as the reduction of the pulverulent peroxide of iron may influence it.

(*h.*) Alkaline chlorides in natural waters deprived of air do not corrode lead. (*i.*) Salts, generally, impair the action of waters upon lead, by lessening their solvent power for air, and by lessening their solvent power for other salts.

A coat of greater or less permeadility forms in all natural waters to which lead is exposed. The first coat (*j.*) is a simple suboxide absolutely insoluble in water, and solutions of salts generally. This becomes converted in some waters into a higher oxide, and this higher oxide, uniting with water and carbonic acid, forms a coat (*k.*) soluble in from 7,000 to 10,000 times its weight of pure water. The above oxide unites with sulphuric and other acids which sometimes enter into the constitution of the coat *k*;—uniting with organic matter and iron-rust, it forms another coat (*l.*) which is in the highest degree protective. The perfection of this coat, and of the first above mentioned, may be inferred from the small quantity of lead found in Croton water (New York), after an exposure in pipes of from twelve to thirty-six hours, and from the absence of an appreciable quantity in Fairmount water (Philadelphia), after an exposure of thirty-six hours, when concentrated to one two-hundreth of its bulk.

REASONS WHY THE WATER OF LAKE COCHITUATE SERVED THROUGH IRON MAINS AND LEADEN DISTRIBUTION-PIPES MAY BE SAFELY EMPLOYED AS A BEVERAGE IN ANY FORM.

(*a.*) It has the small measures of air, nitrates, and chlorides, the large proportion of organic matter, soluble, and insoluble and exposure to the sun, above referred to as grounds of distinction in the relations to lead between lake, pond, or river water, and well-water.

(*b.*) In experiments with Croton, Fairmount, Jamaica, and Cochituate waters, made with lead, lead soldered to iron, to tin, to copper, and to brass, prolonged from mid-winter to the middle of summer, the relations of the last of these waters to lead were found to be as favorable as were those of either of the others.

(*c.*) Large numbers of individuals in the daily and unrestricted use of Fairmount, Croton, and Jamaica waters served through lead are not known by physicians of great eminence and extensive practice to suffer in any degree from lead maladies.

(*d.*) A coat forms upon the lead in Cochituate, as in the other waters above mentioned, which for all practical purposes becomes, in process of time, impermeable to and insoluble in the water in which it occurs.

Report of the Water Commissioners of Boston, on the Material Best adapted for Distribution water pipes.

THE Water Commissioners having taken into consideration the order of the City Council by which they were requested "to give their opinion as to the best and most economical mode of introducing water into private houses, in pipes of such materials as the Consulting Physicians may recommend," respectfully submit the following Report.

By an order of the City Council passed at the same date as that above refered to, the Board of Consulting Physicians of the City were requested "to give their opinion as to the material of which the pipes for carrying water from the mains into private houses should be composed, as far as the same may effect the purity of the water, and the health of the citizens."

In compliance with this request, the Board of consulting Physicians made a report.

* * * * *

They have expressed the opinion that "*pipes of cast or wrought iron* may be safely used for the transmission of water as far as health is concerned," but they do not recommend their use. They state, on the contrary, that "iron is easy of oxidation," that it "impairs the purity of the water, and in small pipes is liable to obstruction from the accumulation of its oxide." They have expressed the opinion that *copper pipes* effectually tinned throughout by reliable workmen, are a safe material for the transmission of water, "*so long as the internal coating keeps in repair;* but the guarded terms in which this opinion is stated, imply a doubt of the durability of such an internal coating. They express the opinion, also, that copper in the form of some of its salts, is an active poison, but that in its metalic state it is not very ready of oxidation and solution in water. In giving these opinions of the properties of this material they do not recommend the use of it. They state that *leaden pipes*, in certain waters, and under certain circumstances, are known to communicate a highly deleterious quality to their contents, yet that "a large portion of the population of Boston, Philadelphia, New York, and London, have for years consumed the water introduced from various sources through leaden pipes, with apparent impunity," but, as has been remarked above, they do not recommend the use of this or any other material.

The Waters Commissioners, therefore, in giving an opinion as to the best mode of introducing water into the dwelling houses of the City, in compliance with the request of the City Council, and in making choice of a material to be used in the execution of the work entrusted to their charge, are under the necessity of deciding independently of any such recommendation, by the aid of such information as they have been able to obtain from the above report, and from other sources.

In coming to a decision upon this question, we have given careful attention to the information and opinions of the scientific gentlemen who have given replies to the inquiries addressed to them by the Board of Consulting Physicians, and particularly to the results of the very thorough investigation and experiments of Professor Horsford of Harvard University.

These results appear to us to be of great value, and in corroboration of the great mass of evidence derived from a very extensive observation of the use of leaden pipes for the supply of cities and towns, for a long series of years, entirely satisfactory and conclusive.

While this subject was undergoing the investigation of the Consulting Physicians, and of the eminent chemists who had been invited to aid them in the inquiry, the Water Commissioners were under the necessity of beginning the work of laying down the distribution pipes. They deemed it improper to make use of a material which might in the result be proscribed, as dangerous to the health of the citizens

They accordingly procured iron pipes of one and a half and two inches in diameter, to be cast, which have been laid down for carrying the water from the street mains to the sidewalks, and in part to the dwelling houses, so far as this branch of the work has been yet accomplished.

The cost of pipes of this description, including the laying down, is considerably higher than that of pipes of lead, independently of the cost of making additional joints, where they are required. There is also a further objection to the use of these pipes, that with the greatest caution which can be used in laying them, they are more liable to be broken, than pipes of lead, or other flexible metal.

In the mean time, we have given attention to experiments which have been made of pipes constructed of various other materials. Tin has been used for coating the internal surface of pipes of iron, lead and copper, for the purpose of preserving them against the action of the water upon those metals. Pipes of each of these descriptions have been strongly recommended on some limited experience, but we are of opinion that there is not sufficient evidence of the durability of the coating, in either form, to justify its adoption for general use. Pipes of block tin appear to be in some respects preferable to either description of those formed of other metals, and merely coated with tin. The cost of tin per pound is about four times that of lead, but as it is of greater tenacity than lead a smaller quantity of metal serves to give the pipes a sufficient degree of strength, so that pipes composed of block tin, of a suitable thickness, can be procured at about double the cost of pipes of equal strength composed of lead. But the experiments detailed in the reports of Professor Horsford, as well as information derived from other sources, show that tin is gradually dissolved by the Cochituate and other similar waters; and that the decomposition does not in a short time cease, like that of lead in the same water, but continues as far as any experiment has been made, indefinitely. It is also liable to rapid decomposition, by being brought in contact externally with certain acids and gases, to which in various positions it will be exposed. Whether any sensible deleterious effect upon the water is produced by the gradual decomposition of the tin pipe, is a question which has not been satisfactorily determined. But for the reasons briefly stated, we are of opinion that, independently of the question of comparative cost, tin is no better adapted for the distribution of the water of Cochituate Lake than lead, and that probably it would prove less durable.

Pipes manufactured of malleable iron are used to some extent in various places, for the distribution of water for domestic uses. They are in every respect well adapted to the purpose, with the exception of their liability to corrode, by the action of the water within, as well as the effects of moisture on the external surface. They are stronger than lead, and not more expensive. They can be made of any desirable dimensions, and are not liable like cast iron to be broken, by an unequal pressure on the different parts. The experience of their use, however, so far as it has come to our knowledge, is too limited to enable us to form a positive judgment of the force of the objection above mentioned. It has been apprehended, that the effect of rust would be such as to render the water unfit for use, in the washing of clothes and linen, and in process of time, to close the aperture of the pipe.

Pipes formed of sheet iron, coated internally with hydraulic cement, have been recently introduced, and they promise to be highly useful under certain circumstances. When laid in the earth, and in situations exposing them externally to moisture, they are protected by a covering of hydraulic cement, which besides preserving the iron against rust, gives an additional strength to the pipe. Whether they can be economically used for the distribution of water from the mains, has not been fully determined by any experiment within our knowledge.

The Consulting Physicians, in their report above referred to, although they did not recommend the use of distribution pipes composed of lead, strongly intimated the expectation that the doubts which they entertained might be removed by further experiments. It was important to reconcile the fact, that on immersing lead in water taken from the Fairmount, Croton and Jamaica Pond Water Works, it undergoes a perceptible partial dissolution, with the well attested evidence, that a large portion of the population of the cities of Philadelphia, New York and Boston, are in the constant use of water from those works, drawn through leaden pipes, without experiencing from it any injurious effects. The experiments which had at that date begun by Professor Horsford, and have been since more thoroughly prosecuted by him, afford in our opinion a satisfactory solution of this apparent contradiction. These experiments demonstrate that the action of the comparatively pure water of lakes and rivers, upon bright bars of lead, which on their immersion in it, is distinctly perceptible, ceases after a period of a few days; and that this immediate action of the water, upon the surface of lead, forms a coating, which, for all practical purposes, is impervious to water, and entirely insoluble in it. This coating remains unchanged during any period in which it has thus far been immersed; its appearance after some months or years of immersion, in the case of the Croton, is quite the same, as within three or four days from the first immersion. The water on the first or second days in which the lead is so immersed, and during the continuance of any perceptible action on the surface of the leaden bars, shows traces of a mixture of lead, on trial by the ordinary tests; but on the repeated removal of this water, and substitution of other water from the same source, after the coating is formed, no trace of lead is discoverable by the most effective tests, after any length of exposure of the water in contact with the lead, which will ordinarily occur.

It has, however, never been doubted by those who have investigated this subject, that the water of wells and springs of certain descriptions, and in certain situations, exerts a much more powerful and continued effect upon lead with which it comes in contact; and that cases of paralysis, colic, and even death, have been traced to the drinking of water contaminated by this poisonous mixture. The negative evidence that no well authenticated cases of these diseases have occurred, in consequence of drinking the waters furnished by public water works of the cities of London, Philadelphia, New York, and many other places, when distributed through leaden pipes, authorizes the belief, that the scattered cases of disease of these descriptions, which have been usually traced to the use of water from wells and springs, have arisen from some property peculiar to the water from those sources, and not common to water derived from lakes and rivers. Attempts have accordingly been made, to discover the nature and source of the mixtures, which impart to water the power of acting more energetically upon lead. It is observed that nitrates possess this power, and that they are frequently found in well water. The observations of Professor Horsford have led him to the conclusion, that the unequal proportion of these salts constitutes the chief distinction between different waters, in their relation to lead. These salts are often, if not uniformly found, in the water of wells and springs, so situated as to be replenished by the filtration of water through a soil enriched from the stable, or by the wash from collections of animal substances, of any description. A small solution of saltpetre, or of a nitrate of any description, in water, is found to impart to it the property of dissolving lead, and thereby forming the nitrate of lead. This substance renders the water undoubtedly deleterious, and dangerous to the health of those who drink it, or use it in the preparation of their food. This explanation, which seems to be fully confirmed by ample experiments, accounts sufficiently for the fact, that the water of wells situated, as are a large portion of those in towns and cities, and of springs situated in the midst of richly cultivated fields, or in the vicinity of animal deposites of any description, may produce the chemical effect here described, upon the leaden pipes used to conduct it, while the waters of rivers and lakes, not particularly exposed to contact with substances of that nature, will be destitute of any such power.

So long as it remained unknown what ingredients imparted to water the property of acting upon the surface of a leaden pipe, in such manner as to convert it into an active poison, the fact that the water flowing from a particular source was harmless at one time, did not afford a satisfactory assurance against its becoming dangerous at another; especially when it was fully ascertained, that it possessed the property of dissolving lead in a sensible degree, on its first immersion in it. But since it has been discovered as the result of repeated trials, that the effect of the waters of the Schuylkill and Croton rivers, and of Cochituate and Jamaica lakes, upon lead, is limited to a short period from its first immersion, and that by this temporary effect, there is invariably produced an indissoluble coating on the surface of the lead, which permanently protects it against any further action of the water upon it, and consequently preserves the water against imbibing any poisonous property; and since it is further ascertained that the more efficient power of disolving lead, which is found to reside in certain waters apparently pure, is imparted by a substance rarely if ever found, except in a very minute degree, in the water of lakes and rivers, but which is often found in the water of wells and springs, there appears to be no longer any good ground to apprehend injurious effects upon water, of the former description, from its being transmitted through leaden pipes. A perceptible line of distinction is thus drawn, between a class of waters which are liable to acquire the property of imbibing a poisonous substance, by its contact with lead, and another class, which, in a very wide experience of their use for domestic purposes, have been found not to possess that property.

* * * * *

The ample testimony, founded on the continued use of the waters from the three first named sources, for a series of years, by thousands of families, without a single distinctly proved case of lead poisoning, although the water is served from the mains to the dwelling houses almost universally through leaden pipes, affords as satisfactory a demonstration as the nature of the case admits of, that the Cochituate water may be safely distributed in the same way.

* * * * *

Authorities of this description, derived from experience in the use of leaden pipes in other places, might be increased to an almost indefinite extent. On the other hand, a great number of cases might be cited, and many of them have been made known to the public, in which the water of wells and springs either conveyed through leaden pipes or received into cisterns lined with lead, has not only rapidly dissolved the lead, but has proved seriously detrimental to the health of persons who have habitually used it with their food. Repeated cases of both these descriptions have occurred, from the use of the water of certain wells in Boston, and in Worcester, Dedham, Cambridge, and other places. It is not possible to prove, in reference to all these cases, what ingredient the waters contain capable of producing the effect, which is not contained in the water of rivers and lakes. In many of them, however, the effect is distinctly traced, as is above stated, to the presence of nitrates in the water; and in other cases, the situation of the source from which the water is derived is such, as to justify the presumption that this ingredient is to be found in it. For example, the water of two wells in Cambridge, situated near each other, (those of Rev. Dr. Walker and Mr. Buckingham), drawn through leaden pipes, were sujected to experiment by Professor Horsford. In the former, a trace of lead was discovered, and in the latter, none. The use of the water of the former had also proved injurious to the health of the family. On subsequent inquiry, it was ascertained that the well of Dr. Walker was shallow, and was supplied from springs near the surface of the earth, and above the clay substratum. The well of Mr. Buckingham, after a discovery that the surface springs were insufficient, had been sunk deeper, and the water at the time of the experiment was drawn from a depth below the clay, which is impervious to rain water.

Upon a careful examination of this mass of testimony, we regard it as satisfactorily proved that tho water of Cochituate Lake, which is about to be introduced into the City, may be safely distributed to private dwellings, by means of leaden pipes, without danger to the health of those who may freely use it with their daily food.

* * * * *

We have, therefore, resolved to use leaden pipes, for conducting the water to houses, except in cases in which the owners or occupants shall make known their preference of iron pipes, and announce their determination to make use of pipes of iron, or some other material than lead, for the conveyance of the water through their respective houses, to the place of delivery, for use for culinary purpose. Persons making such request will be furnished with the water by means of pipes of cast iron.

* * * * *

We recommend that when leaden pipe is used, it should be five-eighths of an inch in diameter, weighing about three pounds to a foot in length, and that it be conducted through such part of the cellar, as will afford the best protection against frost, to the kitchen or sink-room, where the most constant supply will be required.

* * * * *

Respectfully submitted by

NATHAN HALE,
THOMAS B. CURTIS.

Boston, Aug. 14, 1848.

Water Commissioners.

On the use of Metallic Lead and Cast Iron, to convey and distribute the Waters of Quebec.

To George R. Baldwin, Esq., Charlestown, Mass.

Dear Sir,—Since you intrusted to my care the samples of water from the vicinity of Quebec, I have devoted to them such time and attention as I could command, directed in my inquiries into their chemical character by my former researches and the published results of others. The number of samples received from you was nine, numbered consecutively, but being taken, as I am informed, from the rivers Montmorenci and St. Charles at different points and different seasons. Four of them, (viz: Nos. 1, 3, 4, and 5), are from the Montmorenci.

The geological character of a country will in a great measure determine the character of the streams flowing through it. It must be remembered, that water is one of the most powerful solvents known to chemists, and that it cannot fall upon the surface of the earth without becoming impregnated, to some extent, with the soluble matters of the rocks and soils over which it runs. In a country of granitic rocks, of feldspar and quartz, and the various minerals which constitute the aggregate, which geologists know by the several names of granite gneiss, mica slate, and other rocks of the same family; the streams will dissolve out the silica and allumina, the magnesia and lime, the potash and soda, and the various acids which are combined with these constituents, and a careful analysis of the waters of a given region may enable an acute chemist to judge with considerable certainty of the mineral nature of the country from what he finds in its waters. In a limestone region we look principally for lime and magnesia in the natural waters, and have little reason to expect the presence of many other ingredients which are found in the various minerals of a primitive country. The waters of a limestone region are generally, hard, or at least not so soft as those of a granite region. The quality of hardness is one of great importance to be known, and is owing, usually, and I believe I may say always, to the presence of soluble salts of lime and magnesia in the water. Soap forms an insoluble lime compound, lime-soap, in hard waters, which fills the water with a white curdy precipitate, harsh to the touch, and a serious impediment to the use of the water for many domestic purposes. The familiar fact that a small dose of wood-ashes, or of sal-soda, will remedy this defect in hard waters, is owing to the union of the lime with the carbonic acid from the alkali of the ash or sal-soda, and the production thereby of an insoluble, and hence innoxious compound of the lime. Perhaps no single character is of more importance to be known than that of the hardness or the reverse of a natural water.

In this particular the Quebec waters were examined by means of what is usually known as the "*soap test*," which is a saturated alcoholic solution of fine hard soap.

This test, when added in a minute quantity to soft and pure water, produces only a delicate, opaline hue, and the water containing it will immediately yield a bubble or froth on agitation. If on the contrary the water be hard, the addition of the soap-test to it at once produces a decided precipitate of a curdy white appearance, which is not dissolved by the addition of any larger quantity of water. The harder the water more of the soap-test must be added to bring it to that point when all the lime salts are decomposed and the water becomes capable of bearing a bead or bubble. A carefully conducted experiment will enable the chemist to form an accurate estimate of the relative value, in point of softness, of a given number of waters.

For the convenience of a general comparison of the several determinations, which have been enumerated with other waters of known celebrity, the following table has been made. The analyses of Croton, Cochituate and Schuylkill water, were made by the writer in 1845, for the city of Boston. One fact of some interest appears from the analysis of the Lake Cochituate water, namely, that the water taken up from near the bottom of the lake contains much more impurity than that upon the surface. A similar observation has been made regarding the water of the ocean; but I am not aware that attention was ever called to this inequality in the higher and lower levels of bodies of fresh water, until the publication of the report by the author, from which these results are quoted.

TABLE,

SHOWING THE QUANTITY OF FOREIGN MATTERS IN QUEBEC WATERS, AS COMPARED WITH OTHER SOURCES IN THE UNITED STATES.

Number of the water......	4.	5.	6.	8.	9.
Solid matter in 100,000 parts by weight	4.20	3.63	5.77	8.10	1.192
Volatile at redness........	2.58	2.32	2.26	2.72	4.38
Leaving solid.............	1.62	1.31	3.50	5.38	7.54
Number of water.........	A.	B.	C.	D.	E.
Solid matter in 100,000 parts by weight	18.714	3.168	5.770	9.417	87.85
IN ONE GALLON. Volatile at redness	4.28	1.85	1.16	1.24	1.218
Leaving solid in 1 gallon...	6.66	0.63	2.21	4.26	50.055
Grains in 1 gallon	10.93	1.85	3.37	5.50	51.274

Nos. 4, 5, 6, 8 and 9, are the waters of this report.

A, is the Croton, in New York; B, Lake Cochituate, or (Long Pond), from the surface; C, the same, from a depth of sixty-two feet; D, the Schuylkill, at Fairmount, Philadelphia; E, a well on Beacon Hill, in Boston, showing the general character of most of the wells in that city.

* * * * * * *

The most important consideration in reference to the supply of water to a great city, next to its original purity and abundance, is to guard against its being contaminated by the means employed in its distribution to the consumers. The calcareous matters dissolved out of the masonry conduit, through which the Croton river runs for forty miles before reaching New York, were found to alter materially the purity of that water, and render the total amount of its solid contents considerably greater after the water reached the city than they were in the river, or great reservoir at the commencement of the aqueduct. This, however, proved to be a very limited evil, and soon corrected itself. Not so, however, the effect of the water on the leaden pipes, employed for its distribution from iron mains to the houses of the customers. The writer, in 1845, made a carefully conducted set of experiments on several waters now used in our larger cities, and among others on the Croton in reference to its effect on leaden pipes. The general result was, that the Croton water only very slightly attacked lead. But it was impossible, in a single set of experiments, to meet all the conditions found in the actual distribution of water to a large town; and one of these conditions which was not taken account of, was the effect of the iron pipes in altering the electrical or chemical relations of the lead. It has since been found in practice, that this condition is a very important one, and must always be regarded.

Pure water has a very remarkable power in dissolving the oxide or rust of lead; so much so, that a pint of pure distilled water will dissolve a grain or more of this oxide. The common air and carbonic acid, always found in natural waters, materially aid in the solution of the lead, by first oxidizing the clean surface and thus placing it in a condition to be acted on; while on the other hand, it has been confidently asserted that the presence of various impurities in water, such as sulphate of soda or sulphate of lime, and other saline ingredients, would wholly or partly arrest the corrosion of lead. It is certain, that natural waters vary very much in their power of acting on lead, and very many are so nearly exempt in this particular that they have been drawn for years with impunity through leaden pipes. This may be owing to the non-action of the water, or to its producing an insoluble and innoxious compound with lead. Thus water, highly charged with organic extractive matter, has, in some cases of my own observation, been brought into contact with lead without being at all contaminated therewith, while abundant evidences of action was found in the precipitation from the water of all its organic matter in an insoluble state, and by the gain of weight in the lead itself. The lead may, even by this process become, as it were, varnished over with a film of organic matter, and the water escape unharmed. The chloride and nitrate of lead salts, the former of which may often be found in waters that have passed through leaden pipes, are both represented as being quite harmless when taken into the system. It is the sub-oxide and carbonate which are the most deadly forms of lead; for although the carbonate is a white powder, insoluble in water, it is easily dissolved in the acids of the stomach, and is the form in which most cases of lead poisoning occur.

To try the effect of the Quebec waters on lead an experiment was instituted, in which a thin and bright strip of lead about one foot long was exposed in a close glass bottle, with a sample of each water for a long time. The lead was perfectly bright when the water was added to it, and frequent observations were made for such changes as might appear. The weight also of each slip was carefully noted before the experiments, that any change which should happen might be discovered, either of increase or of dimunition. Another series, in a distinct set of bottles, was also prepared, similar to the first, in all respects except in the attachment of a small slip of brass to one end of each leaden strip. This was for the purpose of imitating more closely the condition of a leaden acqueduct pipe, with a brass stop-cock on its end. This arrangement, of course, alters the electrical relation of the lead, and places it in a situation to be more easily acted on by corroding agents. Common air, except such quantity as was dissolved in the water, was excluded, as it is in the general use in aqueducts. In this particular, the leaden pipes of wells and cisterns differ in their situation from those of acqueducts. Since in the former there is a line where the water, the metal, and the air join, and at that point is the greatest activity of chemical action. At the conclusion of the experiments it was found that each of the waters had become more or less impregnated with lead. Within twelve hours after the first experiment was instituted, it was evident, from simple inspection, that some action had taken place in Nos. 7, 8, and 9. Each of these slips had become tarnished, and particularly No. 9, while the others remained bright and untarnished. This effect did not appear to increase at all after the first twenty-four hours, during many days and even weeks in which the experiment was continued.

The second series, in which a slip of brass was soldered to each, became acted on after two or three hours, especially in Nos. 4, 7, 8, and 9, while in Nos. 5 and 6 the lead remained quite bright to the end of the experiment. The results of these trials are given in the following tables.

TABLE, SHOWING THE EFFECTS OF WATER ON LEAD.

No. of the water	1	2	3	4	5
Weight of slip before experiment	7.0150	7.34825	7.5430	7.5318	7.490
Weight after exposure	7.0011	7.34760	7.5419	7.5315	7.492
Difference + or —	+.0139	—.00065	—.0011	—.0003	+.002

No. of the water	6	7	8	9
Weight of slip before experiment	7.355	7.5042	6.9265	7.4960
Weight after exposure	7.355	7.5061	6.9290	7.4985
Difference + or —		+.0019	+.0025	+.0025

When samples of all the water which had been in contact with the lead were tested with sulphureted hydrogen water, immediate coloration from sulphuret of lead was seen in each, but in very different degrees. Those which, to appearance, had acted most upon the lead were found to be almost free from taint, (viz: Nos. 8 and 9), showing that while the lead was tarnished, the compound which was formed was an insoluble one, and this was also indicated by the increase of weight in these slips. The degree in which the contamination from lead was observed is expressed in the following order of numbers, beginning with that which gave the least evidence of lead, viz: Nos. 8, 9, 7, 3, 5, 2, 6, 1, 4. Nos. 1 and 4 assumed a clove brown color from the larger quantity of sulphuret of lead which was floating in them from the addition of the test. In the second series, with the brass slips, the action was increased in intensity, while the order was a little changed, as is here expressed: Nos. 9, 5, 7, 6, 8, 4. No. 4, in this case, was more than twice as intense in color as before. These results clearly indicate the propriety of avoiding the use of leaden pipes, if possible, in the distribution of the Quebec waters. They show that one of the purest (viz: No. 4), is contaminated most of all by this poison, and that those which are least pure have escaped nearly unharmed. The action on the lead, it is seen is most to be dreaded, when no indication of it is found from the tarnishing of the metallic surface. Indeed, it may be safely inferred, that the tarnishing of the lead in Nos. 8 and 9, is the principal cause of the water of these samples being saved from contamination. It may be said, that in actual use, the aqueduct water never stands long in contact with lead; but in answer to this it is remarked, that in the experiment here detailed, but little change took place after the first few hours. It is also a fact under the writer's observation, that aqueduct water may be contaminated with lead, even when the stream of water is passing through the leaden pipe unceasingly. A. B., a respectable farmer in this vicinity, had for many years suffered from indisposition of an anomalous character, and was subject to occasional paroxysms of acute and distressing pain, resembling painter's colic. As there was nothing in his occupation to authorize any inference that he was the victim of that disease, the real cause of his sufferings lay for a long time concealed, and he was treated by his medical attendants for various complaints, and with little or on amelioration. By the advice of an eminent surgeon, who, in his practice, had met with similar cases, the inquiry was made in what way water was procured for his domestic use, when it appeared that a spring of water upon a hill, at many rods distance, was brought to his door in a leaden pipe. A sample of the water was procured, and brought to the writer for examination. It proved to be strongly contaminated with lead; the use of this water was immediately discontinued, the patient treated with the proper antidotes to lead poisoning, and his amendment confirmed the correctness of the diagnosis. This case is cited out of hundreds of cases of lead poisoning, to show that it may not always be necessary for the water to remain any considerable time in contact with lead in order to produce contamination.

But it remains to consider how the union of leaden pipes with the iron mains may affect the predisposition of the water to act on lead. As iron is more easily rusted than lead, so it might be inferred with some plausibility that the union of the two would, on well-known galvanic principles, aid in protecting the lead. We shall see that this inference cannot be safely trusted. I have kept the waters of 5, 6, 8, and 9 for some time in contact with cast iron in close vessels. It was immediately and deeply rusted in all, and little lines of concretionary oxide and carbonate of iron were formed in ridges over its surface, while the water became in each case quite turbid from the floating particles of free oxide of iron suspended in it. Water is deprived of all, or nearly all, of its carbonic acid by the action of iron and the oxygen of the dissolved air, (which is known to be present in larger relative proportions to the nitrogen than in the air) is also nearly all removed. From the abundance of the bulky rust of iron produced in this way and from its adhering so feebly to the walls of the iron pipes, it cannot fail of being carried forward by the current of water moving through the pipes, and come into contact with the leaden conduits. As the water has, by the action just described, lost its carbonic acid, that substance is no longer present to aid in forming a coating of carbonated oxide of lead, which (as has been seen in Nos. 8 and 9), would materially aid in protecting the lead. Moreover, the contact of the pulpy free oxide of iron with the leaden pipes, must result in the production of oxide of lead at the expense of the oxide of iron, which will thus part with a portion of its oxygen to unite with the lead, and the water at once takes up its quota of this deadly compound.

We confidently state, therefore, the important fact, that the passage of water through iron pipes, prepares it for a more speedy and certain action on lead. To this cause I look for an explanation of the fact, that several alleged cases of lead poisoning have happened in the city of New York; although the experiments made by me with the Croton water on lead, had appeared to authorize the inference that it would be safe to employ lead for the distribution of that water.

It must be admitted, however, that as far as our present knowledge of facts goes, the cases of poisoning with lead in New York have been rare exceptions : but the public attention has as yet, not been fully awakened to the subject, and when it is, probably more evidence of deleterious consequences will be made known. At least, one well attested case has been recorded in England, in which water that had for years passed uncontaminated through leaden pipes, and been collected in leaden cisterns, was afterwards passed through *iron* pipes, and received as before, in leaden cisterns, when it was found that the lead was rapidly corroded. The view already presented of the action of water on iron, in connection with lead, will explain this case.

I have dwelt thus fully on the subject of conducting water through leaden pipes, because it appears to me that too much attention can hardly be given to a question which is of such momentuous consequences as regards the health of the community. And surely no great city in this enlightened age will propose to supply itself with water in this manner without at first demanding all the facts.

In conclusion, I may be permitted respectfully to ask whether the possibility—may we not say almost certainty—that the waters of both the Montmorenci and St. Charles will be seriously contaminated by contact with lead, is not a sufficient reason why the authorities of Quebec, as the guardians of the public health, should prohibit the distribution of its waters through this dangerous metal.

Doubtless the skill of their engineer and the fertile invention of our countrymen will contrive a safe and economical substitute.

All of which is respectfully submitted by

Your obedient servant,

B. SILLIMAN, Jr.

Analytical Laboratory, Yale College,
New Haven, March 27, 1848.

P. S. The writer may be permitted to add, that by his advice, a pipe of copper, well coated with pure tin, has been in use for some years in a well in New Haven, with entire success. Should the Quebec waters fail to coat over the inner surface of the lead pipes with the covering of organic matter, before alluded to, thus rendering a substitute not necessary—this description of copper pipe would probably be the best resort.

On the Action of Water on Lead Pipes, and the Diseases proceeding from it.

By Horatio Adams, M. D., of Waltham, Mass.

The subject referred to your committee embraces two distinct propositions, to wit: 1. The action of water on lead pipes; and, 2. The diseases proceeding from it. A distinct section of the report will be devoted to each of them. The committee will proceed to consider them in the order above designated.

SECTION I.—ON THE ACTION OF WATER ON LEAD.

On this subject, the committee would report only well known and well established facts. . . . .

It may be stated, in the outset, that pure water exerts no effect on pure metallic lead. Pure water is never decomposed by pure lead.

By pure water, the committee understand that which is free from all uncombined oxygen, acids and alkaline, earthy and metallic salts. Such water exists not naturally. . . . . The action of natural water on lead is due to foreign matters contained in water. All natural water contains air, acid, gas and salts. These all exert an effect more or less direct on lead. The salts cause water to be hard or soft, and these qualities modify the chemical relations of lead and water. The salts in natural water are either neutral or non-neutral; the last are all alkaline. The neutral are, sulphate of lime, common salt, earthy and alkaline nitrates, and chlorides. The alkaline consist of bicarbonates of lime and magnesia, sometimes of bicarbonate of potash and soda.

These several substances act, either singly or combined, on lead. Single action is generally direct, combined action is always indirect. Hence the foreign matters in water may be divided into direct and indirect agents. The first class comprises oxygen, chlorine, and compounds of sulphur and hydrogen.

The second class comprises the alkaline, earthy and metallic salts, and organic or inorganic acids. Among the foreign matters, oxygen exerts, perhaps, the most important influence in determining the action of lead and water; when absent from water, action will rarely occur; its action is primary. With the exception of chlorine and hydrosulphurous compounds, no other agents act primarily, and direct action always precedes indirect, primary always precedes secondary action.

Pure metallic lead cannot be put in contact with any direct agent in water without being acted on by it, and the results of this primary action are OXIDES, CHLORIDES, and SULPHUROUS COMPOUNDS OF LEAD.

The degree of oxidation depends on the amount of common air, carbonic acid, and oxidizing agents in the water. If only a small amount of air or free oxygen is present, a compound of two proportions of lead to one of oxygen, or a suboxide, is formed. If carbonic acid and oxidizing agents are more abundant, then a higher degree of oxidation, one portion of lead to one of oxygen, or a protoxide, occurs. All natural water contains oxidizing and decomposing agents, which readily change the lower oxide into a higher oxide of lead; hence it may be said that the result of direct action is the formation of protoxide, chloride, and sulphurous compounds of lead.

Water containing hydrosulphurous compounds is never used for domestic purposes; hence, practically, the only compounds of lead here to be considered are the protoxide and chloride. Bearing these principles in view, it is evident that, since all natural water contains direct or indirect agents, ALL NATURAL WATER ACTS ON LEAD. The result of this primary action is the production of an oxide or chloride of that metal.

The properties of these compounds are highly important. Their mere formation could demand no further investigation, did not their behavior towards the water in which they have been produced give that water characters of the utmost importance in its hygienic relations.

Among the most important properties of oxide and chloride of lead is their solubility. Both are soluble in natural water. That oxide of lead is dissolved by pure distilled water, to the extent of about eight grains per gallon, is beyond question. Hence the solvent power of natural water varies in proportion to its purity.

If natural water contained only pure, common air, it would dissolve as much oxide of lead as would distilled water. Hence, in aqueduct service with lead pipe, where natural water flows freely and continuously, oxidation and solution of lead will occur. In this view, it may be said that the purer the water and the greater its aeration, the greater is its action on lead.

On the other hand, natural water aerated contains carbonic acid. This compound, by its behavior with suboxide of lead, converts that into an oxide, and by its combination with this, produces carbonate of lead. This salt, insoluble in pure water, is readily solved by an excess of carbonic acid, or by supercarbonates existing as alkaline or earthy salts. No natural water is so nicely balanced in its relative proportions of absorbed air, oxygen, and carbonic acid, as to form carbonate of lead alone, and hence it may be said that natural water necessarily dissolves a portion of the carbonate of lead which it has formed. Failing of the due proportion of carbonic acid, solution ceases. Failing of air, action ceases.

One may easily understand then, that, in experimenting in a limited quantity of water, the formation and solution of oxide cease, and hence, apparently, lead becomes insoluble. It is so actually only when retained in *that* portion of water in which it was originally immersed.

Natural water generally contains organic, or sometimes inorganic acids, which convert oxide and carbonate of lead into soluble or insoluble lead salts, while the presence of such acids renders chloride of lead more easily dissolved than by pure water. Mutual reäctions occur among the salts of natural water, whence result products of decomposition by which oxide of lead is converted into a salt soluble in water, or its contained salts; the reäction of the per-salts of iron, and of nitrates, is, in this view, of the highest importance. The influence of salts in causing oxide of lead to be dissolved by water is very unequal. Nitrates increase the solubility in a greater degree than do other salts. Sulphates and silicates alone do not dissolve oxide of lead. Viewed singly, the lead solvent power of salts, common in spring water, is as follows, as determined by Spencer, of Liverpool; the highest being first named:

Supercarbonate of Magnesia.
" " " Lime.
Chloride " Sodium.
" " Magnesium.
" " Calcium.

Oxidation of lead and solution of the oxide in water are independent of the degree of hardness; hence the hardness being equal, oxidation may be very unequal. This seems, however, dependent on the quantity present of some particular salts, for a large amount of one salt renders lead soluble, when a smaller amount renders it insoluble. Hence, though the total of hardness may be equal, the solvent power may be very unequal. It may, however, be stated generally that salts causing hardness usually dissolve oxide of lead.

It is easy to determine what is the lead solvent power of each salt. In this question we deal not with single or individual salts. There is an inherent difficulty in determining by experiment what are the effects due to the combination of the various salts in natural water. Analysis may accurately determine the amount of each salt element in water, but the *mode* in which they exist in combination cannot be ascertained. Our arrangement of the union of these elements is arbitrary. It is the *mode* of combination which doubtless influences the solvent power of salts. The weight and solvent power of each salt having been determined, the total solvent power will not be represented by their sum. The *mode* of combination probably varies with the quantity of each salt present in the water; hence every variation in the quantity of any one salt alters the lead solvent power of the water, and gives to the combined salt elements new properties. Hence, it is not improbable that, though analysis may detect the same elements in different waters, and as rigorously as our means of analysis may permit, apparently in the same proportion, yet, a variation in the amount of any one element, too slight to be detected, may influence the *mode* of arrangement of the salts, and the lead solvent power of the water. Temperature exerts also a marked influence on the mode of arrangement.

A *mode* of combination of salt elements of natural water may possibly render that perfectly inactive on lead. It is only on this supposition that such a natural water can be admitted to be found.

But no previous analysis of water for domestic use will allow a prediction as to what its exceptions to the usual relations of lead and water may be. That can be determined only by actual aqueduct service, continued through a series of seasons, as it is well known that the action of water on lead has been intermitted. Hence, water apparently free from lead to-day may become charged with that metal to-morrow.

The actual amount of lead-solving power of any water is of little moment. It will become important only when it shall have been determined what is the minimum of lead which can exist in water, when used as a beverage, without detriment to health, a question as yet wholly undecided. The committee have yet to learn upon what facts, by what experiments this minimum has been placed by those eminent chemists, Professors Hoffmann, Graham, and Miller (see Report on the Supply of Water to London, *Quarterly Journal of Chemistry* No. 16), so high as one-fifty-seventh of a grain of lead per imperial gallon of water. "So minute a trace of lead," continue the above-named chemists, "remaining in the water could have no possible influence on the health;" and they seem disposed to adopt, if they do not in fact adopt the opinion of Dr. John Smith, of Aberdeen, "that less than one-twentieth of a grain of lead per gallon produces no deleterious effect on the health of those using it for dietetical purposes."

In numerous cases of well-defined, unmistakable lead disease, which have come under the observation of some of the members of the committee, the water suspected to be the cause of disease has been chemically examined. While, generally, it may be said that the amount of lead in solution would not fall below one-twentieth of a grain per gallon, yet, the cases have not been rare, where disease has been produced by less than one-one-hundreth of a grain of metallic lead per gallon in solution, or one in seven millions of water. One hundredth of a grain of lead is easily detected by a simple stream of sulphuretted hydrogen. Water has sometimes caused disease, under the eye of a part of your committee, where this test showed no trace of lead: yet, lead was abundantly evident after concentration of the water, and the sulphuret thus obtained has been converted into salts of lead, which have been again examined to confirm the hydrosulphurous test. Small as the amount of lead—less than one-seven-millionth of the weight of water—in solution thus appears, the committee are disposed to place it still lower. The Tunbridge well may be adduced, whose water, flowing through a lead pipe, disordered many who drank it; and it contained so minute a trace of lead in solution, that some of the most acute and eminent chemists of the day, men full of chemical tact and laboratory experience, failed to detect its presence. Happily for the afflicted, lead was at last detected, the pipe was removed, and health returned.

The salts of natural water were at one time thought to be protective against its lead-solvent power. To a limited degree this is true of water holding in solution bicarbonate of lime, a deposit of carbonate of lime gradually incrusting the interior of the pipe. But as we have no analysis recorded of the water thus flowing through a pipe lime-coated, it is impossible to say whether bicarbonate of lime has ever prevented gradual corrosion of the lead.

The doctrine of protective power has been much extended within a few years. It has afforded, and still affords to many minds an argument for the safety of water lead-transmitted. This doctrine has assumed various phases, which may be reduced to the three following:—

1. Protection by certain salts of the "right kind," present in water in a limited proportion, or by salts artificially introduced for the purpose of producing compounds of lead known to be insoluble in pure water. In the latter case, the pipe filled with a solution of the protective salt must be left closed for some months to allow a protective coat to be formed.

This may be called the Edinburgh doctrine, having been promulgated and advocated by Dr. Christison, of that city.

2. Protection by the formation of an insoluble coat of suboxide of lead after a few days, or at most a few weeks contact with water. This may be termed the Boston doctrine. It was there adopted as the ground of safety of using lead service pipes for lake water; fortified as it was by the belief that the inhabitants of other cities, using river or lake water lead-transmitted, had been protected from lead disease by the formation of an insoluble coat.

3. Protection by the presence of a limited amount of carbonic acid present in the water, forming insoluble carbonate of lead.

This is the latest, and it may be termed the London doctrine.

It is assumed by the eminent professors of chemistry named above as the ground of their belief, that the present distributing lead pipes in London may safely be continued if that metropolis should hereafter be supplied from the newly proposed sources with a constant supply of soft water.

The advocates of protection seem not to have duly considered that their several protective coats, however insoluble in pure water, are decomposable and soluble by the salts contained in natural water. The Edinburgh doctrine has been practically abandoned by its author. The Boston doctrine has been disproved by the results of analysis of water at present flowing through the lead service pipes earliest laid down by the city authorities. The London doctrine is yet to be proved, but its authors admit that an excess of carbonic acid will dissolve the coat of carbonate, and thus the water will be rendered deleterious if the solved lead exceeds one-twentieth of a grain per gallon.

The whole doctrine of the protective power by the formation of an insoluble, impervious coat on lead by the action of the impurities of water, is set aside by the fact that, however this coat may be formed, lead transmitting water is constantly dissolved. No limit of time has yet set bounds to this action.

This is a lesson of experience taught by the erosion of lead pipes and cisterns. It is the result of experiment that, where no perceptible action is visible, chemical examination detects lead in solution. Without going into details, adducing evidence on these points, by citing the statements which within a few months have been made to learned associations by scientific men, or to parliamentary committees by practical plumbers, of the ceaseless corrosion of lead by water, the committee would remark, that the doctrine of protection is no longer tenable on scientific or practical grounds. Still it is a doctrine which has many advocates, and exerts an influence on many minds, which is much to be deplored, viewed as a question of public hygiene.

This influence can be destroyed, not by reason, scientific argument, or practical experience of the erosion and destruction of lead pipe, but it will be counteracted —

1. When a substitute for lead of some material which, while it has all the practical working advantages of lead, will be equally *cheap*. It is a question of *price*, which always determines and will determine the preference for lead. This consideration with the many will continue the use of lead, however little faith may be placed in the doctrine of protective coating.

2. This doctrine will gradually be overthrown by the numerous cases of disease occurring where lead-transmitted water is used. These cases will be marked in proportion as the knowledge of lead malady, so much misunderstood, becomes more general and searching.

No argument for the safety of lead-transmitted water, founded on the absence of lead malady, ought to be admitted, which does not add to the non-occurrence of disease the fact that the pipe is not acted on, and that the water repeatedly, and under all circumstances examined, has never shown the presence of lead. Such pipes and such water are unknown to your committee; and they would, therefore, proceed to lay before the Association the facts they possess which prove the danger in the use of lead for transmitting and containing water, by the disease which the use of lead-water has caused.

SECTION II.—ON THE DISEASES WHICH PROCEED FROM THE USE OF LEAD-WATER.

This is by far the most important, and most difficult part of the duty assigned to your committee. They will, however, lay before the Association such facts as they have been able to collect, feeling that they have but just entered upon a subject which they hope those who have a wider field of observation may, ere long, more fully develop.

Science has not probably yet revealed all the diseases which proceed from lead taken into the human system. Several serious diseases, however, at the present time, are well understood to have their origin in the absorption of this poison, while others, scarcely less severe and distressing in their character, have not as yet been definitely proved to be thus produced, although many of them have fallen under strong suspicions of having a saturnine origin. Several of these, as some forms of dyspepsia, neuralgia, and rheumatism, from their well-known resemblance to other forms of lead disease, have been so classed by many very intelligent and observing physicians.

The earlier writers considered lead colic as the only form of disease produced directly from the introduction of lead into the system. Later authors have given more accurate discriptions of *saturnine colic*, and some of the characteristics of several of the other forms of lead disease. . . . .

Tanquerel was the first to present to the public the true pathology of these diseases. He classes lead diseases, so far as he has observed them, under four distinct and well-determined forms, viz: colic, arthralgia, paralysis, and encephalopathy. . . . . . .

These affections, he considers, have an independent existence, and have no real or necessary relation, except their common origin. . . .

Lead introduced into the system, from whatever source, may manifest its presence in various ways, before any of the usual forms of disease ultimately produced by it becomes apparent. These manifestations Tanquerel calls "*primary effects of lead.*" . . . . . .

These premonitory symptoms are rarely all produced in any one individual. . . . .

The first of these premonitory symptoms which we shall notice is, the *discoloration of the teeth and gums.* . . . . . .

This coloring matter is the *sulphuret of lead*, and is formed by a change of chemical affinities; when food, which always contains more or less sulphur, is masticated, same portions of it adhere to the roots of the teeth. A species of decomposition very soon takes place, and sulphuretted hydrogen is formed, which at once combines with any particles of lead that may be taken into the mouth, and forms sulphuret of lead, which is deposited on the gums and teeth precisely where the sulphuretted hydrogen was evolved.

(See *Tanquerel, Primary Effect of Lead*).

The next most frequent manifestation of lead is the *lead taste, breath, and odor.* Those who have been long exposed to the influence of lead often complain of a sugary, styptic, and astringent taste. The breath has also a peculiar fetid odor, which it is not easy to describe, but which can never be confounded with any other, by one who has ever been obliged to experience its effects; it is as marked as the mercurial breath, but is unlike it, and may be called the "lead breath."

The sense of smell is often affected; persons who have been much exposed to the influence of lead soon experience a smell of metallic lead; they seem sometimes to smell their own breath.

Another premonitory symptom of lead disease is what has been called *lead jaundice.* "When lead jaundice," says Tanquerel, "exists in the greatest degree, the skin is of a foul, earthy, yellow tint; if the disease is less severe, it appears of a pale, slightly ash yellow.

*   *   *   *   *

The discoloration of the skin in lead diseases is not from the ab-orption of bile. The liver performs its functions as usual, as is shown by the absence of bile in the urine, and its presence, in the usual amount, in the excrements. It is produced by the presence of lead in the system, precisely in the same way that nitrate of silver produces a change of color in the skin, when used internally for any great length of time.

Lead emaciation very soon follows the jaundiced appearance just noticed, and, like it, does not show itself till the system is highly charged with the poison. . . . . . .

Lead colic is the most frequent form of lead disease, and is the one most generally known, and perhaps the best understood. . . . .

Pain is the first and most distressing symptom of lead colic. It is generally situated about the umbilicus; sometimes it occupies the epigastrium, but rarely the hypochondria or the iliac fossæ. "These regions seem only to be the centers from which the flashes of pain radiate to other parts of the abdomen."

* * * * *

Arthralgia is the next most frequent form of lead disease. "It is characterized by pain in the limbs, without swelling or redness." The pain is constant, but subject to exacerbations; motion generally increases it, but gentle pressure diminishes it. The patient is often seized with severe cramps in the affected parts, on making any motion.

* * * * *

Paralysis is of less frequent occurrence than arthralgia, but is oftener seen than encephalopathy. According to Tanquerel, "the paralysis produced by lead preparations may consist in the loss of motion only, in parts at once enjoying both motion and sensibility. In other cases, on the contrary, the sensibility only of these same parts is affected, and they are rendered unfit to receive impressions from external bodies, the power of motion being unimpaired. The first kind of paralysis is called the paralysis of motion, or simple lead paralysis; and to the second is given the name of anæsthesy." These two kinds of paralysis may be combined, so that the parts affected may have neither motion nor sensibility.

* * * * *

Encephalopathy, according to Tanquerel, is a distinct form of disease arising from the noxious influence of lead upon the animal economy, which would seem to depend immediately upon some lesion of the brain. It embraces all the various forms of cerebral affections which have been observed to arise from lead poisoning. The same author considers that it requires the absorption of a larger proportion of lead particles to induce this disease than is requisite for the production of colic, arthralgia, or paralysis. He establishes four distinct forms of cerebral affection: 1, delirium; 2, coma; 3, convulsions: and 4, a combination of delirium, coma, and convulsions.

* * * * *

From what has already been stated, it appears that, in the present state of science, all known lead diseases are referable only to alterations in the brain or nervous system; and that pathological anatomy reveals no organic changes whatever that can account for the phenomena of these diseases. Where anatomy fails to demonstrate disease, we are naturally led to the only resource left us to ascertain its seat and nature; viz: observation and reasoning on the symptoms it presents. . . . . . .

Chemical analysis has given us more positive results than pathological anatomy. It has demonstrated not only the presence of lead naturally in the human system, but that it exists in much larger quantities in persons who die of lead diseases than it does in those who die from any other cause. Lead, in such cases, has been found in undue quantities in all the tissues of the body, and also in the blood itself; consequently, it must pervade every part of the system. Its poisonous effect is manifested in a remarkable degree in the brain and nervous system. This is demonstrated by the functional changes in these parts; as has already been shown, in the derangements of the functions of all the organs to which the great sympathetic nerve is distributed, as in lead colic; by functional alterations of the organs which derive their power of motion and feeling from the spinal nervous system, as in arthralgia and paralysis; also by a disturbed state of the brain in encephalopathy.

Lead diseases induced by drinking lead-transmitted water do not differ in their general character from the same disease produced by other forms of lead exposure. In their course, they are often complicated with each other; for instance, colic is often found in connection with arthralgia, sometimes with paralysis, and even with encephalopathy. Most of the cases, which will be reported by your Committee, present some of these complications. In fact, it is unusual to find a well-defined case of any form of lead disease unaccompanied by symptoms of some other form of disease, produced by the same poison. The following case is one in point: While it presents most of the phenomena of colic, those of arthralgia and paralysis are displayed in a very marked form.

It occurred in the person of a distinguished scholar and eminent divine, Rev. Dr. Lamson, of Dedham, Mass. The case is reported as drawn up by the patient himself, who, in describing his own feelings, has given an admirable delineation of the extreme suffering, the depressed nervous feelings of a person affected with lead disease.

Dr. Stimson, a distinguished physician in Dedham, informs your Committee that, in 1836, water was brought to the village from a spring upwards of half a mile distant, through leaden pipes, and distributed from them, through small service pipes of the same material, to most of the houses in the place. Dr. Stimson further states "that the Rev. Dr. Lamson was the first person who became diseased from drinking the water. It was used in his family both for drinking and culinary purposes. His case was one of the most interesting that occurred, was very insidious, and for a long time baffled the skill of other physicians besides myself. The cause of his severe illness was finally detected by accident. One day, when at his house, his wife asked me to taste their water, said it had a sweetish taste, and brought me a pitcher full that had stood over night. (The acqueduct water was not received at my house). I observed on its surface a scum of leaden color, resembling drops of lead; it had decidedly a sweetish taste. I had two bottles of it, one drawn early in the morning, to obtain the water that had remained in the pipes over night, and the other taken some time after, and sent to a chemist to be analyzed; saying, if lead was found in the solution, we should no longer be in doubt as to the cause of her husband's illness. The chemist analyzed the water, and found it to contain lead in solution."

Rev. Dr. Lamson, in a letter addressed to the chairman of your Committee, says:—

"My dear Sir: In compliance with your request, I will describe to you, so far as I can now distinctly recall them, the symptoms and history of the disease or diseases under which I suffered some years ago, from the introduction, as I confidently believe, of lead into the system, by means of water brought in lead pipes. I cannot, after the lapse of several years, determine the precise point of time when my attention was drawn to the malady which, most insidious in its approach, afterwards developed itself in so strange a manner.

"I am not positive as to any decided traces of a diseased state of the system before the early part of the summer of 1838; though I have an impression that the sensations I am about to describe commenced the preceding summer.

"The first symptoms which I can recall (I now speak of my first attack) are a peculiar uneasiness or moderate pain in the bowels, with a sort of feeling that there was required, or would be some action of them, but no effect of the kind ordinarily followed, or could be induced by a natural effort. Yet there was at that time no violent constipation. This uneasiness, or these sensations, were not constant, but grew in frequency, the pain gradually creeping round to the lumbar region, when it became fixed and constant; by degrees, however, diffusing itself over the system, particularly the lower limbs. I do not recollect any pains in the head. But by the middle or latter part of the summer of 1838 I became greatly debilitated, yet was without fever, the pulse not elevated. An uneasiness or pain in the lumbar region now caused me continual suffering. I had a feeling of great misery; could walk but a few steps without wanting to stop and sit down; and if I did so, it was a great effort to rise again. I had a sense of constant lassitude or weariness, and an indisposition to motion. I was perplexed by the symptoms. The least fatigue—and all motion fatigued me—aggravated the suffering.

"I have now a very vivid recollection of going, with two or three friends, to pass a day or two at Natasket Beach. This must have been late in July or early in August. We went out in a boat, and I well remember my sufferings as I lay listless in one end of it, trying, by various changes, to put myself in a posture of some ease, which I could not succeed in doing. I remember distinctly the question asked me by one of my companions: "Are you in pain?" I was scarcely able to get home. We rode from the beach to Dedham in a carryall. I remember the difficulty I had in supporting myself, holding on, as I could, by different parts of the carriage. As soon as I reached home, I threw myself on a bed, and sent for Dr. Stimson.

"The bowels had now become wholly inactive, and it was, I think, two days at least, before they could be moved, and then very imperfectly. During this time I was in a most restless state, day and night. There was no sharp pain, but a constant, dull, gnawing pain, more particularly in the lumbar region and bowels, and a tired feeling in all the limbs. I was every moment changing my position, seeking ease, but not, for a moment finding it. I would get out of bed every little time, and sit in a chair, or attempt to walk the room, but it was all the same. There was no relief to be had. After the bowels had been effectually stirred, I found myself in a degree relieved. From this time, the duties of my pulpit were suspended. I gradually gained, however. I now kept out as much as possible."

In the latter part of August, Dr. Lamson went to the sea-shore, and, about the 20th of September, to Eastport and the Provinces; and subsequently traveled, by easy stages, through the interior of Maine and New Hampshire, reaching home in the autumn. After this he walked, or rode on horseback, a distance of ten to twelve miles every day. Exercise did not now fatigue, but seemed to invigorate him, so that he entered his pulpit and preached on Thanksgiving Day. "This, you will recollect," the Dr. continues, "was in the latter part of November of 1838."

"I went through the next year very well, keeping up my system of out-door exercise so far as my duties allowed. In the latter part of winter, or early in the spring, I think it was winter, I had an attack, mainly in the left side, apparently in the intercostal muscles. From this I recovered in no long time, and went on till late in the spring of 1840. Then, and in the early part of summer, I had a return of the old symptoms described as occurring in 1838; only with this difference, that the development of the disease was much more rapid. I went through the same process of active medicines, injections, &c., before the bowels could be stirred. I became more debilitated than before, the countenance assuming, in a more marked degree, the peculiar earthy yellow described by M. Tanquerel.

"Then came on the pure arthralgic pains. They seemed to be deep, as if in the very bone, and were seated more particularly in the flexor muscles, as the inside of the elbow joints and the joints of the knees.

"Soon after, that is in July, there commenced a trembling of the fingers, which soon passed into decided paralysis, the paralysis increasing for about three weeks. This paralysis was in the extensor muscles of the fingers, wrist, forearm, and arm of both the upper limbs; the lower limbs, with a slight exception I shall hereafter notice, not being affected. My arms, when left to themselves, hung loose and dangling at my sides, as if turning on a pivot. Using only one at a time, I could elevate them only in a slight degree. I could not get my hand to my chin or mouth.

"But what puzzled me at the time was that there was certain motions which I could perform; for example, placing the palm of one hand against the back of the other, I could get them to my face, the flexor muscles of the hand, which were not paralyzed, being thus brought into action. So, too, I could draw on my boots almost as well as ever, the same muscles acting. If my arms were elevated to a right angle with the body, the palm of the hand being turned downward, the whole hand fell at the wrist, hanging loose as a piece of cloth, and the will had no more power over it. I could not, without help, raise the hand in the least, nor so much as one of my fingers, in the slightest degree. When I took a tumbler to drink, I clasped it with both hands fully spread, and could so get it to my lips. When I ate, I rested my right arm, below the elbow, on the edge of the table, and grasping the wrist with the left hand, and then bringing my mouth down to within three or four inches of the table, I could get the food to it. The backs of the hands became prominently arched; the fingers when left to themselves, became bent and half shut, the natural consequence, I suppose, of loss of power in the extensor muscles. The rotatory motion of the arm was entirely lost, a fact to which my attention was directed, when they attempted to assist me to put on my coat.

"I tried all I could to exercise the poor lame muscles, but all fatigue, that is, all use of them, seemed to be attended with injury. They had totally lost their contractile power. The abdominal muscles were similarly affected, though not in the same degree. If I had any, it was only a very slight power over them, which gave me great trouble when an action of the bowels was needed, though they could at this time be readily moved by medicine.

"All the while there was more or less of arthralgic pain, more particularly at this period, in the inside of the knee-joints.

"The pain seemed to have no connection with the paralysis, and was greater in the parts not paralyzed than in those which were. The intercostal muscles on the left side were now affected; for months

I could not sneeze; the moment the process began it was arrested by these muscles. The sensation was a very unpleasant one.

"We were at this time entirely in the dark as to the nature of this disease; my physician seemed perplexed at the very extraordinary character of the symptoms.

"I got down to Nantasket Beach, and passed four weeks there with some slight benefit; that is, I became in a trifling degree, less debilitated. I could not but remark at the time, that, whenever I left Dedham for a few days, I gained a little strength, but relapsed on my return, an effect which I afterwards ascribed to drinking the water, as I at the time used no other. I recollect asking myself at the time, what could be the cause? Was it the atmosphere of the place? That seemed an insufficient solution of the problem. At this time I had some appetite; I could eat enough, in fact, and in general with a tolerable relish. I had no constant thirst, though I felt thirsty at times, especially in the afternoon, or when unusually fatigued. I had little or no fever, though at one time a highly nervous pulse.

"I have spoken of the loss of the power of motion in certain muscles, or their loss of contractility. The sensibility of the muscles or nerves, with a slight exception, was not impaired, but the reverse. This sensibility became intensely acute. There was a soreness or peculiar tenderness in all my flesh. Sitting in a common wooden chair and leaning back, the parts of the chair seemed to penetrate to the very bones. The exception referred to was a small muscle in the inner part of the left thigh; I never ascertained its name. There was a spot of three or four inches in length, and two or three in breadth, which had lost its sensibility. There was, at times, a sensation of a peculiar and unpleasant kind at the bottom of my feet, a sort of burning, which I used to relieve, when in bed, by drawing up the covering, and pressing the soles of my feet firmly against the foot board, which produced a cool and agreeable sensation. I had also, at times, a violent pain in the back between the shoulders, rather nearer the right than the left shoulder, which I would relieve by getting on my bed, and lying flat on my back, bringing as much pressure to bear on the part affected as I could. This method mitigated the pain before a long time. In a multitude of ways, I was a great sufferer; but the brain I did not think was affected, and I do not now think that it was. There was no appearance of encephalopathy."

Soon after Dr. Lamson's return from the beach, the latter part of August, he was induced to visit the Sulphur Springs of Virginia. The journey was with great difficulty performed. He remained about two weeks at the White Sulphur, and about the same length of time at the Hot Mineral Springs. Returning by the way of Washington, he reached home after an absence of about six weeks.

To resume the narrative. "About this time I heard some talk of lead as the probable cause of my disease, and attention was directed to the water. It was at this time, or a little before, I think, that Dr. Stimson expressed a conviction, or an opinion, that lead might be, or was, the cause. I did not myself think that it could be so, and, in fact, at first treated the suggestion rather lightly. I remembered to have heard it stated, at the time the pipes were laid, that the water being soft and pure would not act on lead. I had, therefore, rested secure. I did not then know what I afterwards ascertained from reading, that the pure and spring waters were quite as likely as others to act on lead. It happened, however, that about this time, a volume, treating of mineral poisons, being mainly an epitome, I think, of Dr. Christison's work, was put into my hands. Some symptoms, which he described as those of lead disease, caused me to pause and reflect. About ten days or a fortnight after this, we heard the result of the first chemical analysis of the water drawn from my branch-pipe. This analysis was made by Prof. Webster, of Cambridge. He found the water decidedly impregnated with lead; enough so, in his opinion, seriously to endanger the health of those who should habitually use it. He found acetate of lead, and, I think, carbonate. A quantity of the water was afterwards sent for analysis to Dr. Hayes, and with the same result.

"At this time I was very slightly improving, as I thought. Still I could not be quite sure that the paralysis was leaving me, or was, in fact, essentially better. I may say that I had yet remaining some little skepticism as to the nature and cause of the malady. But the last vestige of it was soon to be put to flight.

"I received from Paris the two volumes of Tanquerel on diseases occasioned by lead; the work subsequently so faithfully translated and abridged by my friend Dr. Dana. I fell to reading it with great eagerness, and there I found all my symptoms minutely and accurately described, under the heads of arthralgia and paralysis. I could hardly persuade myself that it was possible for one who had not felt the symptoms himself to describe them with so much minuteness and truth. All mystery now vanished with regard to the nature of the disease. I can never feel more certain of any fact whatever, than I was, and am still, that all my suffering came from the use of water conveyed in lead pipes.

"It was impossible, as it appeared to me, to doubt it. I know the power of incredulity, but there are cases in which incredulity itself must yield. I deem this one of them.

"Still my recovery was exceedingly slow; I could perceive no change from day to day; but from week to week I flattered myself that I could. Electricity was tried, but without any perceptible advantage.

"Time and the open air, in which I kept as much as possible, and nourishing food, seemed to me to do the work. The pains gradually left me, and the muscles became strengthened, and returned to their normal state.

"The arms, which had become greatly emaciated, and the wrists and hands, were the last to be restored. By the first of January, 1841, I was able to enter my pulpit, and go through the services. But I had then a very imperfect use of my hands; I could write a little, but my chirography looked like that of a very old man. My pen would jump and go all sorts of ways, and was tremulous. In the course of the winter I improved gradually, but for some years occasionally felt the effects of the disease, particularly in the wrists.

"The above is a simple narration of facts and sensations as they now rise up to my memory, I have many times regretted that I did not write a description of my case at the time. I have done it now. at the request of your Committee, and in the hope of benefiting my fellow-beings. You will excuse the length of my communication, and believe me, with sentiments of great respect,

Very truly yours,

"(Signed) A. LAMSON."

* * * * * * *

"There was another person in Dr. L.'s family who became diseased, and presented symptoms similar to his, but of less severity; a colored female domestic, who had drank the water for eighteen months. Her symptoms were arthralgic and neuralgic pains about the trunk and extremities, impaired appetite, loss of flesh, with a peculiar anxious and distressed countenance and constipated bowels; was obliged to leave her place, in consequence of her indisposition; after she left, she soon began to mend, and in a few weeks regained her usual flesh and health."

"It appears also, from the Doctor's report, that many other cases occurred similar to the one above; for many of the inhabitants continued to drink the water, although warned that it contained a deadly poison, until they began to feel the evil effects of it, when it was abandoned. Most of the cases recovered after the water was discontinued.

The following cases we give in Dr. Stimson's own language:

Lead Arthralgia with Paralysis.—"April 18, 1849. I was called to visit a patient in a neighboring town, a Miss Mayhew, aged about 14 years. The following history of her case I received from her mother and the attending physician. She had been confined to her bed for several weeks with what they supposed to be chronic rheumatism. It came on gradually, without fever, with severe pains in the inside of her upper and lower extremities, more particularly about the inner angle of the elbow and knees; then about the loins and chest. The mother said she had pains all over her: sometimes they appeared more severe in one place, and sometimes in another; but when moved she complained of its hurting her everywhere; that she was very nervous, unwilling to be touched, or have any thing done for her; much depressed in spirit, and unwilling to see any one. Nothing she had taken done her any good; she had continually been growing worse and worse; her appetite was very poor, and she had lost much flesh; and her bowels were constipated from the morphine she had been obliged to take to get any sleep.

"The first thing that attracted my attention, as she lay curled up in the bed, was that specific physiognomy peculiar to persons poisoned by lead. Skin cool; pulse moderate, soft and feeble; much emaciation. It was difficult to make a thorough examination, she was so fearful it would put her in pain; for, when still, she said she was comparatively easy. On gently moving the limbs, both upper and ower, I found it was the flexor muscles that caused the pain on motion; the abdomen was small; the muscles were rather firm, not soft and pliable. The fingers of one of the hands were curled up into the palm, and I could not persuade her to move them. She breathed naturally, and I could discover no disease of the heart or lungs. I suspected the disease was caused by lead; that somehow or other it had penetrated the system. I questioned the parents about their water, whether it came through leaden pipes; and was informed that it did. It was brought, they said, some distance to the house for washing, as the water was very soft, and their well-water was hard. They had generally used their well-water for drinking and for culinary purposes; but their well had been out of order the last six or eight months, and the water from the aqueduct had been used constantly during that time for all domestic purposes. This water was frequently used in the family while the well was in order, as it came into the house and was so handy; but oftener they thought for cooking than for drinking. These facts confirmed my diagnosis. I gave my opinion that the disease was lead arthralgia, caused by the aqueduct water, and advised an immediate discontinuance of it.

"*August* 29, 1849. Saw her again; her parents brought her to Dedham; she remained here a week under my care. Her general health had much improved; she had gained in flesh and strength; suffered little or no pain; slept without anodynes; appetite good; and the countenance had recovered its normal expression. The extensor muscles of one of the upper and one of the lower extremities of the same side were paralyzed. When she raised the arm, the hand hung pendulous from the wrist. Pronation or supination could neither be performed; the fingers were still drawn into the palm of the hand; no one of them, nor the thumb, could be moved in the slightest degree; they retained their sensibility. When she walked, she shoved the foot on the floor, not being able to raise the toes, which gave her a peculiar and unsightly gait. I prescribed strychnine in pills, commencing with 1-12th of a grain, and increasing 1-12th each dose, till she felt the tetanic shaking; 4-12ths produced the desired effect. The next day she slightly moved the forefinger. She continued to take 4-12ths of a grain, every second or third day, for several weeks, with much benefit. I did not see her again till the summer of 1850. She then was quite fleshy, her health good, had entirely recovered the use of her foot, could walk or dance without any perceptible difference in the movement of her limbs. She could rotate the lower arm and hand, and move it in all directions, as well as the other, but could not straighten the fingers; the thumb had also recovered perfectly. She played on the piano, using the knuckles of that hand, instead of the extremities of the fingers, with a facility that surprised me. Whether she will ever be able to use these fingers, time alone must determine. She could not the last time I heard from her, six months since."

Lead Paralysis with Encephalopathy.—"J. Guild, aged fifty-four, a resident of this village, engaged in mercantile pursuits, of rather feeble constitution; had always been able to attend to his business; had never been severely ill previous to May, 1847, when he was attacked with pleurisy, which terminated in effusion into the left pleura. In about two months, the water was absorbed, and he gradually recovered such a degree of health, that he returned to his business in the latter part of the following July. His system was shattered by his long sickness, and his health never so good afterwards as before. Early in March, 1848, he began to falter, complained of being easily tired, walked feebly, said he had no pain, and could not imagine what ailed him; thought he might have more water in the chest, and wished me to examine him. I did so, by auscultation and percussion, and was satisfied there was no disease about the chest, and could discover none any where about him. His pulse was feeble, his appetite failing, and flesh declining; but what caused his indisposition, at that time I could not divine. A few days after this examination, strabismus supervened; one eye turned in toward the nose, and he could not roll it out; the external muscle of the eye was paralyzed. He could see as distinctly as ever with either eye separately; but, whenever he looked with both, the object appeared double. He continued about his business several weeks after this, much in the same state, though rather declining; he had some slight pains about the chest at times, and was apprehensive his old difficulty would return, and wished me to examine his chest frequently, which I did, but could discover no disease there.

"I advised him to take a journey; he did, to the Sulphur Springs, in New York; he remained absent but a short time, feeling too unwell to be from home. Soon after his return, he complained of numbness in his fingers; it soon increased to such a degree that he was unable to button his clothes; and soon after this, there was evidently paralysis in the extensor muscles of the arm. The countenance began to put on that expression so peculiar in all who suffer from lead disease. I was satisfied that lead had penetrated his system in some way; but how? The acqueduct did not come to his house or store; he believed it unhealthy, and never used it. He had his store painted and grained in the inside; the workmen were a fortnight doing it, in the month of March; he was in the store every day, with the doors and windows closed, while they were about it. The strabismus occurred during this time. Did he inhale the poison of lead in a sufficient quantity to cause the disease? I thought not, as the earlier symptoms appeared some weeks previously. On further inquiry, I learned that the water he drank and used for culinary purposes came from his well through leaden pipes. We had two junk bottles of the water, one from the pump, and the other from the well outside the leaden tube, sent to Dr. Hayes, a distinguished chemist, formerly of Roxboro', now in Boston, for analysis. Lead was found in both bottles, but less in No. 2 than in No. 1. How long the leaden pipe had been in the well could not be certainly ascertained; they were sure it must have been in a number of years, probably five or six; no one else of the family had suffered from it. We were now fully satisfied the cause of the disease was discovered.

"The patient was put under the treatment recommended by Tanquerel, viz: sulphurous baths and pills of strychnine. The baths were prepared by putting five ounces of sulphuret of potash to each bath; they were taken six days in succession, then omitted; gr. i of strychnine was made into twelve pills, beginning with one, and increasing one every day, till the tetanic shakings were produced; four pills generally affected him, and caused as severe shakings as he was willing to bear, continuing two or three hours before they entirely ceased. This course was interrupted, then again repeated, as long as it was thought best, without apparent benefit; at any rate, he gradually grew worse, with the exception of the pains about the chest; they were better. The paralysis increased in the extensor muscles of both the upper extremities, and soon after, one of the lower was so severely affected, that he could neither dress nor feed himself, nor walk without assistance. The debility and emaciation increased, also the tremor; the complexion, a pale dirty white, and the physiognomy peculiarly marked. His spirits greatly depressed; if a neighbor called to see him, would burst into tears, and be unable to speak, for some time. This state of mind appeared in all the severe cases; the stoutest hearts seemed to succumb, become passive and non-resistant. Bowels constipated, readily moved by medicine; pulse normal, but feeble.

"He continued with little alteration till early in October, when encephalopathy supervened;* he became delirious during the night, talked incoherently; countenance wild and staring. This continued ten or twelve days; at times would talk rationally, and answer questions correctly, then wander and be quite insane. After the affection of the brain terminated, his general appearance was much as it had been previously, only more debilitated. He continued from this time gradually to sink, and became very much emaciated before his death, which took place January 2, 1849."

We have selected but two of Dr. Stimson's many cases of the well-marked and well-defined lead diseases, which appeared in Dedham, Massachusetts, a few years since; so common were these diseases, at one period, that they might have been considered in the light almost of an epidemic.

But as soon as the inhabitants were convinced that they were caused by the use of lead water, *most* of them abandoned it, and the great frequency of the disease disappeared.

But some of them were sceptical, and continued to use the acqueduct water, and were unwilling to believe in the poisonous quality of it, until forced to do so by their personal experience in the diseases caused by it.

The Doctor himself, at a subsequent period, suffered a severe attack of arthralgia in his lower extremities, from using water drawn from a well through a lead pipe.

His wife also had an attack of paralysis in the lower extremities, which prevented her from walking; she could not rise from her chair without taking hold of something and pulling herself up; she was also unable to raise her toes from the floor. The disease continued to increase till the cause was discovered and removed; since which the Doctor has had no return of the pain, and his wife has gradually recovered the use of her limbs. His case had some points of peculiarity; the pain always came on in the night, was seated in the in-

* The chairman of your Committee first saw this patient, in consultation, on the last day of September, 1848, when he began to show some symptoms of the aproach of encephalopathy.

side of his knees and legs, and seemed to him as if it extended to the marrow of the bones, and was always relieved by pressure.

The Committee regret that their limits will not allow them to give the Doctor's minute description of these two cases entire.

The following cases, communicated by letter to your Committee by Dr. Challiss, of Moorestown, Burlington County, New Jersey, will show, that the liability to disease does not always cease immediately on abstaining from the cause. One case of colic occurred two months after the patient ceased to drink the water; and the case of paralysis did not show itself till three months after the use of the water had been discontinued. The first case of colic was also attended by some symptoms of encephalopathy.

"The family of William Clark commenced making domestic use of water, transmitted through lead pipes, on March 20, 1851; with the exception of his son George, who commenced in September, 1850. George, who was a man of robust and plethoric constitution, was taken with colica pictonum, April 3, 1851, and after a severe illness of three weeks, convalescence commenced. Lacinating pain in the bowels and severe cephalalgia were the prominent symptoms. He was at times delirious, very restless, and manifested great concern for his affairs. But, as soon as ptyalism was produced, the severity of the symptoms abated. But, before leaving this case I would state that, in the September following he had another attack, and died under the care of a homœopathic physician; the only case, out of five, in this family, that was treated homœopathically, and the only one that died. April 7, 1851, Mrs. Clark, who is old and anemic, was taken, and did not fully regain her health until June 12, 1851. Her symptoms were, in character, the same as her son's, but not so acute. Susan (the daughter), who is a young woman, of ruddy countenance and full habit, was taken May 3, 1851. She did not remain ill after May 15. The onset of the disease, in this case, was threatening, but the recovery was rapid. The symptoms were in the main, the same as in the preceding cases.

"William Clark was taken October, 1851, with paralysis of the left arm, but which, in about four weeks after I began the treatment, was restored to use. For the particulars in regard to this case, I would refer you to the January number of the *New Jersey Medical Reporter*, (from which we gather the following facts: 'The appearance of the patient was very much changed from what it was a short time previous. His countenance was pale and sunken, his expression melancholic. That vivacity which was a marked feature of his character was gone, and sadness and silence sat enthroned.')

"He was able to make flexion and extension but to a slight degree; but, what is singular, the grasp was as perfect, and as strong as in health. The condition of the left side was involved in great obscurity. To the touch, that part, extending from the false ribs to the crista ilii, and from the dorsal vertebræ to the left rectus muscle, presented a hard and indurated feel. The hardened mass lay immediately beneath the skin, and could be traced only to the muscular system. His general system was not at all deranged. This attack came on three months after the water, which had poisoned his family, had been discontinued for domestic purposes."

The following cases are extracted from a letter addressed to the Committee by Dr. J. T. Garrison, of Swedesboro', West N. Jersey:

"In the autumn of 1847, Mr. C. laid a train of one inch lead pipe from his residence to a spring about a mile distant, for the purpose of conveying the water from it to his house and barns. The spring being on a hill which was more elevated than the buildings for which the supply was intended, no machinery was required to impel the water through the pipes; it made its way along them, by its natural gravitation, into large wooden tanks provided for it in the kitchen and cattle yard. When the spring was very low, as sometimes happened in warm weather, the pipes were but partially filled by the current, room being thus left for the entrance of air into the unoccupied space. I cannot ascertain the exact time at which the water was first used by the family more nearly than that it was in the latter part of the summer, or the first of the autumn; but from this time it was used constantly; and, as it was esteemed peculiarly pure and good, none other was ever employed for culinary purposes or drinking. The cattle and horses were also supplied exclusively from the same source.

"There was no illness in the family during the winter of 1847; nor the spring of 1848, until the middle and latter part of May, when several members of the family began to complain of feelings of uneasiness in the abdomen, with pains over the body generally, accompanied by constipation in some, and in others, by tenesmus and small bloody stools. Mr. C. himself was especially effected, and became gradually worse, suffering from violent colic pains, with unrelenting constipation, until June 20th, 1848, when we were called on to visit him. Dr. Garrison (senior), who first saw the case, found him in excruciating pain, which was located near the umbilicus; it never left him for a moment, and seldom even remitted decidedly; this was attended with intense retraction of the integuments of the abdomen towards the spine, and a hard knotty feeling of the muscles in various places over its surface.

"The bowels had not been moved for five days previous to the visit, although there was a frequent and urgent tenesmus; his pulse was rapid, his skin hot, his countenance anxious, his tongue furred, and his gums fringed along their edges with the strongly marked blue line, said to be pathognomonic of the presence of lead in the system. His stomach was also disordered; so much so as to induce a frequent desire to vomit.

"The peculiarity of the symptoms, joined to a knowledge of the facts above mentioned, respecting the water which he was in the habit of using, left no doubt of the nature of his ailment. He was treated by bleeding and the administration internally of calomel and opium, followed by senna and salts, cream of tartar, and jalap, and other purges, which were, however, one and all rejected; nor was the constipation overcome until the morning of the third day of our attendance, when it was effected by the use of croton oil, assisted by enemata. After this, he gradually improved, and on the tenth day (June 30th) was decidedly convalescing."

"Mrs. C. and several of the children had also been suffering in a similar manner, though not so severely; and, on examination, we found the gums of six others of the family distinctly marked with the blue line along their edges; but, by suspending the use of the water, and some slight medication, they were soon made quite well. Since this time, the family have entirely discontinued the use of this water for cooking and drinking; but the cattle and horses have been allowed to take of it freely, and as yet without any injury to their health that is notable."

A gentleman from New Hampshire called to consult the chairman of your Committee, a few months since; but, being absent, he did not see him. Soon after this gentleman's return home, he sent by a friend a bottle of water to be analyzed, and the following history of his own and his wife's case—two very well defined cases of arthralgia, accompanied by slight paralysis of the muscles of the extremities. It is quite remarkable that he should have noted most of the prominent symptoms of the two diseases above mentioned. The water contained traces of lead, sufficient, in all probability, to produce the state of the system which he describes. They had no suspicion that lead poison was the cause of their troubles until this was suggested to them by a friend, who had known something of the effects of it in other instances.

We give the letter in his own language, which is eminently descriptive of the diseases from one not familiar with the phraseology of medical science :

"In 1843, we began to use hard water, drawn through heavy, one and a half inch lead pipe; in 1851, renewed the pipe, the old being very badly corroded, in fact, eaten through in several places. At the time we began to use the water, Mrs. G. and myself were in good health and spirits; previous to which, neither of us had labored so hard as we have since; both of us have been troubled, more or less, during the whole period since 1844, with numbness in our hands and arms. Mrs. G. for most of the time has been in good health and spirits, has generally slept well; the exceptions are, the numbness, before mentioned, and more particularly in 1850–51, was much troubled with *lame*, *weak*, and *painful* limbs, particularly in her knees; she is now nearly recovered in this particular; yet she is, from numbness or something akin to it, now frequently unable to write, sew, or knit. We discontinued using the water in August last.

"My own case is substantially as follows: In the first place, I have drank very freely of the water, particularly in warm weather; it is quite cool, and I have indulged copiously in the luxury, and, as a general thing, my health and spirits have been bad; generally worse in autumn, often down or very near it at this season; better in the winter. My back has been lame, weak, and painful; my knees and legs at times nearly useless, or in other words extremely feeble; very troublesome dreams almost nightly; generally restless; on rising in the morning, often (not always) completely enervated, with neither energy, strength, nor courage; depressed exceedingly; stirring about, however, soon, in a degree, remedies the difficulty.

"In 1849–50, I was greatly troubled with pain in my leg; frequently awoke in the night in most intense agony; a sudden jump, with hard rubbing, would very soon cause relief.

"I also had thirty or forty sores, something like boils, on the back of my thigh and above; 'push boils' in the commencement, but they enlarged and discharged very much. My teeth began to work loose and come out before I left Boston; they, however, went rapidly after I came here; the last that were firm, say four or five, the dentist took away in 1849.

"I have described my feelings as nearly as I can; you will bear in mind the *hard work*, and also the ages, being now fifty-four and fifty-six."

The cases which follow fell under the immediate observation of Dr. Dalton, a member of your Committee from Lowell, Mass.:

The case which I shall first describe strongly illustrates the intractable character of lead affections, so long as the cause remains unsuspected, and in continued operation, and also how liable this is to be overlooked by even the most sagacious members of the profession, in the absence of suspicious circumstances.

"E. M. Read, a mason, 35 years of age, married, of a fine constitution, and in the enjoyment of perfect health, removed from one of the factory boarding-houses (supplied with water, for domestic purposes, through a wooden pump) to a residence on Gorham St., Chapel Hill, in 1836. His health remained good until the early part of 1839, when he began to have attacks of colic, with constipation, attended with a disagreeable sense of heat in the bowels; loss of flesh and color—his skin assuming a yellowish dingy aspect; pains in his lower limbs, with a sense of weakness, stiffness, and numbness, with frequent, indeed almost daily, attacks of colic. Eructations; loss of appetite, with all the variety of dyspeptic symptoms. Naturally cheerful, his spirits became depressed, and he became very nervous. These symptoms, which came on very insidiously and gradually, in the course of a few months were much aggravated, and from their frequent return, after partially yielding to active cathartics, alteratives, bitters, &c., became alarming.

"The treatment, which relieved in the early stages, failed to be of any benefit as the case advanced. Practitioner after practitioner was consulted, with equally unsatisfactory results. The costiveness became constant, while cathartics and even laxatives aggravated his sufferings; colicky pains recurred almost daily, and he suffered from a sense of stricture, as if a cord were drawn permanently tight around his body at the navel.

"At this juncture, he consulted Dr. James Jackson, and remained a week under his care, in Boston; by him leeches were applied twice freely to his abdomen, and with immediate, but transient relief; in a few days, the pains, &c., returned, and leeches were ineffectually repeated. Dr. Jackson dissuaded from the further use of medicine, advising him to a strict course of diet, and such as was calculated to produce a soluble state of the bowels, without resort to purgatives. This course was strictly followed, but the disorder remained substantially unaltered.

"No inquiry or reference, up to this time, was made by any one, as to the true cause of the difficulty. Some five or six months previously to his own ill health, the health of his wife and of his only daughter had become impaired; the former suffering from frequent attacks of colic, pain in the limbs, nausea, vomiting, numbness and stiffness of the lower extremities—the latter from spinal irritation, dyspepsia, fetid breath, and covulsions.*

"About this time similar cases, in this same neighborhood, had occurred; and several in my own practice. The result was a suspicion as to the true cause; which was at once confirmed by chemical examination of water in the wells, which was found to be supplied to all the families in that portion of the city through lead pipe, in some cases several hundred feet in length; of course no time was lost in substituting other material for lead in supplying the family of Mr. R.; which example was very soon followed in the case of the other sufferers.

* In about a year after their removal to the Ch. Hill, Mr. R's son, a child about two years old, began to be affected with anomalous symptoms in his bowels, terminating, after a few week's illness, in fatal disorder of the brain, which, at the *post mortem* examination, exhibited, however, no tangible traces of disease. The father feels a conviction that the child owes its death to the influence of lead in the water of the house, which he says, constituted its constant beverage. I did not see the case.

"From this time, Mr. R.'s symptoms began to mitigate; the attacks were less and less severe; and, although his recovery has been slow, he is now in the enjoyment of nearly the same amount of health as when he first removed to the district. His wife and daughter also soon recovered."

"Similar cases, of a more or less pronounced character, continued to occur in this, as well as in other parts of our city, all of which were traced to the use of water impregnated with lead; not a small number of them terminating fatally, either before the cause was detected, or from an obstinate incredulity on this subject, which prevented its removal at a sufficiently early stage of the affection to admit of recovery. But, eventually, this incredulity was overcome; lead pipes were generally removed; block tin or iron substituted—and forthwith the intractable character of the disease disappeared; protracted cases began to permanently mend; new ones became less frequent, and finally very rare, occurring only now and then, here and there, where the avarice of a landlord had refused to listen to the voice of humanity, by submitting to the trifling expense required in the exchange of the material above mentioned. When cases did occur, they were at once identified, and the cause being immediately removed, recovery began, and was soon established, with very little, and in some cases with no medication. In one of the cases above alluded to, the water for the uses of the family was brought through a lead pipe more than 400 feet in length; scarcely one of its members, domestics, or visitors, however transient their stay, escaped attacks of disease, bearing evident marks of their saturnine origin; the visitors being attacked with nausea, vomiting, constipation, and colic; the more permanent members with the same as well as with the more severe and dangerous symptoms; yielding but imperfectly to treatment as long as the cause remained undetected, but recovering rapidly and permanently so soon as this was removed. One of these cases terminated in complete paralysis of both lower extremities, which eventually disappeared under the use of strychnine.

Although, as I have above intimated, there were here and there cases of the affection in other localities within the city, yet by far the larger number, and most severe ones, took place in that portion of Lowell embraced by what is called Chapel Hill; a fact readily explained by its peculiar geological structure, abounding in those chemical agencies, which, in their various plays, act with energy upon lead, producing either soluble compounds, or suspending it in indivisibly diffused particles, throughout the water; these, prevailing less abundantly elsewhere, the affections under consideration were less both in amount and severity. In a very large majority of cases, the suspected water was subjected to appropriate tests, by competent chemists, principally by Dr. Dana, and invariably found charged, in a greater or less degree, with the noxious principle.

The following letter, from a manuscript lecture of the late Dr. Howe, of Billerica (having allusion to one of the fatal cases which he saw, in consultation with Dr. Bartlett, and which occurred in the Chapel Hill district), may not be without interest:—

"In the year 1836, I owned a house in Lowell; the water supplying it was drawn from the well through lead pipe some forty feet long; my patient was a man of a broken-down constitution—he sickened and died. During his illness, I saw him occasionally in consultation with Dr. Bartlett, his attending physician. The case exhibited some peculiarities; the symptoms were obstinate and unyielding; and from them I was induced to fear that our patient was suffering from the use of the water. Without expressing my apprehensions to the physician and friends, I determined to ascertain whether the water might not be contaminated with lead; *the pump forthwith got out of order, and would not go at all.* I procured privately, through a friend, two junk bottles of water, drawn from the same well, and in the same manner; one bottle contained water which had stood in the pipe over night—this marked No. 1.

"The other bottle was filled directly fresh from the well—this I marked No. 2. Both bottles were sent to Dr. Jackson, (C. T.) to be analyzed, &c.

"In due time, he wrote me that bottle No. 1 contained lead in sufficient quantity to enable him to reduce it to the metalic state; that bottle No. 2 contained some traces of lead, but in much smaller quantity than No. 1.

"We then, without assigning any reason for so doing, immediately removed the pipes from the well, and introduced wooden pumps in their places.

"On the 2d July, 1842, I was called in consultation with Dr. H. of Lowell, to visit a young lad belonging to a respectable family in that place; it was a case of real Devonshire colic, attended with symptoms too clearly defined to be mistaken by any medical practitioner; one other member of the family was suffering at the same time but under a milder form of the same disease. The boy died in a day or two after I saw him."

In the following case, although the symptoms were unmistakably those of arthralgia and colic of lead, I was for a long time baffled in my attempts to ascertain the fact, in conseqence of my patient's want of good faith towards me; who, either because he had no belief himself in the poisonous qualities of lead, or from a fear of the expense which might be involved in the acknowledgment, concealed from me, not only the important fact that the well water used in his family was drawn through some twenty feet of lead pipe, but also the far more important one, that, about a year previously, he had caused the water from a neighboring hill to be brought into his tannery through lead pipe, a distance exceeding two thousand feet; which water, in consequence of its "superior freshness, coldness, and *sweetness*," he had been in the habit of drinking when about his work; of course, he was warned against a repetition of his error, and, since his recovery, has enjoyed perfect health, having become himself convinced of the true origin of his complaint.

"H. T., aged forty-five, a tanner; after suffering for several weeks from pains in his limbs, shoulders, neck, face, and head, attended with costiveness and abdominal distress, was seized on Nov. 26, 1850, with violent colic, when I was called to him. I then learned that, for several weeks before the onset of the above train of symptoms, he had loss of flesh and appetite, frequent nausea and occasional vomiting, and the skin had become sallow and dingy. I found the abdominal walls drawn in and perfectly rigid; pulse weak, and but little quickened; little or no feverish action, indeed his skin was rather inclined to be cool. Although naturally patient of suffering, he was importunate, nay, clamorous for relief, uttering himself in terms of agony far stronger than his general appearance and symptoms seemed to warrant; active and frequently repeated cathartics alone afforded him any satisfactory relief, the distress recurring the moment the bowels ceased to be kept in a perfectly soluble state. The effects of opiates were transient; sulphuric acid drinks were freely used, and after a fortnight (the active symptoms having been subdued), sulph. quinine and other tonics were administered."

In the following case, the patient was but little inclined to acknowledge the habit to which his repeated attacks of the characteristic symptoms were mainly due.

"Alva Eaton, aged forty-four, carpenter, has generally had good health; in 1848, had severe typhoid fever, from which his recovery, though protracted was perfect.

"In the —— of 18—, he entered the Lowell machine-shop, and continued in the enjoyment of his ordinary health, until the fall of 1851, when he began to suffer from "rheumatism" of the back, hips, and lower extremities; his knees became weak and stiff, making locomotion painful, particularly the going up and down stairs; to these were occasionally added colicky pains, which repeatedly confined him several days at a time, partial recovery following the use of cathartics, sweats, liniments, &c., self-prescribed and administered.

"In August last, an attack of these symptoms, under an aggravated form, attended with rending, twisting pains about the umbilicus, shooting through to the back and down the limbs, and with obstinate constipation, nausea, and vomiting, compelled him to call in medical advice. In my absence Dr. D. attended him, and after repeated and continued cathartics, the severity of the symptoms gave way, and an imperfect recovery took place in about three weeks. His appetite however did not return. Some pain in his bowels, weakness and stiffness of lower extremities, with dull pains in the back of his head, extending upwards from the spine, remained; the true nature of his case having been overlooked, the cause was unsuspected, and of course allowed to continue in operation. He, however, went to work, when, after the lapse of about five weeks, another attack of equal severity with the last took place, with which he was confined about ten days, taking as a cathartic, principally castor-oil and calomel; the last producing a slight constitutional effect. Getting out, he continued at his work until Jan. 11, when he began again to complain of abdominal pains, and on the 5th, was seized with all the symptoms marking his previous attacks—yielding, as did the last, and under similar means, in about ten days. As strict inquiry elicited no source of the suspected poison within the family, we, were forced to the conclusion that it was derived from the white lead with which, to prevent rusting, the pieces of iron machinery were smeared, previously to being packed in boxes, to be sent away, it being his principal employment to perform this duty.

"Before he got out from this last attack, however, the much more probable cause was ascertained to be his habit of stopping at a beer-shop, on his way to and from his work, and indulging in potations of that villanous compound, which was drawn through lead pipe. At any rate, he has since abstained from this habit, and has remained, ever since, entirely free from any vestige of his former symptoms."*

The case of which I will now proceed to give a brief account came under my notice recently, and occurred in the persons of two families, occupying a house in the extreme north-western part of our city, quite removed from the locality of those already detailed.

"I was called to Mrs. R. on Friday, Jan. 9th of the present year, and found her laboring under symptoms of approaching abortion, of which, however, she was not aware, inasmuch as (she said) her present sufferings were only an aggravation of what she had suffered for many months. She was thirty years old, the mother of one child, and considered herself now advanced about four a half months; abortion took place in two or three hours; size of fœtus justifying this estimate. She then gave me the following history: Having previously, always enjoyed good health, in January, 1850, gave birth to her first child—got up well, and continued in good health during the whole period of lactation, weaning her child on the last of Sept., 1851. About the third week in October, began to experience a "tired," heavy feeling of pain in her lower limbs, particularly her knees; the same pain was soon felt about the navel and in the groin, giving the sensation of a cord pulling down, and extending to the very lower part of the bowels; soon a similar pain was felt in the shoulders, back, hands, fingers, feet, and toes, particularly over the tops of the feet and hands. She suffered the characteristic nausea of pregnancy for the first two months, none afterwards, until Dec. 31., when she was seized with vomiting, with an increase of all the symptoms just named, until it closed with abortion.

"Has occupied the same house for a year and a half, and used the water from the well until a fortnight since. After her confinement, the pains in her limbs, &c., disappeared, and at the present time she is quite well.

* For another case of lead disease, viz: the dropped wrist, which was traced to its causes only after the most thorough inquiry, see Watson's Lectures, Philadel. edition, page 811: the cases of Mary Ann Davis.

"Mrs. B. and four adult children, three girls (one married) and one boy, occupied the lower story of the same tenement, where they have lived for four years.

"Mrs. D., the married daughter, aged 23, without children; enjoyed good health until about last October, when she began to have dull, aching heavy pains in her feet, which gradually extended to her legs and bowels; in December, was seized with severe pain in the stomach, radiating thence to both groins, striking down both limbs, particularly the left; also a dragging pain from the chest, as if a string was stretched from it to the groin; severe nausea and vomiting, with obstinate constipation, nervous restlessness, thirst, coldness of feet, cold chills, frequent desire to pass urine—which was painful; urine often high-colored, and depositing a lateritious sediment; pains also in the back, hips, and down the spine, extending occasionally up the neck to back part of head; also in hands and feet, and numbness of the same; loss of flesh, with dirty yellowish color of skin and eye.

"Mrs. D. called for medical advice about Dec. 1, but obtained only partial relief; it being difficult to persuade the family that their illness was caused by the water. This, however, she consented, after a while, to give up; was put upon a course of sulphur and sulph. acid; and, after one or two relapses, began permanently to mend.

"I found her, on the 14th Jan. last, as follows: Pulse 88, soft; skin has a dry feel; tongue slightly coated with white; gums, where they run up between the teeth, bluish, but no regular distinct line: appetite good; sleep quiet; bowels regular; has now occasionally attacks of pain in the bowels and limbs, but, on the whole, is much improved within the last fortnight. March 19, has now scarcely any remains of former symptoms.

"Thryphena B., sister of the above, has suffered precisely in the same way, but less in degree, commencing about the same time; but, supposing her symptoms owing to long confinement and over-work at her business (factory harness-making), went into the country in September and returned, after a month's absence, relieved of her pains, stiffness of limbs, &c.; but, after a few weeks' residence with her mother, had a return again of all her symptoms—was put under same treatment as her sister, and with similar results, carefully abstaining from the suspected cause. She is now (March 15) quite well. The blue line, at first much more marked than in Mrs. D., still continuing perfectly distinct.

"Amos B., the son, has, within the last two years, had repeated attacks of lead colic pains in both arms; numbness and stiffness of lower limbs, so that frequently he was not aware when they touched the ground; dysuria; blue line well marked, which still continues at this date (March 15), although he has been quite well for two months, and has not used the water since.

"Sarah B., aged seventeen, youngest member of the family, went away to school in June last; similar temperament and constitution with the above; has never had any symptoms, however, of lead disease, and the gums are entirely unstained.

"Mrs. B., the mother, aged fifty-eight, has frequently suffered from arthralgic, colicky pains, and costiveness; blue line marked; has been decidedly in better health, since she omitted the use of the well water, than for several years."

The water, for all domestic purposes, was supplied to both families from the same well, through lead pipe. Dr. Dana, at my request, tested the water, and found it highly impregnated with lead.

In my own practice, I have never met with any cases of decided encephalopathy. In consultation, I have seen two or three; one, Dr. Huntingdon's patient of this city, and one at Manchester, N. H., under the care of Dr. Josiah Crosby: the former proved fatal; the latter, a very interesting case, recovered. I trust, through the politeness of these gentlemen, you will be put in possession of detailed accounts of both cases.*

Several deaths among children, from affections of the brain attended with symptoms of an anomalous character, were, by the attending physicians, ascribed to the agency of lead water, taken as drink; but no *post-mortem* examinations were had, and I have not been able to obtain reliable reports of the cases.

The two following well-defined cases were received by your Committee, from Dr. Josiah Crosby, of Manchester, N. H.

"Albert Taylor, thirty-eight years of age, of good constitution, and of very industrious temperate habits, an iron-worker in the repair-

* Two cases have been received from Dr. Crosby. No account of the other case has yet been received.

shop on the Amoskeag Corporation, in Manchester, N. H.; moved into a new tenement belonging to the company in the autumn of 1849.

"The water to supply his family was drawn through a lead pipe, 1½ inch in diameter, and 75 feet long, from a well 5 feet diameter, having 20 feet of water and nine lead pipes of the same dimensions as his, reaching to the bottom. His family consisted of himself, wife, and one child.

"The water on this corporation, generally, was not good, being impregnated with iron, some of it largely—but was generally denominated *hard*. This well was an exception; the water was much softer, and considered excellent to drink. Mr. Taylor was very fond of water, drinking nothing else, and drank very freely, and with so small a family they probably did not generally pump all the water from the pipe before using it.

"In January, 1850, Mr. T. began to complain of constipation, colic, and pain in the limbs and thorax; with loss of appetite and occasional vomiting. During this month and the two following, he was under my care, and a part of the time at his work, but too sick to attend to his business much of the time. In April, he went into the country; after a few weeks he returned very much improved, and went again to his work in the shop; in a short time he began to feel all his former difficulties return upon him, and so he continued through the first year of his residence in this tenement. Up to this time, his disease had been considered by his friends as resulting from his long confinement to the shop. 'The shop is killing him!' was the language of all his shop-companions, notwithstanding I had expressed my opinion strongly that it was lead in the water.

"In August, the colic and neuralgic pains in the thighs, arms, and thorax had become so severe that he was unable to sleep much at night, groaning and twisting himself continually; had but little appetite, and when food was taken, it would produce great distress and frequently vomiting—so much so, that he often took no supper.

"In September, he painted all the lower part of his house, and remained in it with his family during all the operation of painting and drying. This seemed to produce an explosion, and his disease was soon and fully developed; all the symptoms were greatly aggravated; he had three forms of the lead disease—colic, paralysis, and arthralgia, all at the same time—having now, for the first time, the addition of paralysis of the sphincter of the bladder, which allowed the urine to pass guttatim. His case now became alarming; he could take but little nourishment, and this was often rejected; got but little sleep, and this never quiet—always disturbed; often getting out of bed, and wishing to go home; sometimes not recognizing his family; thought they were conspiring to kill him; almost daily vomiting of a green, bilious fluid; the pain in the head, thorax, inside of the arms and thighs, was at times so intense as to produce furious delirium; his bowels all this time were very costive, and not moved but by powerful cathartics; when quiet, he would lie on either side, generally on his left, with his thighs pressing against the abdomen; taking no notice of any thing about him, unless roused by pain or an attendant; the pupils were largely dilated; pulse 45 to 50; about fifteen inspirations in a minute; urine very scanty, four to six ounces in a day, and high colored; *gums very blue.*

"In December he had four fits; two at intervals of several days, and the other two on the same day. The emaciation was extreme; the parietes of the abdomen seemed glued to the spine, with no elasticity; I could grasp the curvature of the spine in the hand, and take hold of the descending aorta with the thumb and finger.

"This case was so severe, and continued so long, it would make a long chapter to give the treatment in detail. I shall therefore only mention those means which seemed to afford the most relief; cathartics, warm bath, in which was dissolved the sulphuret of potassium, and anodynes were the remedies which had the most control over the neuralgic pains, both of the colic and arthralgia, which I consider the same, and requiring the same treatment.

"The cathartics which I found best adapted to this case were castor and croton oils; sometimes they were administered separately, and sometimes combined. I think they afforded more relief when given together.

"I consider the warm bath with sulphuret of potassium a remedy of the greatest value in relieving the pains. Immersing the patient, and also the local application of the solution with flannels, applied hot to the bowels, thighs, arms or thorax, whenever the pain is most severe, and friction with the same solution, was of great service, the patient expressing great satisfaction from its use.

"The whole catalogue of anodynes was tried; morphia was the

best, and the only one that accomplished much. Chloric ether was applied to the head externally, and was also inhaled with benefit.

"The paralysis, so far as manifested in destroying the action of the sphincter of the bladder, was more readily overcome than any other symptom in the case. Strychnine internally administered, in doses of from one-sixteenth to one-twelfth of a grain, three times a day, restored the action of the sphincter in about three weeks, so that the patient could control his water.

"In this case, I could do nothing specifically for the encephalopathy. The patient was so reduced, we could only support as much as possible his strength by nourishment, wine, brandy, cider, &c.; expecting daily that death would terminate the case; but, notwithstanding the extreme prostration and emaciation, Mr. T. has perfectly recovered, and enjoys at this time as good health as ever. He was away from his business six months.

"On the 8th of August, 1851, I was called seventeen miles into the country to see Mr. W., thirty-five years of age, naturally of robust constitution, corpulent, temperate, of active business habits, (farmer, and deputy sheriff), who had been confined to his house and bed for several weeks with what was considered "liver disease," accompanied by yellow skin, severe colic pains, and extreme costiveness and vomiting; pulse slow; urine scanty; *gums very blue:* neuralgic pains in the limbs and back, and sleepless nights.

"On inquiry, I learned that he had never been able to get a good supply of water at his house, on account of a ledge of granite, which came very near the surface of the ground, on which his buildings stood; and that two years before he had sunk a well *twenty-two* rods from them, and had drawn the water that distance through a lead pipe, by a pump in the house, for all household purposes; that it took five minutes smart pumping to bring fresh water from the well. This explained the whole difficulty; the diagnosis was clear, and the treatment too; a supply of pure water, cathartics of croton and castor oil to remove costiveness, and anodynes to abate the pain, constituted most of the treatment, and the patient soon began to improve, and ultimately recovered perfectly.

"From observations made in the management of a large number of cases, I am of opinion that all cases, not complicated with other and older diseases, would recover—perhaps not quite so soon—but would in a few weeks recover, by discontinuing the use of water drawn through lead pipes.

"I have related this case to show how nearly some forms of lead disease may simulate other and very common diseases, produced by very different causes. Here were exhibited all the symptoms of a severe case of jaundice, accompanied by severe colic; and would have been speedily cured by the treatment that had been adopted, had it been the production of common causes. It was only necessary to withhold the lead to effect the cure.

"I understand the opinion has been recently advanced, by some of high medical authority, that there is no such *specific form of disease* as that called 'Lead Disease,' not even in painters, and that the blue margin of the gums is not evidence of the presence of lead in the system; that it is shown in cases where the disease could not be attributed to lead. Now my belief is, that we have had in this city more than a hundred cases of disease, the product of lead taken into the stomach by using water for drinking and cooking that was drawn through lead pipes.

"I consider the fact as well settled as any fact can be; as certainly as that the contagion of smallpox will produce the genuine smallpox.

"I have found *blue gums* in a large proportion of cases exhibiting the colic and arthralgic symptoms, and in every case of paralysis and encephalopathy. I do not consider its presence always necessary so settle the diagnosis of a case, but always sufficient to settle it when it is present. I think I have never seen, certainly never noticed such *blue gums* in any case, where it could not be attributed to lead. I have seen the blue lines present in several members of the same family at the same time, when only one manifested the symptoms of the disease; and by changing the water the blue has disappeared in every one so affected. This has been the result always."

The following are the only two, of numerous cases, brought under the observation of the chairman of your Committee, either as attending or consulting physician, which he proposes to introduce at this time. He has preferred to lay before the Association those furnished from other reliable sources from different parts of the country. By so doing, the fact has been shown that the diseases in question have not been confined to a limited space, nor to a small number of observers. All the cases reported, except those designated as coming under the observation of the Committee, have been furnished in answer to the circular issued by them in the early part of December last.

I was called, in October, 1851, to see A. C., aged 32, of rather slender constitution. It appeared that, about three months previous, he had an attack of pain in the abdomen, which was relieved by evacuations. This was followed by an uneasiness, nearly constant, in the bowels, constipation, and by occasional attacks of pain, like that just described, but less severe; this uneasy sensation led the patient constantly to hold on, or press his hands upon the bowels. The skin had a sallow, dingy appearance; the white of the eyes was quite yellow. These symptoms had led his friends to believe his disease was jaundice; there was loss of appetite and flesh, his spirits were depressed, tongue lightly coated, breath offensive, pulse 76, small; his whole physiognomy was precisely that indicative of lead poison. On examining the mouth, found the points of the gums, which project between the teeth, stained blue. The urine was rather more colored that natural, but on examination (subsequently made) did not present that peculiar play of colors with nitric acid, said to be indicative of the presence of bile; the excrements were rather darker than usual, showing a sufficiency of bile. I did not hesitate to pronounce it a case of lead poisoning, from some source or other. On inquiry, I found that he had been drinking lead water for something more than two years. The treatment consisted in regulating the alimentary canal, which was done with a moderate amount of medicine, and abstaining entirely from the use of the water. In one week, his countenance began to clear up; the distressing sensations about the bowels were soon mitigated, and finally entirely relieved in about three weeks; had no attack of severe pain after the discontinuance of the water; has remained well since, a period of five months.

This case is reported as showing a well-marked case of lead poisoning; its physiognomy could never have been mistaken by any one who had ever been familiar with lead maladies. More of the premonitory symptoms were present than are usually observed in any one case, viz: the blue gums, the fetid breath, the jaundiced appearance of the skin and eyes; yet no one of the four forms of lead disease laid down by Tanquerèl was ever well developed.

The intelligent and reliable record of the following case was furnished me by the patient himself, who is a gentleman of wealth and education, and a graduate of the Boston Medical School; but he has never entered upon the practice of the profession. He was under my immediate observation during the continuance of the treatment, and at my request he kept a daily record of his own case.

Dr. Adams:

My Dear Sir—At your request, I write down what I recollect of the state of my health before your treatment of me for lead paralysis, in the summer of 1848. My health had not been very good for many years, but my strength failed more perceptibly during the two years previous to that summer; and, in the winter previous, I felt an increasing unwillingness to make any physical exertion, and great listlessness. This was made evident in working the foot-treadle of a lathe, which had furnished me exercise for three or four years. I could not keep at work long, and found on comparing myself with others, that I was unable to turn it so fast as they.

I spent three months of that winter in Boston; our rooms being in the fourth story, and the staircase long and rather steep, I never went up without fatigue, and often sat down to rest. I remember, too, an uncertainty in going down, and more than once slipped (as I then thought) and should have fallen but for the banister.

In the latter part of March, being in the saddle, my horse fell with me, and my shoulder was dislocated. Had I been as vigorous as formerly, I could have held him up, but I felt conscious that I could not brace myself up from the stirrups.

I recovered the use of my arm, and we returned to our home in Waltham towards the end of April; from which time to the first of July, it became still more evident that my lower limbs were failing. On one occasion, I started to run a short distance, and fell forward flat; my legs seemed not to obey the will. Two or three times, while standing or walking on the smooth floor, my knees suddenly bent and I fell. I fell repeatedly while dressing. And during that spring I complained, after an hour's drive in a gig, of a cramped feeling in the thighs—so uncomfortable that I seldom drove in any vehicle in which I could not stretch the limbs straight.

All these symptoms I detailed to you on the evening of the last day of June, and added that I began to feel a numbness over the left thigh and buttock, with a diminished sensibility.

You inquired about the water used in the house, and I told you that that for cooking passed through 140 feet of lead pipe to the kitchen-pump, and that I had used it for nine years; that for some months past I had made my breakfast of crushed wheat, which, after soaking in water all night, was put on to boil the first thing in the morning, and probably the water which lay in the pipes all night was used for this purpose. The drinking water chiefly used was brought through forty feet of lead pipe from another well to another pump.

You then said that you believed that I was suffering from lead held in solution in this water, and asked me to let you have some of it in the morning for analysis. On the following day I called on Dr. James Jackson, to ask him about other matters, and before I left his study I told him of the symptoms I had detailed to you, and also of the opinion that you had expressed, Dr. Putnam being present. He said that it might be so, and that he had great respect for your judgment; but that he had not observed in his practice any case of paralysis of the lower limbs from lead which had not been preceded by some affection of the other parts of the body, particularly colic.* He examined my spine thoroughly, with Dr. Putnam, and found no evidence of disease there. Still he recommended, as a matter of prudence, the application of twelve leeches to the lower part of the spine, and to be followed by a blister on the same spot; which was accordingly done.

The next day (the first of July,) you took for examination two phials of water, the first pumped that morning from both pumps. On being tested with sulphuretted hydrogen, that from the kitchen-pump became *very* dark; and, after standing still the next day, looked like ink and water. That from the other pump was colored, but less highly. I discontinued the use of both waters from the first of July.

* The experience of Dr. Jackson on this point differs from that of the chairman of your Committee. Of eleven cases of lead paralysis falling under his observation, in six paralysis was the first form of lead disease observed; and in five cases it was seated in the lower extremities.

Out of 102 cases of paralysis observed by Tanquerel, 39 were not preceded by any other form of lead disease; and in fifteen only was it seated in the lower extremities.

The day after my blister had been dressed, I called on Dr. Jackson again, and took with me the phial of blackened water, at the sight of which, he confessed that he believed that your opinion was well founded, and that he thought I might safely omit the treatment for disease of the spine.

I remark in this connection, though anticipating a little, that another gentleman, equally eminent in his profession, examined my spine, a few weeks afterwards, to whom I had also mentioned your diagnosis, and though he found no tenderness in any spot, he suggested the application of caustic to the lower part of the spine.

For two, or perhaps three weeks, I walked every day a little for exercise, though with great and increasing difficulty. A spasmodic working of the feet from side to side troubled me, and they would often draw back out of the shoes. I was unable to draw on a boot. While sitting still, the legs would insensibly draw back on the thighs, till the feet got entangled under the chair. This involuntary drawing back of the leg made it very difficult to go up stairs. I recollect that the last time I went up (Aug. 10,) a man held the foot on the first stair, while a person behind assisted me to rise so as to place the other foot on the next stair ; and then the man would hold that foot in place, or it would certainly have drawn back so as to have thrown me down. While going down stairs, I straightened the whole limb before planting the foot upon the next step, and with the help of a man and the banister, could get down safely. But on the 11th August my bed was moved to the lower floor, and I did not attempt the stairs again till the 25th October.

The numbness, before spoken of, affected the *right* limb a day or two after, and soon extended over the whole of both limbs, from the buttocks to the toes ; and, for a long time, I so lost the sense of feeling in them, that I had no consciousness where the feet were, unless I saw them; for many weeks I did not know whether one foot touched the other in bed. There was also an unnatural coldness of the lower limbs, uncomfortable to myself, and perceptible to the touch of others. I wore my warmest winter clothing all summer, and always had a blanket shawl over my lower extremities, even the hottest days, when taking my drive, which I did almost every day that summer. In the house I used an India-rubber water cushion to sit upon, and had it filled with warm water every day. Since my re covery, I have felt more warm than before the crisis, and have especially observed that my feet are not so cold as formerly.

It was very perceptible to me, as well as to yourself and others, that the glutei muscles on the buttocks, and the large extensor on the front of the thigh, were greatly wasted; while the biceps and flexors, from the trochanter of the ilium to the tibia, were unusually strong and active, indeed, in a constant state of contraction; and I suffered much from cramp in this muscle, and in different muscles of the leg and sole of the foot. And when I found that Tanquerel lays down a principle, established by facts, that, in lead paralysis, the extensor muscles are always weakened and more or less wasted, while the flexor muscles continue in their usual vigor, I was convinced of the correctness of your diagnosis.

The difficulties in the different motions, as before described, agree with this law: I could not run, because I could not throw forward the leg, nor push forward, by straightening out the foot and rising on the toe. The foot drew back on the stair, and the leg drew up under the chair, because one set of muscles was more vigorous than the counteracting set. And, in walking, the foot would twist about and draw out of the shoe, and the muscles of the sole contract even to a painful cramp, because there was no balance of power.

On the 6th August, I began a daily minute of the symptoms and the treatment which I kept till the second week of November. From the 8th of August to the 25th, I could not get up out of my chair without assistance, nor stand alone even on crutches. On the 28th, I raised myself erect by placing my hands on my knees and let myself down again pretty well.

Aug. 29. Walked with ease and confidence on crutches without other help.

Sept. 14. Manifest improvement in walking and standing; since two or three weeks, I can do many things alone that I could not do without help. Indeed, until a short time before this date, I was quite unable to put on my clothes, or to wash myself, or to undress, without help.

16*th*. Walked round the garden with a cane (discarding the crutches), and holding upon another person's left shoulder with my left hand, bearing almost all my weight upon my legs.

Same day, in the house, walked about a dozen steps entirely alone, without crutches or cane, and back again.

17*th*. Walked about alone on crutches more than I have done any day for many weeks. Glutei muscles said to be very perceptibly enlarged, especially the left.

18*th*. Could stand while I washed my face and hands without taking hold and without help, which I have not done for five or six weeks at least.

20*th*. Walked out of doors on crutches, without other help.

21*st*. Walked half a mile with my wife and a cane; carried a lighted candle in my left hand from one room to another, using cane with right hand.

24*th*. Went to church in Boston in the afternoon, not much fatigued.

Oct. 1. Went to church in Boston all day; not more fatigued than other days. In the morning took my douche standing, for the first time.

2*d*. Played two games of billards, one hundred each, and beat both.

19*th*. Walked a mile with my wife and a cane.

20*th*. Walked a mile with cane only.

25*th*. Out of doors on my feet with a cane only, for three hours, besides driving myself in a wagon about four miles.

During the following winter I walked every day, and often from four to eight miles with a cane, but I have not ridden on horseback with confidence till this winter, and, even now, have not a very firm seat. I can walk as fast as ever I did, but am very awkward in my movements in a room and in running. I cannot walk a single plank steadily. I never go down stairs now without taking hold of the banister, if there is one, or resting on a cane. If I attempt to walk in the house in the dark without a cane I totter; out of doors with a cane, I am unsteady. While washing my face in a wash-bowl, my eyes being shut, there is a tendency to draw back; and to this day, I never for a moment forget the existence of the flexor muscle on the back of the thigh; it is, indeed, developed out of proportion to the other muscles, and seems to be in a constant state of contraction, and this I believe to be the principal cause of the unsteadiness and awkwardness that remains.

I have, from time to time, very sharp neuralgic pains, which I first felt in the winter of 1846–47, owing, I believe, to the state of the stomach; but it is a singular fact that they are always seated in the lower limbs, though not limited to the joints, nor to any particular spots.

There is one fact which I have omitted; the bladder was very much weakened. It was slow in recovering, and has not yet its full natural power.

The treatment was chiefly the use of strychnine and of electro-magnetism. With the last I began early in July, applying it to the whole limb from the buttocks to the foot, putting on the metallic slipper. The effect was not good, for it increased the spasmodic action of the limb, and especially of the foot. But afterwards, on applying the wires to the extremities of the weakened muscles, and under the influence of strychnine, I found a happy result; for it stimulated *them* into action without affecting the healthy muscles. Early in August, I read Dr. Dana's translation of Tanquerel's invaluable work, and proposed to you to try the effect of strychnine, and with your approval I began, I believe, on the 2d or 3d day of August, first with a pill of one-sixth of a grain, the next day a pill morning and evening of one-sixth grain each, and on the 6th one-third of a grain in the morning and one-sixth at night. The effect of the first dose which I took was very similar to that of electro-magnetism, particularly the feeling in the foot; it was like the rapid succession of little electric shocks in the foot, with a sort of creeping sensation through the limb. The larger dose on the 6th, I took at ten A. M.; at noon, the muscles about the mouth twitched spasmodically; at half-past two P. M., there were very strong contractions of the muscles of the lower limbs till three o'clock. Twitchings about the mouth continued till between four and five, whenever I attempted to speak.

On the 7th, I took half a grain.

On the 8th I took two-thirds of a grain at ten minutes past ten A. M. In twenty minutes I began to feel light-headed, with great difficulty of breathing, which led me to suppose that I was fainting. I laid myself flat on my back on the floor, and got no relief. I raised myself on end, which caused a strong convulsion. The man-servant took me up to lay me on the sofa, and, while in his arms, there was a powerful spasm of all the muscles of the body (as it seemed to me), intensely painful for a moment; this subsided on being laid down. I could hardly breathe while the head was down; breathed a little easier on being bolstered up. I found that I was instinctively raising the shoulders at every inspiration. Sensibility was extreme; so much so, that the resting of a fly suddenly on the nose caused a spasm, which lifted the whole body from the sofa, arched up, as in locked-jaw cases. The same convulsion was caused by any one touching me unexpectedly. A person who came into the room and sat down opposite to me, caused such a commotion in my whole frame that I was obliged to request that she should go out. The pulse was eighty-four, intermitting about every tenth stroke. Great twitching and jirking of the muscles round the mouth. I could speak only in a whisper. The jaws were held tight together, so that, even after some time, it was very difficult to get a little water into the mouth; after I got it into the mouth, I swallowed it. Occasionally there was involuntary gritting of the teeth. Pain in the nape of the neck very severe, so that a man's whole force was exerted in pressing against it. At eleven A. M., I began to inhale chloroform; from two to four full inspirations at a time, repeated as often as the spasms became more violent. This acted like a charm; it kept the spasms under, relieved the breathing, and in an hour or two after first taking it, the intermission of the pulse entirely ceased. The symptoms continued, though gradually diminishing, till between two and three o'clock. At a quarter before four I was able to sit up and eat some dinner, and between five and six o'clock, I took a drive in the carriage.

My minute in the evening was, excepting weakness, not much worse than the last few days. The pill to-day was from a new parcel of strychnine and fresh made. The next day I took one-third grain in the morning and one-sixth grain in the evening, and I continued the same dose until the 31st, except the evening pill, which I took only two or three times. Twice, during that month, I took five-twelfths of a grain with symptoms similar to those on the 8th, but much less violent. In both instances, I found great relief from chloroform. During the rest of the treatment, I took usually, during the month of September, one-sixth of a grain daily, and until the 9th of October; from which day till the 9th of November, I used daily one-third or one-fourth of a grain, and twice only one-half of a grain, omitting it for a few days when very much reduced. The electro-magnetism was applied generally three times a day, once to the glutei muscles for half an hour, and twice to the extensors of the thighs, one-quarter of an hour each.

On the 7th and 9th, I took a sulphurous bath at 98°, three-quarters of an hour each time. But it reduced my strength so much that it was given up. I took daily a dose of flowers of sulphur. I continued the use of strychnine till Nov. 9; and, in the following winter and spring, I used it for a short time, at three different periods only, twice in pills as before, and once sprinkled on a blistered surface; in both methods with effects similar to those before experienced. While under its influence, there is much more vigor in the lower limbs, but I observe nothing similar in the upper extremities. It affects my general health to such a degree that I have not the resolution to persist long in the use of it again.

The result of my experience of it is, that it has more effect on the weakened than on the healthy muscles, though it does not act *exclusively* on them. I observed this especially as I began to gain control over the limbs. I could feel at every step that I had a power over the glutei muscles and the extensors on the front of the thighs which I had lost. Under full doses of strychnine there was a feeling of great tenseness and rigidity, and an indescribable sensation of compression of the whole limb. I speak of them on the 31st August, in my journal, as feeling stiff and hard almost as iron. When under the full influence of the medicine, I usually slept a heavy, lethargic sleep, from which I was roused, every now and then, by a sudden jerk of the lower limbs, as if an electric shock had passed through them. The spasmodic motions of the foot gradually diminished, after a week or two from the first dose, and disappeared towards the end of August.

The general effects of the medicine I found very remarkable. Under its full influence, the pulse was usually 96; never observed lower than 84, and in two hours it would fall to 64 and 60. There was also a tendency to intermit, though never so frequently as on the 8th of August.

The breathing became difficult, and this appeared to be caused by a contraction of the diaphragm, as shown by the extreme difficulty of breathing, while flat on the floor, and, when raised, by the action of the shoulders and intercostal muscles.

There was always more or less twitching of the muscles about the mouth, particularly on attempting to speak, eat or drink. Pain in the nape of the neck was caused by the larger doses only.

There was always great nervous sensibility, amounting, sometimes, to a sense of distress impossible to describe. All these effects became more violent under the slightest mental excitement. After a long use of strychnine, the system seemed to run down, the appetite diminished, costiveness increased; and constant headache, stupor, lassitude, and weakness were produced.

I cannot conclude, without an expression of my sincere gratitude to you, for discovering the true cause of my complaint, and for your unwearied attention and kindness in the treatment of it. Nor can I refuse to recognize, that, under the blessing of our Heavenly Father, you have been the instrument of saving my life. For, had I been treated for disease of the spine, without a suspicion of lead, I cannot but think I should have sunk under it.

I am truly and gratefully yours,

WALTHAM, *April* 12, 1852. J. S. COPLEY GREENE.

* * * * *

It has been shown that natural water, when brought in contact, *always acts on lead*, and that the *various theories of the cessation of action, after a certain length of time, are not true*, and are in no case supported by the facts of experience. The Cochituate water, drawn through lead pipes laid four years ago, continues, at this time, to present very notable traces of lead. In New York, the Croton water, even at the present day, drawn from leaden hydrants put down ten years since, is impregnated with lead, and your Committee are credibly informed that diseases which can only be ascribed to this poison are not of unfrequent occurrence in that city. Dr. George H. Kingsbury has published, in the *N. Y. Journal of Medicine* for May, 1851, four cases of obscure disease fairly attributable to the use of Croton water drawn from lead service pipes. We make the following quotation from his report:

"Since the introduction of Croton water into the city, cases simulating lead colic have occasionally been met with; yet, in the absence of the usual and well-known causes of that disease, and the seeming improbability of a sufficient amount of lead poison being held in solution by Croton water from passing through lead pipes, the symptoms have usually been ascribed to other causes or left altogether unaccounted for."

In two of the cases reported by Dr. K., the patients suffered repeated attacks of lead disease, before the true cause was suspected; when suspected and removed, there was no return of disease.

In New Orleans, the inhabitants appear to have suffered more from lead diseases than those of any other large city within the knowledge of your Committee. According to Dr. Fenner, who has published two elaborate reports—one in 1850 and another in 1851—the first on epidemic colic in New Orleans in the summer of 1849; the second, on lead poisoning, in the same city, in 1850; it appears that colic was epidemic during both the summers of 1849 and 1850, and that it presented the appearance of lead colic, which led Dr. Fenner to investigate the cause of it. From this investigation he came to the conclusion that it was mainly due to lead poisoning, derived from three different sources, viz: soda fountains, where this beverage is drawn through lead tubes, and the hydrant water of the city, which is delivered through lead service pipes, which were put down in 1837, and the cistern water, which is collected from the tinned roofs of the houses.* Lead has been frequently detected by him in all these different varieties of water.

According to Dr. Fenner, the colic of 1849 bore a close resemblance to lead colic, and was frequently attended or followed by rheumatic pains, as they were then denominated. The disease was not inflammatory, but was generally considered a neuralgic affection.

It appears, by the report on lead poisoning in New Orleans, that the same disease again prevailed during the warm season of 1850. There were admitted, during this year, into the Charity Hospital of that city, 137 cases of colic, of which 51 cases are recorded as colic, and 83 as colica pictonum, and 3 as bilious colic. A large proportion of these cases occurred between the first of May and the last of October. It also appears, by the same report, that some other diseases, known to proceed from lead poisoning, were very prevalent. According to Dr. Simond's statistics of mortality in the city for the same year, the number of deaths from apoplexy were 115, from congestion of brain 101, from epilepsy 16, convulsions 354, from paralysis 19. Of these, 403 occurred in the summer and autumn, and only 202 during the winter and spring; corresponding in this par-

* The so-called tin used for covering buildings is made mostly of lead.

ticular with the cases of colic. The above-named diseases, according to Tanquerel, are often produced by lead poisoning; and all lead diseases are more common in warm than in cold weather. Of the 354 deaths from convulsions, 330 were children. It is not unfrequently the case that the first development of disease among children from lead poison is in the form of convulsions.

Dr. Fenner, in a letter addressed to the chairman of your Committee, in speaking of the diseases of New Orleans in 1851, says:

"I am decidedly of opinion that *encephalopathy*, *arthralgia* (*vulgo*, *rheumatism*), *neuralgia*, and *paralysis*, arising from *lead poisoning*, prevail in this city to a considerable extent. In our large Charity Hospital, in the year 1851, the number of cases admitted for the various affections that are known sometimes to arise from lead poisoning are as follows, viz: colica pictonum 72, bilious colic 17, colica convulsiva 1, apoplexy 19, epilepsy 12, amaurosis 3, congestion of the brain 19, convulsions 9, paralysis 29, neuralgia 17, rheumatism 358.

"Knowing that the exposure to lead is very great in this city, I have no doubt that it had the chief agency in the production of a large majority of the above cases. The colics marked *bilious* were precisely like the *painter's* colic; and a large number of those marked *colica pictonum* did not occur among *painters*. The conjestion of brain cases may have arisen from a variety of causes. The *convulsions* occurred mostly among *adults*, and I have no doubt mostly depended on lead poisoning."

In support of this opinion, he adds:

"In one patient, immediately after recovery from convulsions, the *wrist-drop paralysis* supervened, establishing the character of the disease. Other cases like this have been observed at this hospital; as also cases of colic and convulsions, which could not be indubitably traced to lead, but which yielded alone to the treatment appropriate to lead poisoning.

"Neuralgia prevails in this city to a great extent, and lead may certainly have something to do with it. As to rheumatism, it is certainly very remarkable that it should prevail here chiefly in the warmer portions of the year, as I have shown in my report."

* * * * * *

In Cincinnati, as appears by a letter from R. Jay Kittredge, M.D., published in the *Southern Medical Reports*, vol. i., lead diseases are not unfrequently met with, although often treated under another name, and that notable quantities of lead are found in the water drawn through lead pipes. . . . . . .

The next point your Committee will notice is the great difference in the length of the exposure of individuals to lead influences before disease is developed—varying from a few weeks to something more than nine years. This may in part be owing to the intensity, or degree of strength of the poison introduced into the system. Extremely minute quantities may be taken for a great length of time, before there will be sufficient accumulation to produce disease. The minuteness of the quantity of poison in water, which may in time produce disease, cannot be limited; less than 1-100th of a grain per gallon has been known to produce it. The chairman of your Committee has now under his care a case of *paralysis* of the muscles of the forearm, hand, and fingers of one limb, produced by lead water, where no trace of the metal could be detected by the most delicate tests, till the water had been concentrated fifty per cent. By the tests above used, 1-100th of a grain of lead per gallon can be detected in natural water.

By this discrepancy in the length of exposure before disease is produced may be mainly owing to difference of susceptibility in the exposed. This difference of susceptibility is due, no doubt, to different degrees of constitutional vigor or energy; and it is possible that this may in some cases be so great as to render the *individual comparatively impregnable* to the action of this poison. Dr. Dana, in his report on this subject to the City Council of Lowell, makes the following opposite remarks:—

"The constitution is only a greater or less degree of vital force. Life is vital force, manifested under the control of a higher influence; the nervous influence, it may be, too spiritual for the cognizance of our senses. The vital force is as much a power as is electricity, magnetism, light, and heat. All agents act chemically on the tissues of the living animal body, as they would upon dead matter. Their agency is limited and controlled by the vital force. If that is strong, so much less is their action. One man differs from another, as a horse, for instance, differs from a man. A horse may take daily, for weeks, several grains of arsenic, without other effect than a softer and more silky skin. In this sense of the constitution, a difference, in degree only, of that agent called vital force, it is found by experience that the young, the delicate soonest succumb under the effects of lead drank in their daily drink, and like the dews of heaven, descending on all, the gentlest and fairest feel the chill which soon closes in death."

* * * * *

In conclusion, your Committee will only add that the settled conviction to which their labors, in preparing this report, have conducted them, is this: that it is never safe to use water drawn through lead pipes, or stored in leaden cisterns for domestic purposes, and that any article of food or drink is dangerous to health which, by any possibility can be impregnated with saturine matter. It may possibly be done in some cases with impunity, but it is *impossible to predetermine* the cases of safety where so many are fraught with danger.

Report by Dr. Samuel L. Dana, of Lowell, on the mutual action of Lead and Well-water.

1. The true answer, to the first part of your letter, is to be found in the knowledge of the action of water, and of salts, upon lead.

2. Lead, scraped bright, and exposed to air, or water, soon tarnishes. This tarnish is the rust or oxide of lead. It forms fast when lead is heated in air, and still faster on melted lead. This rust, or dross, or oxide of lead, is dissolved by pure water, by alkalies, as potash, soda, ammonia, by lime. It is readily dissolved by various acids, particularly by nitric and acetic acid, or aqua fortis and vinegar, and by several vegetable acids. It rapidly forms in contact with fermenting matter, and is dissolved by the acid thus formed.

3. Pure water alone, will dissolve the rust of lead. One pint dissolves a grain of lead. Hence, the purer the water, the greater the amount dissolved.

4. The action of pure water is modified by the presence of carbonic acid. No natural water is pure. All contains carbonic acid. If the carbonic acid alone existed in water, that would change the dissolved lead into white lead, which would thus be diffused through the water, in small and invisible particles, requiring long repose to settle.

5. The presence of salts, also modifies the action of pure water.

6. The salts in the natural water of Lowell, are common salt, copperas, alum, saltpetre, salts of lime, such as sulphate of lime or plaster of Paris, muriate of lime, and nitrate of lime, or saltpetre lime. It is a variety of saltpetre having the same acid as that, but its potash, replaced by lime. There are also small quantities of salts of magnesia, and of ammonia. The most abundant salts, are copperas, alum, the varieties of saltpetre, and common salt.

7. If the salts only modified the action of water upon lead, or if one salt alone existed, which soon of itself acted as a protector, which is the current opinion, then the presence of a salt would be a positive benefit; for 1-2000 parts of plaster of Paris would prevent the action of water. The salts themselves exist not single in water, but mingled. They act on each other, giving rise to products which act on, and dissolve lead. They act in some classes, themselves on lead, and the substance so produced, is dissolved by well-water.

8. The action of salts contained in Lowell water, though somewhat complicated, is easily understood. The most active among the salts, are those which have been said (section 6), to be most abundant. These are copperas, common salt, and the variety of saltpetre called lime saltpetre. To understand how these act, let their composition be briefly stated.

1st. Copperas. It is composed of oil of vitriol and of iron. Exposure to air, rusts the iron, and a portion of the acid becomes free.

2d. The lime saltpetre is composed of lime and of aqua fortis. The other varieties, of potash, or ammonia, or soda, and aqua fortis. The effect of mingling the free acid of the copperas, with these, would be, to set free their aqua fortis, which would then immediately dissolve the lead. Copperas alone, would act on the lime saltpetre, but in this case, no free aqua fortis is formed. The compound of iron and aqua fortis, now formed, is liable still to act on lead.

3d. Common salt is composed of soda and chlorine; muriate of lime, of lime and chlorine. The effect of free acid of copperas is, to let loose the chlorine, or to form muriatic acid. This acts to dissolve lead.

9. The action of common salt, or muriate of lime, does not depend upon free acid of copperas. Lead decomposes common salt. It unites with its chlorine, and thus forms chloride or muriate of lead, which, if heated, would be King's, or patent yellow. This compound, thus formed, as also that produced by the action of free muriatic acid, is easily soluble to a small extent in water, more soluble in acid water, and quite soluble in alkali. When lead then decomposes common salt, the soda, if no free acid is present, renders this compound more soluble.

10. From the variety of salts present in water, the soda produced as above, (9) is usually converted into sulphate of soda; or if muriate of lime, is decomposed by lead, there is also usually formed, in like manner, sulphate of lime. If free nitric acid, formed as stated, (8, 2d) is present, we have only formed the varieties of saltpetre.

11. When lead is dissolved in salt and water, the process continues till the salt is all used. After some time standing, the lead is re-deposited, in little distant, white knobs and threads, varying from the size of a pin's head to that of a pea. If these are removed, the lead is found to be pitted, and very bright in these places.

12. The facts to be chiefly remembered in (9, 10, 11,) are, that common salt corrodes lead, that the substance so formed is soluble in water, that it is still more soluble in nitric acid, whose presence in water has been shown possible, and in free vegetable acid.

13. That a large amount of such acid exists in Lowell waters, has been found by repeated analysis. This acid exists also in the rivers which flow through the city, and it rapidly corrodes and dissolves not only lead itself, but also particularly the white substance produced by common salt and lead.

14. All alkalies, as potash, and soda, and lime, dissolve the compound of lead and salt. They decompose and dissolve the compounds of lead and oil of vitriol, or that formed by the action of copperas.

15. Were the salts of limited amount, it is evident that they would soon, in contact with lead, destroy their own action. But their supply is as unlimited, as that of the water. Their origin may be here referred to. Those only, whose effects on lead are greatest, need here be regarded.

1st. Copperas. It arises from the natural decay of iron pyrites, or a compound of sulphur and iron.

2d. Saltpetre is well known to be constantly formed on the surface of the earth, wherever animals or vegetables decay. These form the acid, and the soil affords the lime and alkali. I have, in no one instance, and my analysis have been extensive, found nitrates or the various forms of saltpetre, absent from the well-water of Lowell. I have detected nitrates in several small streams in the neighborhood of this city, and once in the Merrimack. Probably nitrates will be found always in it during a freshet.

3d. Common Salt. It comes down with every rain. I find this to have been the case in every fall since March last. It is probably a universal ingredient in rain water. Salts of lime, as muriate, perhaps sulphate, and of ammonia, also accompany rain. It is evident then, that the supply of salts is as exhaustless as the rain itself. Small in quantity to be sure, yet bountifully and beneficiently supplied for natural operations, especially vegetation, and injurious only when man subjects his contrivances to those laws which regulate the action of salts on other matter.

16. The great and efficient cause of the action of these on lead, will be found in the natural decomposition of copperas, whose free acid then acts on the nitrates and muriates of lime.

The next most powerful corroder is common salt. The vegetable acid acts least in ordinary cases; though occasionally, I have found it so abundant in the Merrimack river, as to dissolve in twenty-four hours, as much lead as would pure water.

This explanation of the cause of the corrosion of lead, will be seen at once, by those conversant with the usual chemical books of the day, is counter to the current opinion. It would be offered with greater diffidence, were it not supported by two facts.

1st. Leaden pipes are extensively corroded, and in some cases, rendered thereby useless, in the well-water of Lowell. This fact is well known to many of our citizens. It is not confined to particular portions of the city, and occurs even in hard waters.

2d. Analysis detects lead in the water of Lowell wells, into which lead pipe is introduced. The analyses of the water of a great many wells, in different sections of the city, in no one of which, has lead been absent, authorizes the conclusion, *that lead is dissolved by all well-water of the city.*

17. Lead may exist also in suspension in water (4). If the action of salts is, as has been supposed, to form a protecting coat over the lead, then, the tremulous motion communicated throughout the pipe by the act of pumping and other causes, would detach this first formed coat. It may be added, that lead, in such invisibly diffused particles, has been thought by many, to be the only form in which it is usually found in water, flowing through lead pipes.

18. Whether lead exists in water,suspended, or dissolved, is of little moment. The fact that it does exist, is of the highest interest. Nor is it of essential consequence to state the quantity per gallon which may be found. The quantity varies, dependent on two causes.

1st. Proximity to sources of nitrates and muriates.

2d. The geological character of the underlaying, and surrounding rock.

19. The sources of nitrates, are stables, styes and vaults. It is not to be concealed, but deeply lamented, that the abomination of desolation standeth too often where it ought not. There is good reason for the opinion, that the common receptacle for the water which has been drank, is too near the source from which it was drawn, not to have affected its quality. In the wonderful laboratory of a vault, beautiful changes are going on which excite our admiration. The products of these transformations are harmless in themselves. They no longer remind one of their origin. Acting on metals, in obedience to laws, which were impressed on them at creation, we cannot doubt but that the greater their production, the greater the chance that leaden pipes will there be most acted upon.

20. The geological character of particular districts of the city, affects the quantity of lead dissolved by the well-water. For popular use, Lowell may be naturally divided into three geological districts; each distinct, and which may be termed, 1st, the copperas; 2d, the gravel; and 3d, the clay district.

1st. Lowell reposes chiefly on slate rocks, of those varieties called mica, and talcose, or clay slate. The high ridge called Chapel Hill, extending from Concord river to the Rail Road, and the ridge extending from the Rail Road gap to the foot of Appleton street, are composed of mica and talcose slates, highly charged with sulphur and iron. This forms copperas (8). The water obtained from this ledge is charged with copperas. There are, however, many places in this district, where the water is merely top water, which filters through the bed of covering gravel, down to the ledge, without entering it, and it is as free from iron as that obtained elsewhere.

2d. The remainder of Lowell proper, reposes on a more compact variety of slate, passing into clay slate, much less charged with sulphur and iron, and covered generally many feet in depth, with sand and gravel. The water in this gravel district is chiefly top water, which filters through the gravel, down to the rock; but even in the gravel region, veins of water are occasionally met, charged with the like salts, which are formed in that of the copperas district.

3d. That portion of the city, called Belvidere, reposes on clay, which again is underlayed by a rock, called gneiss. The clay is covered with a fine white, clayey gravel. The water of this clay district contains less copperas than that of the others.

21. Referring to these natural geological districts, and to the proximity to sources of nitrates and muriates, it is evident, that particular situations, and on these particular spots, will be found where lead will be much more corroded than on others. Hence, it is found by analysis, that some well-water is so highly charged with lead, as to be detected in a few minutes, by the simplest tests, while others require an elaborate analysis, and delicate tact, to enable one to perceive that in them, lead exists. No case has come under my observation, in which lead has been absent. It may be stated as a general inference, that lead in water will be in proportion to the copperas, and muriate, and nitrate of lime. If the copperas was entirely withdrawn, the action of the muriates of lime and soda would be the next most active cause of the erosion of lead. The action of these last is much promoted by vegetable matter, in fermentation, or the natural decay of wood. Lead is sometimes corroded, only where in contact with decaying wood.

OF THE EFFECTS OF USING LEAD WATER.

22. The fact so well known to our citizens, that leaden pipes are corroded and destroyed by well-water, would long ago have told them the effects of using such water, were it not that the disorders produced by it are of such slow and insidious character, that they have been attributed to other sources, till chemical analysis has pointed out a cause of disease more to be relied on than doubtful speculation.

23. That lead, in continued small doses, is a cause of disease and death, is the accumulated testimony of two thousand years.

* * * * *

32. Those who have been unwittingly drinking daily, the seeds of disease, whose power is thus unfolded by chemical laws, I trust will not allow themselves to indulge in any unnecessary fears. It were much to be lamented, if the inquiry now set on foot, by our city, should result in alarm. If chemistry unfolds causes for fear, she also, angel like as she truly is, holds out greater cause for hope, to those who think themselves already under saturine influence. Two remedies may be proposed, one acting wholly on chemical principles, the other on the principle of common sense. The last is, abstain at once from the use of lead water. The first is, drink daily for some time, a small portion of sugared water, rendered sour as lemonade, by oil of vitriol. This will decompose the compound of lead, with the tissues, with which it may come in contact, and form a perfectly insoluble salt of lead which is harmless. Possibly, under this course, the poison may be finally eradicated from the system.

OF THE SUBSTITUTES FOR LEAD WHICH HAVE BEEN PROPOSED.

33. The remedy (32) based on common sense, would lead to an abandonment of leaden pipes in our wells.

* * * * *

42. However confident one may feel, of the results of the action of salts and the metals, I was unwilling to discourage the resort to galvanized iron without experiment.

1. I find that the zinc is rapidly dissolved in a very dilute solution of common salt in water, and may be found in the solution, or water as the muriate of zinc. This would be the action of the common salt in rain-water, and it is the source of the corrosion of zinc roofs.

2. Galvanized iron, introduced into a solution of copperas in water, very dilute, acts thus: I soon found iron rust rapidly falling on the galvanized pipe. In a short time, *all* the iron was precipitated from the water, and fell in a coat of rust, while its place in the water was supplied by zinc. In other words, copperas or green vitriol was exchanged for white vitriol.

3. Galvanized iron, in a mingled solution of salt and of copperas,

such as is found in several wells in Lowell, is rapidly destroyed, the water becomes charged with salts of zinc.

43. I should therefore recommend:

1. Wood, wherever it can be used;

2. Cast iron, or wrought iron tubes;

3. Copper, protected either by pure tin, or still better, perhaps, with pure zinc.

The use of all other metals and alloys of these, in the present state of our knowledge and experience on these subjects, ought to be abandoned.

Reports furnished to the Directors of the Gorbals Gravitation Water Company, Glasgow, on the action of Water on Lead.

SECOND REPORT BY DR. MILLER, FOR EVIDENCE.

King's College, London May 5, 1854.

To Robt. Lamond, Esq.,—My Dear Sir,—Since I last wrote to you, I have made a very careful comparative examination of samples of the water of *Loch Katrine*, of the *Dee* as supplied to the town of Aberdeen, of the water of the *Tay* as supplied to the townof Perth, especially as regards their action upon lead, both in the form of sheet and of pipe, under various circumstances. The samples were all collected in my presence. There had been no rain for some weeks previously.

The result of this investigation has fully confirmed me in the conclusion which I drew from my former experiments.

I proceed to give a detail of the trials upon each water separately.

I.—WATER FROM LOCH KATRINE,

Collected from the middle of the lake, above the Lady of the Lake Island, on the 14th April, 1854.

It is clear, brilliant, well aërated, and has an agreeable taste.

During evaporation it assumes a brown tinge, which eventually becomes very strongly marked. It is a beautiful water, the purest I have ever analysed. Hardness on Clark's scale, 0.6. One imperial gallon contains of solid soluble matters 2.28 grains, consisting of

Fixed salts,	1.16
Organic matter,	1.12

The saline matter in the gallon consisted of

Silica,	0.16 grs.
Sulphate of lime,	0.56
Chloride of calcium	0.16
Common salt,	0.29
Carbonate of magnesia,	a trace.
	1.17 grs.

In one gallon of the water I found in solution 6.7 cubic inches of gas, composed in 100 measures of

GAS FROM LOCH KATRINE WATER.

Carbonic acid,	0.8
Oxygen,	34.5
Nitrogen,	64.7
	100.0

This water has a more remarkable action upon lead than any natural water I have had occasion to examine.

For the sake of clearness, I would remark that there are two ways in which water may act upon lead. It may simply dissolve the metal, and in this case the action may not be visible till suitable tests are applied; or it may, besides this solvent action, also corrode the metal, so as to form a sediment which contains the lead, which is at once detected by its appearance.

SHEET LEAD.

The action of the water on lead is most rapid when the metal is in the form of sheet. In three hours the corrosion of the metal is plainly visible in the form of a white crystaline deposit in silky scales. The metal, however, begins to be acted upon immediately, and the action goes on increasing the longer the water and lead are left in contact. In open vessels this action proceeds to a very remarkable extent. The lead is first oxidized by the air; the oxide of lead, owing to the extreme purity of the water, dissolves, and then absorbs carbonic acid from the atmosphere, and is deposited in the silky scales above mentioned, which are a compound of carbonate of lead with what is termed hydrated oxide of lead, that is, oxide of lead in chemical combination with carbonic acid and a fixed proportion of water. A little organic matter is also present. In close vessels the deposit begins to show itself in two or three hours, but it does not proceed to the same extent, and, indeed after the first 24 hours, it undergoes but little increase. A large quantity of oxide of lead, however, is found in solution, amounting to two grains per gallon, and sometimes more.

If this clear water is exposed to the air even after it has been filtered, it becomes milky upon the surface. Shining crystals of the mixed oxide and carbonate of lead gradually separate, and the quantity of lead dissolved eventually becomes very small.

If the water remains in contact with metallic lead, fresh portions of the metal are dissolved as fast as the separation of these flakes takes place. The whole can be watched step by step, with ease in a glass bottle.

Actions of this nature would of course be produced in an ordinary open lead cistern.

LEAD PIPE.

But the action of the water on leaden pipes is not less important. In order to examine this carefully, I took a piece of new ¾-inch lead piping, and had it divided into lengths of 13 inches, so that when closed above and below by corks, and rendered air-tight by India-rubber, I obtained a series of similar pipes a foot long, which were completely filled with the water under examination. Portions of lead were rapidly dissolved. In one hour a quantity amounting to 1-60th of a grain per gallon was taken up; in three hours it amounted to 1-30th grain; and in four hours to 1-6th of a grain per gallon; while in 15 days it was 2½ *grains*.

A similar set of experiments were made with a piece of old lead piping taking up from a court in Glasgow, where it had been used many years for the conveyance of Clyde water. In one hour the lead dissolved amounted to 1-100th of a grain per gallon; in three hours, to 1-40th of a grain; in four hours, to 1-10th of a grain; in fifteen days, to 1-3d of a grain.

The interior of this pipe was lined with a coating which adhered very firmly to the lead. I found it to consist of carbonate of lime, a little carbonate of lead, oxide of iron, a small quantity of silica, and a notable portion of organic matter.

To ascertain how far this coating and its supposed preservative power upon the metal would be influenced by the continued action of a current of water through the pipes, I examined the effect of the water upon the pieces of old pipe (a portion of that operated upon above), which was placed in the outflow from the lake of Loch Katrine, where, as I understand, it was for ten days subjected to the action of the stream which flowed through it.

This piece of piping (4 feet long) was forwarded to me from Glasgow in a sealed box, and was delivered to me on the 2d of May. It was filled, with the exception of about five inches of its length (which contained air), with water from the lake, as I am told, which had been in contact with the lead about sixty hours when I examined it. It was very turbid and had a brown tinge, but became nearly clear on standing for two days in a closed bottle. It contained ¼th of a grain of lead in solution per gallon. I found that from this pipe, in three hours, 1-14th of a grain per gallon was dissolved, when subjected to a trial similar to those previously described; and in 24 hours, 2-3ds of a grain was dissolved.

From a piece of new inch-pipe, which had been placed for four hours in a run from the lake, I found that in three hours 1-14th of a grain was dissolved per gallon; and in 24 hours ¼th of a grain.

This piece of pipe, two feet long, was forwarded to me from Glasgow in the same box with the one last mentioned. I found that it likewise was filled with lake water, which had remained in it for about 60 hours. On examining the water, it had a strong brown tinge and a vegetable smell. It contained half a grain of lead in the gallon in solution.

From the foregoing experiments with pipes, it is obvious that although the action is not so rapid as upon sheet lead, even in closed vessels, yet a solution of the metal to a very dangerous extent takes place in a very few hours, and this action goes on increasing in new pipes to a frightful extent.

Also, that pipes which have become coated by the transmission of a less pure water are not thereby preserved from the solvent action. It is lessened, but still occurs with great rapidity, and proceeds till it reaches a point which would produce most serious mischief, if the water were used for domestic purposes.

Since I commenced writing this report, I have received from yourself a sealed box, containing a sealed bottle.

I examined the contents of this bottle, and found it filled with water through which glistening silky particles were diffused, mixed with some flocculi of organic matter.

I found the water to contain in solution 1-3d of a grain of lead per gallon, whilst in the sediment abundant evidence of the presence of lead was afforded by all the ordinary tests.

ALLOYS, &C.

It appeared desirable, in addition to the foregoing trials, to vary the kind of lead acted on, and to ascertain the action of the water upon cert ain other metals and alloys.

Lead from seven different mining districts was used, but in every case the action of the water, both in dissolving and in corroding the metal, was rapid and very uniform.

An alloy of lead, with 1-20th of zinc, was destroyed more rapidly han lead alone.

An alloy of lead, with 1-20th of tin, was dissolved and corroded, both in open and closed vessels, but less quickly than pure lead.

Zinc was rapidly covered with the white hydrated oxide, both in open and in closed vessels.

Iron in sheets was very speedily covered with brown hydrated oxide, which in a few days became in open vessels extremely abundant.

II.—WATER SUPPLIED TO THE TROSACHS INN.

In consequence of the statement that this Inn was supplied with the same water as Loch Katrine, I examined a sample taken by myself from the brow of the hill behind the hotel, before it enters the stone cistern lined with cement, and a second sample after passing through about 100 yards of lead piping to the cistern at the top of the Inn, from which by lead pipe it is distributed in the house. The sample was drawn from a pipe on the second floor.

The hardness of both these samples was 0-8, a trifle higher than that of the lake. The water contained, also, a little carbonate of lime, which I did not find in the lake water.

This water acts *very slightly* on lead.

The water drawn from the lead pipe contained 1-80th of a grain to the gallon, of the metal dissolved,

In two days, in an open vessel, a slight scaly deposit was obtained from sheet lead, and 1-60th of a grain was in solution. After the lapse of a week the corrosion had scarcely increased, and the quantity of leed was still only 1-10th of a grain.

In closed vessels, in two days, 1-20th of a grain had dissolved, and after a week the quantity in solution was unchanged, though the sheet lead still remained in the water.

The quantity of this water that I possessed was too small to admit of a more detailed examination.

III.—WATER OF THE DEE AT ABERDEEN.

This water also was taken by myself, from the iron reservoir at Union Place, into which it is pumped through an iron main from the Dee, just above Dee Bridge, April 15, 1854.

The water was bright, clear, with very few floating particles, and had a pleasant taste. It was well aërated. It deposited a few flocculi of organic matter during evaporation, and assumed a slight brownish tinge; hardness, 1.4. It contained in one gallon solid soluble matter 3.71 grains, consisting of—

Fixed salts	2.89 grs.
Organic matter	0.82

The saline matter was composed as follows:

Silica		0.56
Carbonate of lime		0.84
Sulphate of lime		0.19
Sulphate of magnesia		0.32
Chloride of sodium and potassium		0.82
Oxide of iron and phosphates		0.10
Loss	0.06	2.83 grs.

7.2 cubic inches of gas were contained in the imperial gallon. 100 parts of this gas contained

Carbonic acid	5.15
Oxygen	30.52
Nitrogen	64.33
	100.00

No deposit occurred in the bottles with lead during the 17 days that this water was under trial. The surface of the lead, however, became coated with a blueish crystalline film, which could easily be rubbed off. The water also dissolves the metal in appreciable quantity, and, indeed, by prolonged contact, to an extent which is certainly dangerous.

Sheet lead in an open vessel, in two days, had dissolved 1-20th of a grain; in a week the action had not extended; in a close vessel, in ten days, 1-25th of a grain was dissolved.

Upon lead piping the action seems to be greater.

A new pipe, in three hours, gave 1-14th of a grain of the metal per gallon; in 24 hours 1-10th of a grain: a piece of the old pipe, after submersion in Loch Katrine ten days, 1-8th of a grain by a three hours' exposure. A similar result was obtained by exposing a piece of old pipe for 24 hours to its action, whilst by a fortnight's stay in a piece of new pipe, as much as 1 grain of lead per gallon was dissolved; and in a similar piece of old Glasgow pipe, 1-4th of a grain was dissolved in the same time.

Water drawn from a lead pipe, in the Douglas Hotel, Aberdeen, contained 1-100th of a grain per gallon.

In open cisterns and by rapid use, experience has shown that this water may be used for a town supply, and has been so used for 20 years with safety; but it is obvious that, under certain circumstances, serious consequences might arise from its employment.

IV.—WATER OF THE TAY AT PERTH,

Collected in my presence, April 15, 1854, from the iron cistern at the top of the tower at the Waterworks, into which it is pumped by an iron main below the town.

This water much resembles that of the Dee, but is rather harder. It was clear and colorless, but became brownish on evaporation; hardness, 2.3. Solid soluble matters in one gallon, 5.96, containing

Fixed salts	4.32
Organic matter	1.64

I had not sufficient of this water for a complete analysis. It con tained, amongst other salts,

Carbonate of lime	1.02
Sulphate of lime	0.97
Sulphate of magnesia	0.66.

It acts less upon lead than the water of the Dee. No visible deposit occurred in the bottles; a thin blueish crystalline film formed upon the lead.

Sheet lead, in open vessels, was dissolved

In two days, to the extent of	1-18th	grn.	per gall.
In a week	1-12th	"	"
In closed vessels, 4 days	1-10th	"	"
In new pipe, closed, 3 hours	1-14th	"	"
In new pipe, " 24 "	1-8th	"	"
In old pipe, " 3 "	1-8th	"	"

This last mentioned pipe had been submerged in Loch Katrine for ten days, a treatment which certainly rendered the solvent action more rapid, whatever was the water afterwards placed in it.

The general result of this inquiry may, therefore, be thus stated:

1st. The water of Loch Katrine acts dangerously upon lead whether the metal be in the form of sheet, such as is used for cisterns, or in that of pipe, whether new or previously used for conveying a water like that of the Clyde.

2d. The waters of the Dee at Aberdeen, and of the Tay at Perth, have, under ordinary circumstances, *no* dangerous action upon lead, though even these may at times dissolve the metal to an unsafe extent.

My experiments, however, do not enable me to say whether such action on lead will be modified or affected by changes produced upon the waters by changes of season; and my remarks must therefore be regarded as applicable with certainty only to the sample and the season to which they refer. I am, dear sir, very truly yours,

WM. ALLEN MILLER, M.D., F.R.S.,
Prof. of Chemistry.

THIRD REPORT BY DR. MILLER.

King's College, London, 17*th July*, 1854.

To R. Lamond, Esq., Dear Sir: I have read and carefully considered the "Chemical and Medical Reports and Evidence on the Quality of the Loch Katrine Water," published by the promoters of the scheme, which you were good enough to send me; and notwithstanding the eminent chemical names they bear, must say they have not induced in my mind any change in the opinion I expressed when first I examined the water, viz: that it would be extremely hazardous to supply such water through leaden pipes, with a view to its use for domestic purposes.

It has been suggested that the passage of the water through a channel or tunnel cut for 11 miles through the sandstone rock will materially alter its properties and character, so as to render it unlikely to act on lead. I fully admit the great practical importance of the question thus raised. It, however, does not fall within my province to estimate the amount of hard water springs which would make their way from higher levels into this channel, and contaminate the water of the Loch, nor does it belong to me to calculate (what is not less important) the quantity of water which would drain off through the large exposed surface of this natural filter, and would be diverted to a lower or different outfall to that designed.

I have to deal with plain and undisputed facts: and it appears to me that those which must guide our judgment in this case lie in a very small compass. Let me state them briefly:

1st, It is well known that lead is an active poison to the animal economy, and that its effects are never more distinctly seen than when it is introduced in successive small doses continued for a considerable period.

2d, That distilled water, and many pure and other natural waters do act upon, and dissolve lead.

3d, It is a fact but too well attested by experience that numerous instances of poisoning have been traced to the employment as a beverage, for dietetic purposes, of water which has been become impregnated with lead from the employment of leaden service pipes or cisterns. The case of the ex-royal family of Claremont, and that of the royal hounds of Ascot, are recent instances, on a considerable scale, which have obtained wide publicity, and have undergone most sifting investigation. Indeed, the proportion of lead required to produce serious ill effects in a case where Mr. Herapath analysed the water, was found to be what most persons would, without such proof, consider insignificant, it was less than two parts in a million of water—1-9th of a grain per gallon.

4th, It is conceded on all hands that the water of Loch Katrine acts most remarkably and powerfully upon lead, especially on new lead.

If ever a water should be excluded on account of this action from contact with lead, it seems difficult to conceive a case where such a precaution is more urgently demanded than this. For, lead is a poison; many waters are known to dissolve it, and to act as poisons when used for diet; and the water of Loch Katrine acts violently on lead.

But it is said slight circumstances are sufficient to modify this action on lead. Let us bear in mind there are two modes in which waters act on lead, and these two modes require to be distinguished from each other. 1st, It may *corrode* the metal, and form a white deposit, evident to the eye. 2d, It may *dissolve* the metal, in which case the employment of proper tests would be necessary to render the fact apparent.

I have made a large number of experiments on the Katrine and other waters to ascertain by what circumstances these actions are modified; and the following are some of the conclusions which I have been enabled to draw :—

1st, The action of distilled and of Katrine water goes on uninterruptedly, if the vessel be exposed to the air. I have specimens of the Lake water which have been in contact with lead for nearly four months. The action is *now proceeding* as regularly as it did at first.

2d, Whenever a piece of lead has been corroded, either by distilled water or by any other water, and this lead is transferred to Loch Katrine water, whether immediately or after allowing it to dry in the air, the corrosive action continues as rapidly as before.

3d, Sheet or pipe lead which has been superficially coated by plunging it for a few days in hard water, or some water that does not corrode the metal, is not *corroded* when transferred to Katrine water; but the *solvent* action of the Katrine water *is not prevented*, although retarded. I have invariably found lead in solution, in such Katrine water, after exposure for twenty-four hours, either to old sheet lead, or shut up in closed pipes. Sometimes, in the case of new pipes, I have had a crystalline deposit from the liquid on exposing it to the air, and this deposit has proved to be carbonate of lead.

4th, The addition of 1-20th of tin to the lead diminished, but did not prevent either the corrosion or the solution of the lead.

5th, If slight circumstances arrest, *slight circumstances also renew the action of the water on lead.* It is stated by some of the chemists who examined the water for the Promoters—and I can, from my own experiments, fully corroborate the observation—that Loch water in which coated lead lies without corrosion immediately begins to act upon a piece of new lead, if dropped into it. And it may be added, that *if the old lead be scraped*, that also immediately, begins to undergo corrosion.

6th, The action of Loch Katrine water is not limited to scraped leaden surfaces; it begins immediately upon ordinary milled lead as it comes from the plumber. I have found the metal present in the water which had stood upon the lead not more than a single minute.

In conclusion, I would say that the remedial effects of transmission through the channel or aqueduct must, of necessity, be speculative, whilst the action of water, in its present state, on lead, and the poisonous quality conferred on the water by it, are undoubted. This action occurs to an extent rarely met even in soft water, as indeed might have been expected from its extraordinary purity. I am, Dear Sir, faithfully yours,

WM. ALLEN MILLER.

REPORT BY GEORGE WILSON, ESQ., M. D., F. R. S. E.,

Lecturer on Chemistry in the Extra-Academical Medical School, to the School of Arts, and to the Veterinary College of Edinburgh, for his Evidence in Committee.

Edinburgh, May 2d, 1854.

R. LAMOND, Esq.,—Dear Sir,—On the 17th April, 1854, I received from Professor W. A. Miller, of London, a box containing six Winchester quarts of "Loch Katrine water, taken from the middle of the loch," full, and tied over the stoppers with sheet caoutchouc.

The water was seen through a glass, or examined in small quantities in porcelain, or as poured from vessel to vessel, is clear, colorless, and transparent. It is without taste or smell, and deposits no sediment on standing, or when raised to its boiling point; but when kept in a state of ebulition for some time, it acquires a yellowish-brown color, and this deepens in tint as its volume diminishes by evaporation. The darkening thus occasioned by protracted boiling or heating, points to the presence of organic (*i. e.*, vegetable or animal) matter; and there can be little question that in the water under notice it is chiefly of vegetable origin.

It is only surface or soft waters which have not percolated through porus *strata*, and thereafter issued as springs from levels much lower than those on which the water originally fell as rain, that contain much dissolved organic matter in them; and all such waters are more liable as a class to corrode lead and dissolve it than those spring waters which have become hard by dissolving salts in their passage through beds of rock.

The indication of softness furnished by the darkening of Loch Katrine water when heated is confirmed by other trials. The great majority of waters employed for household purposes, although not coming under the title of *Hard Waters*, contain so much common salt, sulphate of lime, and carbonate of lime (dissolved by carbonic acid) that the mere addition to them of certain simple tests, such as solution of nitrate of silver, of oxalate of ammonia, and of acetate of lead, is sufficient to prove that they contain those salts.

Loch Katrine water, however, is almost proof against all those tests, and acts like ordinary distilled water with them. The quantity of salts, indeed, in it is so small, that it is only after great concentration of the liquid by evaporation that they can be shown to be present at all.

Thus, on evaporating to dryness 5 imperial pints of the water, the residue, representing both salme and organic matter, I found to amount to 1 grain and 47-100ths, or a little less than $1\frac{1}{2}$ grains. A gallon (imperial) would thus contain 2.35 grains of solid matter. This, however, on being raised to a low red heat, loses 0.85 of a grain (in consequence of the destruction of the organic matter already referred to), leaving 1-5th grain of mineral or saline matter, which consists chiefly of sulphate of lime and common salt, and does not contain so much carbonate of lime as to effervesce sensibly with acids.

The water is remarkable for its freedom from carbonic acid, of which it contains so mere a trace that I have not attempted to determine its amount.

Of oxygen, on the other hand, it contains a large proportion. The amount of gas (nitrogen and oxygen) dissolved in the water is 6.83 cubic inches in the gallon. The amount of oxygen in the gallon is 2.28 cubic inches; and the proportion of this gas present in any water is a *datum* of essential importance in estimating its action on the metals made use of in the pipes or tanks employed to convey or husband it.

It thus appears that Loch Katrine water proves on analysis to be a very soft, highly oxygenated water, and one, therefore, which it could not but be greatly feared would rapidly corrode lead. I will freely acknowledge, however, that I was not prepared for so rapid an action on lead as the water in fact exerts.

I have tested its action on the metal in question by placing (1) slips of lead in bottles filled with water to the total exclusion of air; (2) by shutting up the water in lead pipes closed at either end by corks; and (3) by shutting it up in tubes, hammered together at one end, and closed by caoutchouc (without a cork) at the other.

The results have been substantially the same in each case. Within glass vessels, through the walls of which the visible action of water on lead can be watched from time to time, the lead exposed to the water is observed to become soon surrounded by a white haze, and gradually a white powder gathers about it, and goes down to the bottom.

Within a few minutes after shutting up the lead with this water, the metal can be detected in it; and the corrosion of the lead proceeds till the whole of the oxygen of the water has been expended in producing oxide of lead (which is partly dissolved, partly settles as a sediment), after which, if air be not admitted, no further corrosion occurs.

In lead pipes it is of course impossible to observe what changes occur, but the water shut up within them for ten days is found when drawn off to contain a white sediment of pearly or silky crystals, consisting chiefly of oxide of lead, and when filtered from these, still to retain a portion of oxide in solution.

The entire amount of lead thus present (in the pipe water) both in the soluble and insoluble form, amounted, according to my observations, to 1-58 grain in one case, and in another to 2 grains of lead in the gallon. The amount held in solution, after filtration through paper, was on an average from 1-9th to 1-6th of a grain in the gallon.

It is a rare thing to find a water admissable for household purposes *dissolving* lead. It is notorious that waters which only corrode lead into an *insoluble* powder, resembling in appearance and composition white lead (*i. e.*, consisting of oxide and carbonate of lead) are poisonous, although the powder must be changed from the insoluble to the soluble condition before it can affect life or health. The Loch Katrine water, however, developes, by contact with lead, an amount of oxide of lead which it dissolves, and thereafter an excess which appears as an insoluble sediment.

A water which acts thus cannot possibly be conveyed through lead pipes with safety to the health of those doomed to drink it. However full the pipes are of water, lead will be dissolved as a result of the action of the oxygen in the liquid (which the closed pipes do not permit to escape) on the metal, and the oxide thus produced will partly dissolve and partly remain suspended in the water.

I feel persuaded that no passing of the water in question through pipes of a different metal before it touches lead will appreciably diminish its action on that metal. Yours, very truly,

GEORGE WILSON.

SECOND REPORT BY DR. WILSON.

Edinburgh, *July* 26, 1854.

R. Lamond, Esq., Dear Sir: As the paper you have sent me in proof* was not originally intended to form my report on the Loch Katrine water, but simply to convey a general idea of the results which I had reached, I shall, with your permission, supplement it now by a few remarks on some of the points on which the scientific witnesses employed at the instance of the Glasgow Corporation differ from those with whom I was associated.

I.—GENERAL QUALITY OF LOCH KATRINE WATER, AND ACTION ON BRIGHT LEAD.

In the first place, however, I must express my satisfaction at finding, from the reports of the opposite witnesses, that the chemists on both sides are at one regarding the composition and properties of Loch Katrine water, and also in reference to its rapid action on *bright polished* lead. In truth, as any one may satisfy himself, watch in hand, that within a minute of putting such metal into the water, lead can be detected in it, there is no room for difference of opinion on this point.

II.—ACTION OF LOCH KATRINE WATER ON DULL LEAD.

On the other hand, there is a decided difference of opinion between the chemists on the two sides as to the action of Loch Katrine water on old or *dull* lead. Dr. Taylor goes the length of saying, that "if the surface of the lead be dull (*i. e.*, covered with its usual blueish grey coat of suboxide, which is seen on the manufactured sheet, or pipe-metal) there is no perceptible action on lead." (*Glasgow Corporation Waterworks' Chemical and Medical Reports*, p. 32.)

Dr. Anderson and Mr. Campbell, in their joint report, attach much importance to the access of light and air as increasing the corrosion of *bright* lead; and in illustration of the opposite condition of matters in preventing the corrosion of *dull* lead, mention that "experiments were made by enclosing the water in leaden pipes perfectly

* Report for Evidence.

full, and carefully corked, and though allowed to stand for many days, the action was *so* small as to be hardly appreciable."—*Op. cit.* p. 18.)

I experimented exactly in the way described by these gentlemen, and with such lead as Dr. Taylor states to be unaffected by water, but with a totally different result.

The pipes had been long in the possession of the plumber from whom they were obtained, and presented fresh surfaces only at the *edges* of their mouths; where they had been cut across to divide them into equal lengths. To prevent the water from touching these edges, the tubes were closed by tight-fitting corks descending to the extent of half an inch within their mouths, and a piece of caoutchouc having been tied over each cork, the tubes (three in number) were locked up in a drawer, and left there for ten days. On drawing off the water from them at the close of this period, the (action on the lead. so far from being barely appreciable, was so marked, that silky crystals of the oxide of lead were found adhering to the inner surface of the tubes, and were washed out with the liquid from them whilst even after filtration through paper, lead was found dissolved in the water, although it was quite transparent. Similar results were obtained with pipes hammered together at one end, and simply tied over with caoutchouc at the other, after being filled with Loch Katrine water ; and also with plates of dull sheet lead immersed in bottles full of the water and tightly stoppered.

Lead which has been long exposed to the air, and has thereby acquired a very thick and coherent layer of grey oxide may resist the action of soft water for some time, but the ordinary pipe or sheet lead of commerce certainly does not.*

III.—SOLUTION OF LEAD IN LOCH KATRINE WATER.

A point which strongly attracted the attention of all your chemists, but is scarcely referred to by those on the other side, is the fact that Loch Katrine water does not merely corrode, but likewise dissolves

* Lead which has been simply melted and allowed to cool appears to be acted on considerably less quickly than the metal which has been subjected to the mechanical processes requisite for its conversion into pipe or sheet lead. I found newly-cast pistol bullets made from ordinary plumber's lead resist for days the action of distilled water and Loch Katrine water. In the end, however, they as well as bullets which had lain in a gunsmith's shop for months were corroded, although shut up in stoppered bottles quite full of water.

lead. Dr. R. D. Thomson states that when Loch Katrine water which has stood upon lead till scales of oxide of the metal are produced "is passed through a double filter of paper, the oxide is detained on the filter, and little or none seems dissolved in the water which passes through the paper."—(*Op. cit.*. p. 42.)

On the other hand, I found (as already stated) that the *filtered* water from the lead pipes referred to in last section contained as much occasionally, as 1-6th of a grain of lead to the gallon. The amount of metal was determined by reference to a carefully-adjusted chromatic scale, such as was described some years ago by Dr. Smith of Aberdeen, in his analysis of the Dee water. That the lead was in solution, was determined by three tests, which taken together, every chemist regards as conclusive. Before, however, referring to the action of these, it may be well to notice that they were applied to a liquid not in the least degree milky or opalescent, but undistinguishable to the eye from pure water, and which was passed through a filter merely as a precaution against any trace of suspended oxide of lead being present in it.

1*st*,—Infusions of vegetable coloring matter, such as litmus, turmeric, and the red-purple dye separable from the petals of the common wall-flower, were changed respectively to blue, brown, and green, when added to the water from the pipes, after it had been passed through a paper filter. This alkaline action on colors is one of the marked characters of solutions of oxide of lead in soft water.

2*d*,—Sulphuretted hydrogen gave a brown color with the filtered water.

3*d*,—A stream of carbonic acid gas allowed to descend on the liquid, produced silky crystals, first, at the surface, and afterwards throughout the entire volume of water. These crystals, produced by the conversion of the dissolved oxide of lead into the insoluble carbonate, gradually sank to the bottom of the vessel. The same effect was produced more slowly by exposure of the filtered liquor to the air.

Those results I have invariably obtained with Loch Katrine water, which has been for some time in contact with lead. It is manifest, however, that if such water be slowly passed through thick filters, the carbonic acid of the air may have time to convert the greater part of the oxide into insoluble carbonate, so that little of the metal will be found in the liquid which passes through.

But when it is remembered that the water used as a beverage in large towns will be drank by the majority without undergoing filtration even through the thinnest paper, it will be seen that my results do not exaggerate the danger attending the presence of dissolved lead in the water. It is true that this lead would be slowly precipitated from the water by the carbonic acid of the air, if it were left in open decanters or drinking vessels; but as this sediment is as poisonous as the dissolved oxide, the risk attending the drinking of the water containing the sediment would be the same.

IV.—ON THE EFFECT OF PASSING LOCH KATRINE WATER THROUGH IRON MAINS IN DEPRIVING IT OF THE POWER OF SUBSEQUENTLY ACTING ON LEAD PIPES.

Professor Horsford, of America, appears to have been the first to suggest that the contact of soft water with iron deprived it of the power of acting on lead. That iron would act thus, if left long enough in contact with the water to deprive it of all the oxygen dissolved in it, can be readily understood. The lead pipe would be saved from corrosion at the cost of corroding the iron one, and contaminating the water with iron rust. But that the mere passage of soft water through an iron pipe would have the same effect is in the highest degree improbable, especially when the pipe has acquired, inside, a coating of oxide of iron. In the only experiment which I witnessed on this point, Loch Katrine water, after being shut up in an old iron pipe for nearly two days, was transferred to a dull lead pipe, and left there for one day. At the end of this period, it was drawn off, acidulated, and tested for lead, of which it contained above 1 grain to the gallon. I infer from this that the negative results obtained by the chemists on the other side, in the majority of their analyses of the water from the cistern arrangements at Loch Katrine represent only an occasional, not the invariable result of such associations of iron and lead in the construction of pipes and reservoirs.

I would not urge this on the authority of the single experiment referred to above. It can be justified by better proof. The town of Aberdeen presents such an arrangement as was sought to be imitated at Loch Katrine. The soft water of the Dee (which is harder, however, than that of the Loch) is brought into the town by iron mains, and distributed by lead service-pipes, generally connected with small cisterns. Dr. John Smith (formerly of Aberdeen, now Professor of Chemistry in the University of Sydney) found in the water drawn off from various of the pipes, before they communicated with cisterns, from 1-100th to 1-20th of a grain of lead in the gallon of water; and in the cisterns themselves, or the pipes leading from them, from 1-8th to 1-14th of a grain of lead per gallon, when they were in daily use; and 1-5th or even 1-4th of a grain per gallon, after remaining a day or two unused. (See "Chemical Report on the Supply of Water to the Metropolis," by Professors Graham, Miller, and Hofmann, reprinted in *Chemical Society's Journal*, 1851, p. 403; and Dr. Smith's paper, in the same journal, p. 131, "On the Waters of the Dee and Don.") I refer to Dr. Smith's results the more particularly that they are specially noticed in the "Report on the Supply of Water to the Metropolis," from which Professors Graham and Hofmann, and Dr. Anderson and Mr. D. Campbell, have drawn support to their conclusions.

Those gentlemen (see Reports) have themselves drawn attention to the fact that the Ennerdale Lake water, after running six miles in iron pipes, still retains the power of dissolving lead; so that, from their results, and those of Dr. Smith, it appears certain that iron pipes do *not* deprive a soft water of its power to dissolve lead; and Dr. Smith's observations further show that, instead of the action on the latter metal ceasing after a time, it is the more marked the greater the period during which the water is shut up in the pipe, and the greater the length of the pipe.

If such be the case with Dee water, it would surely be rash to expect that the softer Loch Katrine water would be rendered indifferent to lead by any conceivable arrangement of iron mains and old lead pipes and cisterns.

V.—ON THE ACTION OF THE OLD RED SANDSTONE, AND THE MOUNTAIN LIMESTONE, ON LOCH KATRINE WATER.

From the reports of the chemists on the other side, I learn that it was intended to convey the water from Loch Katrine for several miles through a conduit built principally of the old red sandstone of the district; and they have accordingly ascertained the action of fragments of this rock on the water, and report that they deprive it of all power to act on lead. They are not quite agreed as to the mode in which the water is changed in properties; for Professors Graham and Hofmann state, that after agitation with pieces of the old red sandstone, "the water retained its great original softness;" whilst Dr. Anderson and Mr. Campbell report its hardness to be increased by one degree, and the amount of saline matter held in solution by one-third.

On either view, the water would remain of excellent quality; but, to obtain these results, Loch Katrine water was either shaken for some time in shut vessels with fragments of the sandstone, or was left standing on them for 10 or 12 hours. But it would be unwise in the extreme to infer that the same results would be procured by passing a stream of the water through an aqueduct of sandstone.

In the experiments on the small scale, a scanty volume of liquid was exposed to a large surface of the mineral, and left for hours to dissolve all that it could dissolve from it. In the proposed conduit, a great body of water would graze the surface of a mass of stone, itself in greater part totally insoluble in water, and from which, whatever was soluble would be extracted by the first stream of water which was conveyed by the conduit. I will not pretend to decide how many hours or days it would take to exhaust the superficial soluble matter in a mass of sandstone, but it could not take very long; and then the water which flowed over its surface would cease to be affected by it. Were it intended to filter the water *through* fragments of red sandstone frequently renewed, then the results obtained in experiments on the small scale would supply a trustworthy basis for speculations regarding the use of such a filter; but they justify no conclusion as to the ameliorating influence of the mere surface of the stones of the proposed conduit.

Similar remarks apply to the effect of the mountain limestone of the Loch Katrine district on the water of the Loch, in so far as it is expected to prove beneficial by altering the quality of the water which passes over it. It forms, Dr. Anderson and Mr. Campbell tell us, "only a thin bed, with which the water is in contact for a very short time," so that it could be little altered by all that it dissolved from it. That the saturation of Loch Katrine water with carbonate of lime would increase its hardness and render it indifferent to lead, is certain; but the mere passage of the water over pieces of limestone would be a most imperfect way of securing this end.

* * * * *

In conclusion, I would observe that the changes induced on water by lead are, confessedly, still, in several respects, little understood by chemists. Two of the ablest witnesses on the other side, Professors Graham and Hofmann, and one of the ablest on yours, Professor Miller, concurred, in 1851, in stating, in reference to the action of water on lead, that "the subject is one of great difficulty, and is still far from being exhausted;" and, again, "the properties of water which enable it to act at times with unusual vigor upon lead are little understood." Considering all this, I will be content to ask the question, Is it necessary, or would it be wise to expose the inhabitants of Glasgow to a risk, the existence of which is certain, whilst the amount is unknown?

I have thus no change to make in my conclusions regarding the Loch Katrine water, highly though I esteem the very able scientific witnesses on the other side. You will understand, however, that the only question which the short space of time at my disposal before my summons to London, allowed me to consider deliberately, was the advisability of using lead pipes, including cisterns, for the conveyance of Loch Katrine water, *with its softness undiminished*, through Glasgow.

The chemists on the other side have discussed the possibility of changing the quality of the lead, or of the water, so that the one shall not act on the other. The lead is proposed to be altered by alloying it with tin. I have no experience as to the action of water on such an alloy; but I know that my colleagues, although they found it promise well at first, *especially if not subjected to rolling*, were in the end disappointed by finding it fail to resist the action of Loch Katrine water. It cannot, therefore, be considered as decisively ascertained that *pipes* of such an alloy would not be corroded by the water.

The water is proposed to be altered by saturating it with carbonate of lime (chalk or limestone); but to do this would require either the use of tanks, where the water could stand for some time on the carbonate of lime, or an arrangement for filtering the water through the carbonate. I do not find in the suggestions of the chemists on the opposite side methods of altering the quality of the lead or of the water, which can be confidently relied on as certain to do so, and therefore I must decline to agree to more of their conclusion than that Loch Katrine water can certainly be hardened so as not to act upon lead, and that, therefore, there is no reason why it should be sent into any town through lead pipes in such a condition as to corrode or dissolve them. I remain, yours very truly,

GEORGE WILSON.

W. T. BRANDE, ESQ., F. R. S.,

Of the Royal Mint, Royal Institution, &c., &c., was prepared to have given Evidence as follows :—

That on the 28th of April last he received from Dr. Miller of King's College, a glass stopper bottle containing about two quarts, and labelled—"*Water from the middle of Loch Katrine.*—W. A. Miller—April 14, 1854."

That he examined this water and found it *remarkably pure.*

That an imperial gallon, submitted to evaporation, left a residue weighing 1·6 grains only.

That this residue was of a brown color, in consequence of the presence of organic matter.

That the water is nearly free from carbonic acid.

That it acts very quickly and powerfully upon lead—the minute quantity of saline matter which it contains (being, in fact, less than 1-43750) not being of such a nature, or in such a quantity, as to prevent, or even materially to interfere with its action upon that metal.

That it also acts upon iron.

That its actions upon lead and upon iron closely resemble those of ordinary distilled water.

That it would, therefore, be very dangerous to use this water for domestic purposes, after having passed through and remained in leaden pipes and cisterns.

That the proposals for *hardening* this water, or in other words so far impregnating it with such saline matters as would tend to prevent its action upon lead, although feasible in theory, would not be safely or effectually applicable in practice. W. T. B.

REPORT BY MR. WILLIAM WALLACE,

Analytical Chemist, Glasgow, for Evidence in Committee, *and revised for publication.*

ACTION OF THE LOCH KATRINE WATER UPON LEAD.

The principal question requiring chemical investigation that has arisen in the opposition offered to the Loch Katrine water scheme, is the action of the water upon lead. I therefore made a number of experiments in April last, in order to ascertain the comparative action of the Loch Katrine and several other waters. I had previously seen some of the results obtained by Dr. Penny, and was indeed surprised at the very extensive and extraordinarily rapid corrosion of lead by the Loch Katrine water. My own trials gave similar results, and later experiments have fully confirmed the conclusion at which I then arrived, viz:—That the water as it exists in the Loch acts so energetically upon lead, that if it were conveyed through lead pipes or retained in lead cisterns, it would of necessity acquire such an amount of impregnation of that metal, as to render it extremely prejudicial to health, if employed as a beverage or for cooking articles of food. I cannot presume to give an opinion as to what extent the water might be altered after a journey of 34 miles through conduits and iron pipes, nor do I think that any *data*, short of the actual experiment, would be sufficient to establish this point satisfactorily. I am convinced, however, by experience, that the mere contact of the water with iron, even for two or three days, would not materially alter its power of acting upon lead; and even if it did, it would necessarily contaminate the water with iron to such an extent as to render it unfit for washing, bleaching, and many other purposes. It is stated by the Promoters that the bed or seam of limestone over which the water would flow is insignificant; and it is obvious that the action of the sandstone, of which the conduit would in part be constructed, would only be of a temporary nature, for the calcareous matter on the surface of the stone would soon be extracted, and would therefore cease to exert its protective influence. At the same time, it must be borne in mind, that if the water dissolved this protecting agent to any considerable extent, it would no longer possess that remarkable degree of purity for which it has been so much and so justly lauded.

The subjoined experiments will serve to show :—

1st, That Loch Katrine water acts most energetically upon lead, more especially upon new lead, no matter whether it be clean and bright, or in the state in which it is procured from the plumber; whether exposed to the rays of the sun or kept in total darkness; and whether air is freely admitted or altogether excluded.

2d, That in open vessels, with free access of air, a large amount of a light, pearly, crystaline precipitate is formed, consisting of the hydrated oxide of lead combined with variable proportions of carbonate of lead—a small quantity only remaining in actual solution.

3d, That this action goes on continuously for days, weeks and months, and appears in fact to be without limit; and that when a piece of lead which has been immersed for a long time in the water, is transferred to a fresh quantity, the action immediately commences and goes on as before; and therefore, that the Loch Katrine water does not possess the power of coating lead so as to prevent further action.

4th, That in closed vessels the action, although neither so rapid nor so extensive as in those to which air is admitted, is yet of a most dangerous nature, a very large amount of oxide of lead being held in actual solution. This effect is the more dangerous, as the presence of the lead thus existing in solution is not detected by mere inspection, and is only revealed on the application of the appropriate chemical tests.

5th, That many other soft and pure waters, used as sources of supply, do not possess the same property of dissolving and corroding lead to such an alarming extent, and therefore that the Loch Katrine water cannot be compared with them.

LOCH KATRINE WATER.

Exp. I. A quantity of water was placed in a closed bottle, with a slip of clean lead, for two days. The clear solution, exclusive of a considerable sediment, then contained six grains of lead per gallon, The liquid was decidedly alkaline to tumeric and reddened litmus. and gave a copious precipitate with a stream of carbonic acid gas, and even by contact with the air. The lead in actual solution, after exposure to the carbonic acid of the air for a considerable time, did not amount to more than ¼ of a grain, the remainder being merely in suspension. The same experiment, continued with exposure to the air for 2½ months, gave about 200 grs. of lead per gallon.

II. Water in closed vessel, excluded from light, with common plumber's lead, coated at the edges with wax; lead, after 24 hours (including sediment), 7 grs. per gall.

III. Same, but exposed to light, and at a somewhat higher temperature, 8 grs. per gall.

IV. Same, with exposure to air, and in a warm situation, 24 hours, 15 grains; 2 days, 26 grs. per gall.

V. Common milled lead, previously in Loch Katrine water for nearly 3 months, with a fresh quantity of water, 24 hours, 4½ grs. per gall.

VI. Same, lead cleansed by rubbing before immersion in fresh quantity of water; 24 hours, 5 grs. per gall.

VII. Clean lead, previously in Tay Water 2½ months; 24 hours, ½ gr. per gall.

VIII. Clean lead, previously in Brockburn Water 2½ months; 24 hours, 1½ grain.

IX. Clean lead, previously in Trosachs Inn Water 2½ months; 24 hours, ½ grain per gall.

TROSACHS INN WATER.

Bright lead in closed vessels 2½ days; no sediment, but lead corroded and encrusted, 1-15th gr. of lead per gallon; 2½ months, open vessel, ½ grain.

TAY WATER.

Similar experiment to last mentioned. 2½ days, 1-15th gr.; 2½ months, ¼ gr. There was no sediment, and the metal was very slightly tarnished.

DEE WATER.

Common milled lead coated at edges with wax, in open vessel; 24 hours, 1-12th gr. No sediment.

LOCH LOMOND.

Similar experiment to last. 24 hours, $1\frac{3}{4}$; 2 days, 4 g. (including sediment).

RAIN WATER (3d July.)

Similar experiment. 24 hours, 40 grs.; 2 days, 60 grs. (including sediment).

Although it may be said that all soft waters corrode and dissolve lead, yet the quantity dissolved or held in suspension varies from the merest trace to many grains in the gallon. The amount of corrosion and solution observed with the same water is much influenced by many circumstances. Of these the degree of purity of the metal is perhaps the principal; a very small proportion of tin, amounting to not more than 1 or 2 per cent., materially alters the extent to which the action proceeds in a given time, and even smaller proportions cause considerable diversity in the results obtained. It thus follows that different specimens of milled lead give somewhat various results. Lead piping also varies in composition; for it is notorious among plumbers, that there are *hard* and *soft* pipes, the latter being generally those of the larger dimensions. The temperature, likewise, seems to exert some influence, the action being more energetic at high than at low degrees. Thus different quantitative results are often obtained by different operators; nor could it be otherwise, unless the same description of lead were used by all, and the various circumstances were in every respect alike. The general result, however, remains unaffected, viz: that the Loch Katrine water acts so powerfully upon lead as to render its employment for domestic purposes quite inadmissable, after having been brought into contact with this metal.

In selecting a source of supply for a town or city, it is necessary, if possible, to obtain a soft and pure water. It would not be wise, however, to introduce a variety that acts violently upon lead; for, although such a description of water might be suitable for all purposes the effect of conveying it through lead pipes would undoubtedly be to endanger the health of the inhabitants. At all events, where two eligible sources of supply of soft and pure water present themselves, one of which acts powerfully, and the other very limitedly, on lead, it would certainly be a matter of prudence to select the latter.

It is my opinion that the Loch Katrine water could not be introduced through lead pipes, or retained in lead cisterns, with safety to the inhabitants.

CHEMICAL REPORT ON THE EXAMINATION OF THE WATER OF LOCH KATRINE.

By Dr. Penny, Professor of Chemistry in the Andersonian University, Glasgow.

In the course of certain inquiries undertaken at the instance of the Gorbals Gravitation Water Company, my attention was incidentally directed to the qualities of the Water of Loch Katrine. The result of a well-known and simple experiment, made to ascertain the extent of its action on lead, has given rise to considerable discussion.

* * * * *

As my name has been brought forward somewhat prominently in this matter, I feel it due to myself to give a more detailed statement than is usual in a merely chemical report, of the circumstances that led to the present investigation.

In the month of February last, I was requested by Robert Lamond, Esq., solicitor to the Gorbals Water Company, to analyze and examine the water of the Brockburn, from which the Company have hitherto taken their supply, with a view to ascertain whether it still possessed, unimpaired, the excellent qualities attributed to it in the Reports repectively made by the late Dr. Thomas Thomson, Dr. Gregory, and myself, in 1845. I was also requested to extend my examination to the Earn water, as well as to the water in the reservoirs and filters at the Company's works. . . . . .

The results of my investigation of these waters were communicated to Mr. Lamond, in a report dated 11th March, 1854.

On the occasion of rendering the report, and when I was further asked to hold myself in readiness to give evidence on the qualities of the Brockburn water, before the Committee of the House of Commons, I expressed a wish to have an opportunity of perusing the chemical report on Loch Katrine water, that had been drawn up and printed for the use of the Town Council of Glasgow, with a copy of which I was immediately furnished. At a subsequent interview with the Directors of the Gorbals Company, I communicated verbally my opinion of this report, and suggested that, as no analysis of the water had been given, and no mention made of its action on lead, it would be highly desirable, particularly as its degree of hardness was extremely low, to have its qualities and composition more thoroughly examined. In this the Directors fully concurred; and, accordingly, at their request, I proceeded immediately to Loch Katrine, and collected, with the most scrupulous care, the specimen of water, from which I obtained the results given in evidence before the Committee of the House of Commons on the 27th of March.

From the circumstances of my being summoned to London within a few days after my first visit to Loch Katrine, my experiments at that time were necessarily very limited; and the opinion I expressed to the Committee, as well as to the Gorbals Company, was merely to the effect, that Loch Katrine water exerts a powerfully corrosive and solvent action on lead; and that, before supplying such a water to the inhabitants of Glasgow, additional investigations should be made.

On reference to the Notes of Evidence, taken by the short-hand writer before the Committee, I find that in answer to the questions, "From what you have seen of the water, would you consider it safe to deliver that water through leaden pipes to the inhabitants of Glasgow?" I stated, "So far as my experiments go, I should say it would be exceedingly hazardous to supply such water to Glasgow." And again, "Have you seen enough to make you think it absolutely necessary and essential that further experiments should be made, and further tests tried, before the water is introduced?" "Yes, I think they would be highly culpable if they did not do so. As a citizen of Glasgow, I would not use the water until that question had been finally set at rest. I do not say that the Loch Katrine water would be poisonous to the inhabitants of Glasgow, though it should be sent through lead pipes; but I say that my experiments, as far as they have gone, show that great caution should be used, and that further scientific inquiry of the most searching nature should be made. It is one of the finest waters I have ever seen; it is unexceptionable in every respect, and I should be very willing, indeed, that it should be supplied to my laboratory, and would pay a higher rate for it, as it would save me the trouble of distilling water for my experiments; but I should be sorry, in the meantime, so far as I am able to judge from my experiments, which are very limited, to use that water for dietetic and domestic purposes after being in contact with lead."

This statement faithfully expresses the views I then entertained. Since that time, I have made an extensive series of experiments on the subject; and having tested the action of the water upon sheet lead, lead piping, &c., in every way that the time at my disposal would allow—having perused and weighed the chemical and medical reports recently published by the Promoters of the Glasgow Water Bill, having visited and examined their apparatus at the Trosachs, and having for the purpose of comparison, extended the inquiry to several other waters—I am now prepared to give the deliberately-formed opinion, *that it would be in the highest degree dangerous to supply Loch Katrine water for dietetic use, through lead pipes, and to retain it in lead cisterns.*

I feel it also necessary to state that, at very early period of the inquiry, immediately indeed on reporting the result of my first experiments to Mr. Lamond, I urged upon the Directors the desirableness of their obtaining the opinion of other scientific men; stating, as I did in 1845, when consulted on the qualities of the Brockburn water, that in the consideration of so important and responsible a matter as a new source of water-supply to a large community, the opinion of no one scientific man should be relied upon, but that the concurrent testimony of two or more chemists should be obtained before deciding in favor of any particular source. For the present inquiry I suggested that the Directors should obtain the assistance of Professor Graham of London, who, on being applied to, recommended them to consult Dr. Miller, Professor of Chemistry, King's College, London. Dr. Miller at once undertook the inquiry; and after a careful examination of the water (see his Report dated 27th March, 1854), was fully prepaired *on the first occasion of my being before the Committee,* to give evidence corroborative of the opinion I then expressed. The coöperation of Professor Brande of London, Dr. George Wilson of Edinburgh, and Mr. William Wallace of Glasgow, was secured after the adjournment of the Committee.

Since my first visit to Loch Katrine, I have, on four different occasions, personally obtained specimens of the water from different parts of the Loch, including both the east and west end. All those specimens have been subjected to minute analysis and investigation, the results of which are comprised in this Report. I have also carefully examined, with special reference to the present inquiry, the following waters :—

Water supplied to Trosachs Hotel.
Brockburn water.
Earn water.
Water of Loch Lomond.
Water from Inversnaid Hotel.
Water of Loch Artlet.
Leaven water.
Water of the Tay at Perth.
Water of the Dee at Aberdeen.
Annerdale Lake water.
Water from the Reservoir at Whitehaven.
Loch Ness water.
Water from River Ness.
Paisley water
Lanark water.

The results of my investigations I shall now proceed to report—premising that several other waters from various parts of Scotland and Eng are also in process of examination, but which I have not as yet been able to overtake. I shall also embrace the opportunity of offering a few remarks upon the reports published by the Promoters of the Loch Katrine scheme; for although these documents bear the names of several eminent chemists, I feel it behoves me, for the information of the Gorbals Water Company, to express unreservedly my opinion of the leading views and statements they contain.

LOCH KATRINE WATER.

Physical and Chemical Qualities.—The water of Loch Katrine is beautifully bright and transparent; it is well aërated and perfectly inoderous, and has an agreeable taste. It gives no deposit on being boiled. When viewed in small quantities, it is colorless; but when closely examined in a deep vessel, it is found to be faintly, but perceptibly tinged. In color it is very far superior to Clyde water, as used in Glasgow, but decidedly inferior to Perth, Paisley, Lanark, and other waters. By prolonged ebulition, its color deepens; and when the water is concentrated to a small volume, by evaporation, it acquires a well-marked yellowish-brown tint. I found it more deeply colored at the west end of the Loch, particularly after heavy rains, than near the Trosachs. This color is owing to the vegetable organic matter it contains. As regards softness and purity, Loch Katrine water deservedly ranks as a first-class water. It is, indeed, one of the finest of the very many waters, from all parts of the country, that I have had occasion to analyze during the last fifteen years. In the purest state in which I have examined it, there is little more than two grains of impurity, or of solid matter, in the imperial gallon, which is about one-fifth of the quantity existing upon an average in Clyde water, as used in Glasgow, and rather less than one-third of that contained in the Gorbals Gravitation water.

Its degree of hardnsss is extremely low, being only .8°. As taken from the Loch, it it free from iron, and from all other hurtful metallic impregnation. It is unquestionably an excellent potable water, and well suited for domestic and dietetic use. From its extreme softness and remarkable purity, it is admirably adapted for detergent operations, as well as for steam-producing and manufacturing purposes. In a word, there can be no question that so pure a water, if supplied at a cheap rate, and without being brought into contact with lead, must prove a great boon to any community.

Chemical Analysis.—The specimen collected on the occasion of my first visit when the Loch was very full, is the purest I have yet examined. It gave only 2.117 grains of solid matter in the gallon of water, whereas a specimen collected on a subsequent occasion, when the water in the Loch was several inches lower, afforded 2.240 grains per gallon. The temperature of the water on both occasions was exactly 40° F.

* * * * *

The following statement shows the exact results from the specimens referred to :—

	First Specimen, East End. Grains per Gallon.	Second Specimen, East End. Grains per Gallon.	Specimen, West End. Grains per Gallon.
Organic matter	900	96	1.025
Mineral matter	1.217	1.28	1.200
Total solid matter	2.117	2.24	2.225
Degree of hardness	.8°	.8°	.75°

A minute analysis of the solid matter in Loch Katrine water gave the following results:—

	In the Gallon. Grains.
Organic matter	.900
Sulphate of lime,	.381
Chloride of calcium,	.144
Alkaline chlorides,	.433
Corbonate of magnesia,	.216
Silica and phosphates,	.170
Oxide of iron,	Trace.
Total amount of solid matter,	2.244

GASES.

The mean of three experiments, which corresponded very closely with each other, gave 7.277 cubic inches of gas in an imperial gallon of Loch Katrine water, consisting of

	Cub. In. In the Gallon.	In 100 volumes.
Carbonic acid	.080	1.10
Oxygen	2.420	33.25
Nitrogen	4.277	65.65
	7.277	100.

From these results, it is manifest that the total amount of gas in this water is not greater than what is found in many burn and river waters; the proportions, however, of the constituent gases are strikingly different. The quantity of carbonic acid is remarkably small, and the proportion of oxygen correspondingly high. I have estimated the gases in many natural waters, both from lakes and rivers, and I have never found so small a proportion of carbonic acid gas as that existing in Loch Katrine water. The water from the west end of the Loch contained rather less oxygen, and a little more carbonic acid.

ACTION OF LOCH KATRINE WATER ON LEAD.

The action of Loch Katrine water on common milled lead, in open vessels, is so rapid, so powerful, and at the same time so unmistakeable and so easily observed, that it cannot fail to arrest the attention and interest, even of those who have ordinarily but little to do with such matters. The interest, moreover, is greatly enhanced, when there is the power of estimating the steady progression of the action, by the application of appropriate chemical tests.

If a piece of sheet lead be immersed in Loch Katrine water in a common tumbler, the surface of the metal being in the proportion of about 3 square inches to the ounce of water, the phenomena exhibited are marked and continuous. In less than a minute, a notable quantity of lead (1-15th of a grain per gallon) may be detected in the water, by chemical re-agents; in less than an hour, the water immediately around the metal becomes opalescent, and at least 2 grains of lead per gallon will be found in the water; in 24 hours, the whole of the water is decidedly opalescent, and a considerable quantity of sedimentary matter, consisting of the hydrated oxide and carbonate of lead, collects at the bottom of the vessel, the proportion of lead in the water, including the sediment, being now about 7 grains per gallon. This action goes on continuously, and the amount of precipitate increases visibly day by day, so that, in two or three weeks, 40 or 50 grains of lead per gallon are found corroded and mixed with the water. I have never yet observed, in any one of the many experiments I have performed, the slightest indication of any cessation of this corrosive action in open vessels. In several experiments which were commenced four months ago, the action is still proceeding as regularly as at first. In one experiment recently examined, I find 120 grains of lead per gallon. The effects and phenomena are the same, whether the experiment is made with "scraped lead" or unscraped lead, with polished lead or tarnished lead, with milled lead in the state in which it is sold by the plumber, or with pure assay lead; the only requisite conditions being, that the water shall be from Loch Katrine, the experiment conducted in an open vessel, and that the lead shall not contain above ¼ per cent of tin.

In closed vessels completely filled with the water, and from which access of air is carefully excluded, the phenomena are different. The action is not continuous, but soon ceases. The metal is corroded and dissolved, as in an open vessel, but to a limited extent; the water remains clear, and a very small quantity only of sedimentary matter, collects at the bottom of the vessel in which the experiment is performed. So long as the vessel is kept closed, the water appears to he eye as brilliant and as pure as when taken from the Loch; but, on the application of chemical tests, it is generally found to contain from 2 to 4 grains of lead per gallon. The clear water, moreover, after being thus in contact with the metal in closed vessels, is strongly alkaline to test papers, and on exposure to the air, the pearly deposit soon separates, and the action proceeds as in an open vessel.

It is therefore manifest that there are two modes in which Loch Katrine water, in common with certain waters from other sources, acts upon lead. It either oxidizes and dissolves the metal, as in closed vessels, when the presence of the metal in the water can be detected only by the employment of proper tests; or the water may corrode the lead and yield a pearly sediment visible to the eye.

These two actions require to be scrupulously distinguished—the former may be designated the solvent or invisible action, and the latter, the corrosive or visible.

In my first experiment to try the action of this water on lead, *clean* (not *scraped*) plumbers' lead was employed; and in the second experiment, pure assay sheet lead was used; the latter having been immersed in the water in the very state in which it was purchased. I must unhesitatingly acknowledge that I was quite unprepared for so vigorous and continuous an action as that which occurred in these experiments. I had never previously witnessed, in the case of any river, spring, or burn water, or indeed of any natural water, except recently collected rain water, an effect so rapid and *visibly* energetic. Dr. Miller, one of the Government Commissioners appointed to report upon the supply of water to the Metropolis, and whose attention had been specially directed for some time to the action of different natural waters on lead, states most emphatically, "Loch Katrine water has a more remarkable action upon lead than any natural water I have had to examine." The opinion of other eminent chemists is equally strong. It was, indeed, the extraordinary rapidity and extent of the action that led me to employ pure sheet lead in the second experiment, lest there should be in the plumbers' lead any extraneous matter which might influence the effect. The results of both trials, which were exhibited to the Committee of the House of Commons, were precisely similar, and have been fully corroborated by all my subsequent experiments. It is certainly not a little remarkable that there is no published record (at least I have not been able to find any), of this powerful action of certain lake waters upon metallic lead; and though two comprehensive schemes have been proposed for supplying Glasgow with lake water, viz: from Loch Lubnaig and Loch Katrine, no mention was made, before the present inquiry, of the qualities of these waters in relation to their action on lead.

The attempts at first made to refer this extraordinary power of Loch Katrine water to the jar in which the specimen was collected, to the bottle or other vessel in which the experiment was conducted, and more recently to the "scraping" of the lead, to the influence of light, and, indeed, to any cause but the right one, plainly indicate that other parties were as little prepared as myself for so unequivocal and remarkable an action. The smile of incredulity, moreover, which greeted the first results, when exhibited before the Committee in London, and the haste with which the Promoters sent down for a sample of the water, to try the experiment themselves, clearly show the scepticism and ignorance that then prevailed. It was certainly candid, however, on the part of their counsel, to inform me, on the following day, that they had tried the experiment themselves, and got a similar result.

I conceive it perfectly superfluous to offer any observations on the general subject of the action of water upon lead. The paramount importance of the subject, in a practical and sanatory point of view, cannot be questioned. The many recorded instances of poisoning by water contaminated with lead, incontestibly prove that this metal is an insidious and cumulative poison, and that though it may be taken in small doses for a time before any mischief is experienced, its effects are never more strikingly manifested than when it is introduced into the system in minute quantities for a lengthened period.

Dr. Burton observes, "from a careful perusal of the papers of Sir George Baker and Dr. Warren, as well as from considerable experience, I presume to express a strong belief that the unobserved introduction of lead into the human body is continually taking place to a much greater extent than is usually imagined, and that it has often caused an ambiguous assemblage of morbid symptoms; for although the influence of lead on the system is readily detected when the symptoms are severe, and follow each other in the expected order of succession, yet when they are mild, or do not follow each other, in regular stated order of succession, if the mind of the physician is not awake to their cause, or the cause cannot be ascertained, then the symptoms appear ambiguous, and they may be misinterpreted without exposing the physician to the imputation of unpardonable or of culpable oversight."

Many similar statements might be adduced to show how keenly alive some of our astute physicians have been, and still are, to insidious lead poisoning, whether through the medium of water or otherwise. The apprehension of danger from the contamination of our food with small quantities of lead is well shown in the reports by the distinguished chemists and physicians appointed about four years ago to ascertain whether Dr. Scoffern's process for refining sugar, in which preparations of lead were employed, could be used with safety to the public. The following paragraphs from the chemical and medical reports are very significant, and the opinions therein expressed are equally applicable to the present inquiry.

"In conclusion, although our results do not indicate certain and immediate danger from the use of this process in British refineries, still we must deprecate its extension on the general ground that poisonous substances should never be used in the preparation of an article of food where they can be avoided; the object effected in this process by means of a poisonous material, the use of which is unquestionably attended with the possibility of grave accidents, being one which is sufficiently attainable otherwise without danger.

"Even supposing that there were no facts to show that very minute doses of lead poison taken daily for many weeks may seriously endanger health, the risk is too great to be incurred."

A constant and suspicious regard should always be directed to the possibility of danger from the slow and insidious introduction of the poison in water that has been in contact with the metal. It has been well observed that "the avoidance of all possible saturnine contamination should be rigorously regarded, for quantities of lead which would scarcely perhaps be deleterious to the healthy, may be highly prejudicial to those already ill."

It is impossible to say how many cases of unaccounted for disease may be referred to such remote sources; and in the obscurity which involves the first disturbance of the equilibrium of the functions of the body, it is neither trifling nor unreasonable to search out their causes in the smallest tangible shape. The attempt, therefore, to check investigation on so important a question, by terming it a speculative topic, is surely inconsistent with the true spirit of scientific inquiry.

It is no part of my present duty to explain the *causes* of the action of Loch Katrine and other waters on lead, or to enter upon the discussion of the various circumstances by which it is increased or diminished, promoted or retarded. In the case of Loch Katrine water, however, I may briefly explain that, in open vessels, the lead is oxidised by the oxygen gas dissolved in the water; the oxide of lead thus formed dissolves in the water, and then, absorbing carbonic acid from the atmosphere, separates in pearly scales, consisting of the hydrated oxide and carbonate of lead, with a little organic matter. Notwithstanding the many researches that have been made, our knowledge of the conditions that influence the corrosive and solvent action of water on lead, is extremely limited. On taking a retrospective glance of the history of the subject, it is not a little curious to observe how suddenly and frequently the views of chemists have oscillated and changed. At one time it was maintained by Lambe, Thomson, and others, that spring waters were most powerful in corroding lead. Guyton Morveau, Christison, and others, on the contrary, who pursued their investigations in a more comprehensive and scientific manner, arrived at the opposite conclusion, and inferred, speaking generally, that the corrosive influence of the water was in direct proportion to its purity; and that certain saline ingredients in spring water were a means of preventing its action on lead. These contradictory views have been more than once revived and discussed. Our acquaintance with the actual circumstances that retard or accelerate the action is in an equally unsatisfactory state. At one time soluble sulphates and phosphates were regarded as the most powerful protecting agents, and nitrates and chlorides the most active saline promoters. At another, waters which are alkaline, and those which contain a notable quantity of organic matters, and of carbonic acid gas, were considered to be most energetic in their corrosive powers. At the present time some authorities affirm that alkaline carbonates and phosphates are most effectual in destroying this action of soft and pure waters; and very recently, in the case of Loch Katrine water, a touch of the "old red sandstone, and the carbonic acid and carbonate of ammonia of the atmosphere," have been ranked among the curative agents. In a word, we have no fixed or satisfactory principles for our guidance. The whole subject stands much in need of careful and comprehensive research; and until this research has been made, we must be content to make a specific examination of the qualities of each water in relation to lead, and to judge it upon its own merits, independently of preconceived notions and speculations.

With regard to Loch Katrine water, our conclusions fortunately are in no way affected by speculative opinions; the problem is purely a practical one, and accordingly our first object must be to ascertain to what extent it acts upon the several commercial forms of metallic lead.

The principal results of the special experiments I have made upon this part of the subject, I shall now detail:

COMMON MILLED LEAD.

One of the severest trials to which water can be subjected, in testing its action upon lead, is unquestionably, to immerse in the water an extensive surface of recently *scraped* sheet lead. There are very few waters which, when thus treated, will not, after contact with the metal for a longer or shorter period, give evidence to chemical tests of having become more or less contaminated. For the purpose of comparison, therefore, or of gratifying curiosity, this preliminary preparation of the surface of the lead by scraping, may be admissable, but in the investigation of a practical inquiry like the present, such a process is highly objectionable, as likely to lead to very erroneous views. Where scraped lead is employed and found to be acted upon, it is always advisable to ascertain if the action is progressive, and to transfer the lead to a second quantity of water, after contact for several days, to determine whether the action is uninterrupted.

In all the experiments to be described, the milled lead was used in the state in which it is sold by the plumber, except where specially stated that scraped lead was tried by way of comparison. It may, however, be as well to mention that the surface of sheet lead is frequently greasy with the oil used in the operation of rolling, in which case it should be cleaned by wiping with chamois leather or a dry cloth. For scientific research, absolutely pure sheet lead must be employed, as nearly all plumbers' lead contains tin.

With Loch Katrine water, it is perfectly indifferent whether dull lead, or scraped lead, soft plumbers' lead, or assay lead be used; the action is invariably rapid and uninterrupted.

The method employed in my experiments for estimating the proportion of lead in the water would readily indicate, in a colorless water, the presence of a quantity of lead equal to the 100th part of a grain a gallon, or the 7-millionth part of the weight of the water. I made no attempt to detect smaller quantities. This proportion, which I consider sufficiently minute for the present investigation, was the limit of the method applied. By using large quantities of water, and concentrating after immersion of the lead, much more minute quantities could of course be detected, but these operations are not admissable where many experiments have to be made.

It would be unnecessarily tedious to give the details of the many trials I have made as to the action of Loch Katrine water upon milled lead. The following statement, deduced from the results of a great number of experiments made in open vessels, and with common sheet lead, will unequivocally show the rapidity, energy, and continuance of the action of the water upon this form of lead.

Grains of Lead corroded and dissolved, per gallon of water.

In 1 minute, ...	1-15th grain.
In 1 hour, ...	2 to 4 grains.
In 3 hours,........................	4 to 5 "
In 24 hours, ...	7 to 10 "
In 12 days.........................	42 grains.
In 10 weeks, ...	120 "

In a few minutes, a distinct opalescence may be seen in the water near the surface of the lead. In less than 24 hours a decided deposit collects at the bottom of the vessel, and increases day by day.

No one, I think, will, after a careful consideration of these results, venture to deny that water which acts so rapidly and powerfully on lead, must in a very short time become prejudicial to health.

ACTION IN CLOSED VESSELS.

Many experiments were made with milled lead in hermetically closed vessels, both in the dark, and with free exposure to light. The degree of action varied from 2 to 5 grains of lead per gallon, according the temperature of the water, the extent of metallic surface exposed, the purity of the lead, &c.

In one experiment, in which the lead surface was in the ratio of 2 square inches to the ounce of water, 2 grains of lead were dissolved in three days. In other trials, in which the surface was equal to 3 square inches to the ounce. I found between 4 and 5 grains dissolved.

In stating the results of the various trials, I prefer to give the quantities of lead detected in the water, in grains or parts of a grain per gallon.

This method, no doubt, has the appearance of being less minute and less imposing, than when the amount is expressed proportionately to the weight of the water, as "a twenty-thousandth part of the water," instead of "3½ grains per gallon;" or "a millionth part of the water," instead of "about 1-14th of a grain." It is, however, I think, to be preferred, as admitting of a more ready comparison of the results.

In order to prevent any misapprehension, I may also state, that the results here recorded must not be regarded as showing the fixed extent of the action for the time specified, or the actual quantities that will invariably be dissolved by a gallon of the water. The degree of action, or amount of lead dissolved, will be influenced by many circumstances, such as the ratio of the lead surface to the volume of fluid—the purity of the lead—the extent of fluid surface—the position of the metal in the water—the temperature of the water at the time of the experiment, &c. If, for instance, a slip of lead be laid flat at the bottom of a large volume of the water, the pearly sediment soon covers the surface of the metal, and the action proceeds very slowly; but when the lead is placed in a vertical or slightly inclined position, the greater part of the delicate scales fall off and subside to the bottom, thus exposing fresh surfaces. The quantities given, therefore, although the actual results of experiments, must be considered, mainly as showing the relative degree of action, since a greater amount of effect could be obtained by using a more extensive surface of metal, and *vice versa*. Accordingly, if one experimentor states that he obtained, in any particular trial, 2 grains per gallon, and another, that he obtained 3 grains, it must not be inferred that either result is incorrect, since the circumstances may have been more or less different. This remark also applies to different trials by the same operator. In my experiments with milled lead, the metal was placed vertically or slightly inclined, and always wholly immersed in the water.

The following experiment will serve to illustrate the influence of a slight variation even in the position of the lead. Five deep cylindrical vessels were filled with Loch Katrine water, and a slip of milled lead was immersed vertically in each, as explained in the following statement, which also shows the results obtained :—

				In 3 hours.
1st vessel,	slip,	half immersed, ...	$2\frac{3}{4}$	gr. per gall.
2d	"	just below the surface, ...	$2\frac{1}{4}$	"
3d	"	$\frac{1}{3}$ below the surface, ...	2	"
4th	"	midway, ...	2	"
5th	"	at the bottom, ...	$\frac{3}{4}$	"

I refer so particularly to this apparently insignificant part of the inquiry, because I have endeavored most diligently, though in vain, to account for the remarkable discrepancies in many of the statements made in the Promoters' Report, and the results obtained in my experiments, which are fully corroborated by the independent investigations of the scientific gentlemen associated with me. If these discrepancies involved mere differences of opinion, considerable latitude might be allowed : but in simple matters of fact, as in the present case, there should be but one result. I am therefore led, though somewhat reluctantly, to notice one or two of the leading statements that appear to me inexplicable.

At page 17 it is stated of Loch Katrine water, that "when exposed along with bright lead, that is to say, lead which has been recently scraped, so as to expose a fresh metallic surface, a strong action manifested itself in a few hours, the lead being covered with a white film, and a deposit of oxide falling to the bottom of the glass." Again, at page 18, "the action was so small as to be barely appreciable. A similar result was also observed in open vessels with lead in the state in which it is usually obtained from the plumber's shop, and though, in some instances, a slight action was apparent at first, the metal became covered, in the course of few days, with a thin coating, which prevented all further corrosion." At page 28, "Loch Katrine water acts strongly upon bright lead exposed to light and air." Page 32—"If the surface of the lead be dull, *i. e.*, covered with its usual blueish-grey coat of sub-oxide, which is seen on the manufactured sheet or pipe metal, there is no perceptible action on lead."

Page 35—"That this water does not exert any noxious action on lead when the metal is in its ordinarily dull state." Page 42—"Where lead with a clear bright surface is introduced into it, the lead is rapidly acted on."

This language is very plain, and unmistakeably affirms that Loch Katrine water acts very slightly, or to an imperceptible and innocuous extent upon lead, if the metal is in its "ordinary dull state," as obtained from the plumber's shop," leading naturally to the conclusion, that there need be no apprehension of danger unless the lead be "bright," that is, "recently scraped lead."

I have made numerous experiments for the special purpose of ascertaining whether there is any truth in the assertion that Loch Katrine water will either not act at all, or to an inappreciable extent, upon milled lead as sold by the plumber. From the results obtained, I do not hesitate to affirm that the statement is entirely devoid of foundation. In none of my trials have I ever seen the mere tarnish or coating of "*grey sub-oxide*," as it is called, make the slightest difference in the effect produced. I purchased pieces of milled lead from eight different plumbers in Glasgow, and immersed, in separate vessels containing the same volume of water, a slip of each specimen, exposing the same extent of surface, and without the slightest scraping or abrasion. In eighteen hours a notable quantity of oxide of lead had collected at the bottom of each vessel, and on testing the water, I found in it and the sediment together, a quantity of lead varying from 4 to 6 grains in the gallon of water, except in two cases, in which there were respectively 2 and 3 grains only. The action is still proceeding in all the experiments, although they were commenced several weeks ago. The amount of sediment in each case is now very considerable, but visibly less in the two experiments before referred to, the difference arising, as I have ascertained, from the impurity in the lead. To obviate the objection that might reasonably be urged, that, when a slip of lead is newly cut from a sheet, brightly polished edges are exposed, I purposely covered these with wax to prevent contact with water. When the edges are thus coated, the total amount of lead corroded is of course diminished, as there is less surface of metal exposed, but the action proceeds uninterruptedly. In a particular experiment I waxed the sides of a slip, leaving the edges *only* exposed; in one hour I obtained 1-8th of a grain of lead per gallon, in four hours about half a grain, and in three days nearly 2 grains.

I have also seen experiments tried in the laboratory of King's College, London, with Loch Katrine water and common sheet lead, without the slightest preparation of the surface;—the effects were equally decided and energetic. To test the question still further, three slips of milled lead were immersed in vessels containing the same volume of the water; one slip was scraped, the second wiped with a dry cloth, and the other left untouched. The following statement shows the result in grains of lead corroded, per gallon of water:—

	1 hour.		3 hours.		26 hours.
Scraped lead.....	1½ gr.	....	4 gr.	....	about 10 grs.
Wiped..........	2 "	....	4 "	....	" 10 "
Untouched......	1¾ "	....	4 "	....	" 10 "

With Loch Katrine water, therefore, it is indifferent whether the lead be scraped or as sold by the plumber; the first effect may vary, but the ultimate action is the same.

Through the kindness of Mr. Whitfield, manager of Messrs. Newton and Keat's Lead Works in Glasgow, which are the largest of the kind in the west of Scotland, I obtained a piece of milled lead that had been rolled and finished under my inspection. It is unnecessary to give in detail the various experiments. I tried it scraped and unscraped, &c.; the action of the water was invariably rapid, energetic, and unceasing.

I have been the more particular on this point, because it appears to me that a mistake in so simple a matter of fact gives rise to grave suspicions as to the accuracy of other statements in the same documents.

Again, it has been frequently affirmed that the action does not go on in the dark, and at page 18 of the Promoters' Evidence, it is stated that "the sun's rays increased both the rapidity and intensity of the action, while, on the other hand, exclusion from light and air had a precisely opposite effect." My experiments, I am sorry to say, do not confirm this most desirable result. I have tried the water in old pipes and new pipes, and never failed to detect a notable and dangerous quantity of lead in the water. I have tried it with milled lead in the dark, in the sun's rays, and in diffused day-light, but the differences in the results were extremely slight. In the case of the direct rays of the sun, the increase of action is, in my opinion, to be attributed chiefly to the heat, and not to the light. In one series of experiments I obtained the following results with milled lead in open vessels:—

	1½ hour. Per gallon.	3 hours Per gallon.	12 hours. Per gallon.
In the dark......	3 grains.	.. 4 grains.	.. 5½ grains.
In daylight......	3¼ "	.. 4 "	.. 5½ "
In the sun's rays..	3½ "	.. 5¼ "	.. "

In another experiment, a slip of lead was immersed in the water, and carefully excluded from light from the 19th April till the 2d May, when the amount of corrosive action was found to be exactly the same as in a similar trial, in which the vessel and its contents were exposed daily to light. Even in closed vessels I have never been able to detect any marked difference in the results of the experiments made in the dark from those obtained with free exposure to light.

The influence of temperature is well shown in an experiment, in which the vessel containing the water and lead was placed in an air bath, where it was exposed to a temperature of 100 degrees F. The water was cold at the commencement of the experiment. A comparative trial was also made with another portion of water at 60 degrees.

	At 100° F. Per Gallon.	At 60° F. Per Gallon.
1 hour........	3 grains	1¾ grains.
2 hours.......	8 "	2½ "
3 hours.......	11 "	4 "
4 hours.......	12½ "	4½ "

A similar experiment was made with two pieces of lead pipe of the same length and diameter. Both were filled with Loch Katrine water, and securely closed. One pipe was kept in the sun's rays for four hours, and the other at the ordinary temperature. On opening the pipes and testing the water, a notably larger proportion of lead was detected in that which had been in the pipe exposed to sunshine, as the following statement fully shows:

	Temp. of water.	Grains of Lead
Water from pipe in sunshine...	79°	.......1-3d in a gallon.
Water from pipe at 65°......	65°	.......1-8th "

It would therefore appear that lead pipes in kitchens and other warm places would be more corroded and acted on than pipes in less heated situations.

From a careful consideration of these experiments, I feel fully justified in affirming that Loch Katrine water acts *upon lead as powerfully in the dark as in the light, and that the increased action observable in the direct rays of the sun may be referred to the elevation of temperature.*

There are one or two other statements in these Reports at complete variance with the results I have obtained. At page 18 we find it stated that "the metal became covered in a few days with a thin coating, which prevented all further corrosion." This would indeed be a desirable effect. In none of my experiments, however, have I ever witnessed the least tendency to the formation of a permanent or protecting encrustation, as in the case of certain hard waters. In open vessels, with milled lead and access of air, the action of Loch Katrine water, as before explained, is uninterrupted; the pearly scales separate from the surface of the metal, and collect at the bottom of the vessel, new metal is exposed, and the corrosion continues unceasingly. I have now before me several trials, commenced nearly four months ago, in which the lead is still as vigorously acted upon as at first. In closed vessels, as already stated, the action is limited, not however in consequence of a protective coating being formed, for, on the admission of air, the corrosion recommences, and proceeds as regularly as in open vessels. In a scientific point of view, the persistence of this action, when there is free access of air, may be regarded as one of its most interesting features; and, in reference to the practical question, it is of the very highest importance.

Further, at page 22 of the Evidence, we find, "and even common plumber's lead, when kept in the water for a sufficient time, ceased to act on a new quantity." All my experiments tend to the conclusion that no permanent interruption of the action occurs on transferring the lead to fresh quantities of water. In one experiment a slip of lead was immersed in the water during 48 hours, then transferred to a new quantity—result the same as in the first quantity. Another slip of lead that had been in the water for six days was transferred to a fresh portion of water—action precisely similar to the first.

A piece of lead, exposing a comparatively small extent of surface, after having been in the water for a period of six weeks, was transferred to a new quantity. It gave the following results:

In 1 hour....1 grain of lead per gallon.
In 4 hours....2 grains " "
In 3 days....A very abundant deposit of oxide of lead.

It is of course difficult to interpret the expression "a sufficient time;" but a period of six weeks is surely adequate for the formation of a protecting crust. What the effect would be when the lead is nearly eaten away, I have no evidence to show.

A statement in Dr. John Smith's Report* on the waters of the Dee and Don, at Aberdeen, shows that other soft waters acts upon tarnished lead. He says, "From these experiments, it appears that the Dee water acts more readily upon tarnished or crusted lead than upon the bright metal; and that when a crusted bar is immersed for a certain time in water, dried and immersed again for the same time, the action is greater the second time than the first; dried and immered a third time, the action is still greater, so that a lead cistern alternately filled and emptied is more unsafe than one kept constantly at the same level, both being freely exposed to the air."

It is my decided opinion, that *lead immersed in Loch Katrine water does not become covered in the course of a few days with a thin coating that prevents all further corrosion; and that it does not, even when kept in the water for six weeks, resist the action of a new quantity.*

I have also tested the action of Loch Katrine water upon lead, after the metal had been in contact with several other waters. In the Promoters' Evidence we read, "We have particularly tried the action of Loch Katrine water upon lead which had been previously in contact with other water. Already the leads have been in the water for weeks, yet they are not in the slightest degree acted upon, nor do the waters contain the faintest traces of lead." The water first used is not specified.

* Quarterly Journal Chemical Society, vol. iv.

At page 32—"If the lead has been already in contact with water which has acted upon it, then the Loch Katrine water produces no noxious compound of lead with it, even when exposed to a large surface of lead, and under a free access of air." The water of Trafalgar Square, London, is particularly referred to.

I can confirm these statements as regards certain hard waters; but after the lead has been in contact with several comparatively soft waters, I find it powerfully corroded on immersion in Loch Katrine water. I have arranged the particulars of several experiments in the following table:

Waters in which the lead was first immersed.	Time of immersion in first water.	Extent of action in 24 hours on being transferred to Loch Katrine water.	Action in 5 days.
		Per Gallon.	
1. Clyde water (as used in Glasgow)	5 days	6 grains	Very abundant crystaline deposit—action continuous.
2. Brockburn water....	30 days	1-6th grain	No visible action.
3. Paisley water (from Stanley Reservoir)	5 days	8 grains	Very abundant crystaline deposit—action continuous.
4. Lanark water.......	30 days	1½ grain	Patches of pearly flakes on surface of lead.
5. Tay water at Perth..	60 days	1¼ grain	Patches on lead, and small quantity of sediment.
6. Aberdeen water.....	60 days	8 grains	Very abundant deposit.
7. Whitehaven water (from Reservoir)	6 days	1 grain	Small patches of pearly flakes on lead.

In making experiments with common milled lead, it is of the greatest importance to ascertain the amount of impurity it contains, and especially the proportion of tin. The sheet lead used in the construction of sulphuric acid chambers, in the lining of pans for chemical operations, and for other purposes in chemical works, is generally made from pure ore-lead, but the sheet lead commonly supplied to the plumber for cisterns, &c., contains an admixture of old lead, with more or less solder adhering; and accordingly, we generally find that plumber's sheet lead is variable in its degree of hardness. I have carefully analyzed numerous specimens of old lead, slag lead, lead piping, and sheet lead, with the view to ascertain the proportion of tin they respectively contain.

I select several of the results, which will sufficiently show the very varying character of common lead in this respect.

		Metallic Tin per cent.
1	specimen of ingot lead from ore...	None.
1	" of assay sheet lead.....	None.
2	specimens of slag lead...........	.82 and 1.25.
2	" of old lead...........	.6 and 1.34.
6	" of milled lead.........	.75, .52, .40, .31, .16, .15.
2	" of lead piping (¾-in. bore)	1.18, 1.22, &c.
2	" of do (1-in. bore)	.94, 1.1, &c.

These results plainly indicate how essential it is, in any important investigation, to analyze the lead pipes and cistern lead supplied by the plumber.

LEAD CISTERN.

I have further tried the action of Loch Katrine water upon plumbers' lead, by having a small cistern made of hard sheet lead, in every respect similar to those used in our houses. It was filled with water, and the effect examined day by day. The action was very decided, though less in degree than with slips of sheet lead in an open vessel, the proportion of lead surface exposed being smaller. In three days the sides of the cistern exhibited unmistakeable signs of corrosion, they were coated in different places with patches of the pearly scales of the carbonate and oxide of lead, and a notable quantity of the same substance was observed in the form of a flocculent sediment at the bottom of the water. The small masses of silky scales stood out in bold relief on the sides of the cistern, and were separable on the slightest agitation. The water itself was perfectly transparent, but on being tested, it gave indications of the presence of nearly ¼ of a grain of lead per gallon. On diffusing the sediment through the water, the amount of lead was equal to about 2 grains in the gallon. The cistern was afterwards emptied and refilled—the action continued as decided as at first.

EXPERIMENTS WITH LEAD PIPES.

A set of pipes, each 1 foot in length when closed, was made from pieces of new lead piping, 1-inch bore, and another set, each 18 inches in length, from lead piping ¾-inch bore. In each experiment, the pipe was completely filled with the water, and securely closed with caoutchouc or cork, and sometimes with both, and when necessary, the cut edges of the pipe were covered with wax. The water was kept in the pipes for different periods of time, varying from one or two hours to several days. In every experiment there was a powerful, and in my opinion, a highly dangerous action. The results, however, were by no means uniform for pipes of the same bore, purchased from different plumbers. The differences, I am induced to think, are to be mainly attributed to the variable quantity of impurity in the lead. In Dr. Smith's report upon the water supplied to Aberdeen, a similar remark is made:—"In some cases it has appeared to me that old pipes are more acted upon than new; the differences, however, may have arisen from impurities in the lead, or from other special causes not detected." Before drawing any definite conclusion, therefore, from experiments with this or any other water, in which little or no action could be detected, it would be absolutely necessary to analyze the pipes employed. To economize space, I shall give the results of several experiments with lead piping, in the form of a table:—

Experiment.	Diameter of Pipe.	Time of Experiment.	Grains lead per gal.
1	1 inch	1 hour	1-40th.
2	"	24 hours	3-4th.
3	"	24 "	1-6th.
4	"	2 days	3-4th.
5	"	15 "	2.
6	"	22 "	3½.
7	¾ "	24 hours	1-6th.
8	¾ "	4 days	Nearly a grain.

To ascertain the effects produced by a current of Loch Katrine water through new piping, a piece of pipe, 1 inch bore, was kept in the outflow of the Loch for four hours, and brought away filled and closed. In three days the water contained nearly 3-4ths of a grain per gallon, and in six days a grain and a half.

Similar experiments were made with a set of short pipes, made from a piece of old piping, 3-4th inch bore, taken expressly for the purpose, from a tenement in the Garscube Road, where it had been used for conveying the present Glasgow water since 1843. This pipe was covered in the inside with a firm coating, consisting of carbonate of lime, oxide of iron, and organic matter. In 24 hours this pipe gave with Loch Katrine 1-5th of a grain per gallon, and in four days half a grain per gallon. The effect of allowing the water to flow through this pipe was also tried. 4 feet of it were placed in the outflow of the loch for 10 days, and brought away full. It was opened after four days, when the water was found to contain upwards of a grain of lead per gallon. *Loch Katrine water, therefore, acts upon lead piping that has for many years conveyed the present Glasgow water.*

Many experiments have also been made to ascertain the effect of keeping Loch Katrine water in contact with iron before trying its action upon milled lead and piping. The water was kept in closed iron pipes for several days, and then quickly transferred to lead tubes. In a few hours the presence of lead was detected in the clear water. In six days as much as 1-3d of a grain per gallon was dissolved; and including the lead in the sedimentary matter, which is abundantly formed by the action of the water on the iron, I found nearly two grains. In the same way, sheet-lead was invariably corroded by the water after the latter had been kept for many days in closed vessels with pieces of cast-iron. In one experiment, after 12 days' contact with iron, the water, in 24 hours, was found to contain 1-8th of a grain per gallon. Its action on lead, after lengthened contact with iron, is therefore evidently diminished; but, when this is the case, the water becomes charged and foul with oxide of iron, and is rendered thereby quite unfit for use, though it still retains the power of becoming impregnated with a poisonous quantity of lead.

ALLOYS.

My attention has also been given to the effect of alloying lead with tin. This part of the inquiry demands careful consideration, from the circumstance that an alloy of lead containing 5 per cent. of tin has been strongly recommended in the Promoters' Reports, to be used for conveying and retaining Loch Katrine water.

It is an undoubted fact, that the addition of a very small quantity of tin to lead considerably diminishes the corrosion and solution of the lead by pure soft waters. This fact has been long known. The protecting power of tin is, however, very much less than the statements in the Promoters' Evidence would lead us to expect. At page 29 we find the following: "The most absolute protection would be obtained by the use of an alloy of lead with 5 per cent. of tin" I cannot corroborate this statement.

When alloys of lead with 5, 10, or 20 per cent. of tin are immersed in Loch Katrine water, no *visible* action takes place, even after many days' contact; the water remains bright and transparent, and no pearly sedimentary matter is formed; but *dissolved* lead can always be detected in the water. Four alloys were made, containing respectively 1, 5, 10 and 20 per cent. of tin. A piece of each, exposing nearly the same surface, was wholly immersed in Loch Katrine water in open vessels. The results are given in the following table:

Alloys.	1 hour. Per gallon.	3 hours. Per gallon.	3 days. Per gallon.
1 per cent. of tin	....1-15th gr.	....½ gr.	....2½ grs.
5 "	....1-20th gr.	....1-8th gr.	....1-3d gr.
10 "	....1-30th gr.	....1-9th gr.	....1-3d gr.
20 "	....1-40th gr.	....1-10th gr.	....1-3d gr.

No sedimentary matter was formed in any of these experiments, excepting in the case of the first alloy, which, after three days, gave the usual flaky deposit, the water becoming opalescent on agitation. The results in the above statement show that Loch Katrine water acts appreciably upon lead alloyed with tin, and that there is very little difference in the protecting power, whether the tin amounts to 5, 10 or 20 per cent. Again, several pounds of lead were alloyed respectively with 5 and 10 per cent. of tin. Part of each alloy was melted and cast, and the remainder was rolled into sheet at Messrs. Newton and Keat's works. The object of the experiment was to ascertain whether the mere operation of rolling influenced, in any marked degree, the protective power of the tin. The following results were obtained:

Alloys.	Cast. 3 hours.	2 days.	Rolled. 3 hours.	2 days.
5 p. c. tin ..	1-9th gr. ..	nearly 1-3d gr. ..	1-8th gr. ..	nearly 1-3d.
10 " ..	1-8th gr. ..	1-4th to 1-3d gr..	1-8th gr. ..	1-3 gr.

Loch Katrine water, therefore, acts decidedly upon lead alloyed with tin, but much less powerfully than upon pure sheet lead.

Several objections present themselves to the employment of alloyed lead in supplying Loch Katrine water to Glasgow. Not to mention the expense and disturbance consequent on the removal of all the pipes at present in use, it would, I conceive, be absolutely necessary, even granting that 5 per cent of tin would insure perfect immunity from danger, to appoint a qualified assay master to superintend the admixture of the tin, or to analyse the pipes and sheet lead, in order to ascertain that the proper quantity of protecting and more expensive material had been used.

VISIT TO PROMOTERS' APPARATUS AT THE TROSACHS.

I have now to report the result of my inspection of the pipes, cisterns, &c., erected about a mile from Loch Katrine, on the stream issuing from the Loch. The visit was made with the consent of the Promoters, on Saturday, the 29th April. I was obligingly shown every thing that I requested to see, though of course no opportunity could be afforded of examining the interior of 200 or 300 yards of closed iron piping, and of several lengths of lead piping laid in the ground. My attention was, therefore, exclusively directed to the condition of the cisterns.

I may, however, at once state that I consider the arrangements as I saw them, most defective, and unsatisfactory. The chemical experiments made with this apparatus, were, I have no doubt, conducted most zealously and faithfully, but the arrangements themselves, in a scientific point of view, are open to grave objections.

In all the new laid cisterns, I observed unmistakable evidence of the corrosive action of the water upon the metal. At the bottom of each cistern, there was more or less of a flocculent pearly white sediment, which became diffused through the water on the slightest agitation. It was similar in appearance to the deposit formed in my miniature cistern, and the application of chemical re-agents proved it to be the carbonate and oxide of lead with organic matter. On the sides of the cisterns also there were numerous patches of white silky flakes projecting from the surface of the metal, and easily detached when the water was agitated. I am perfectly satisfied that in time the lead at these places would have been perforated by the corrosion. It is the peculiar feature of many waters, that corrode lead cisterns, to attack the metal in particular spots, where the lead gradually gives way and is eaten into holes. This very strikingly obtains with lead containing from ½ to 1 per cent. of tin.

At the bottom of the new lead cisterns communicating with the new iron pipes, I remarked a small quantity of oxide of iron mixed with the lead sediment.

I run off a part of the water from one of the cisterns, and having agitated the water in order to detach the loose scales from the sides, and to mix the sediment, I filled three bottles with the water; one of these I sent to Dr. Miller, the second I gave to Mr. Wallace, and the third I retained. On my return to Glasgow, I subjected this water and sediment to a searching examination. In the clear water I detected between 1-3d and 1-4th of a grain of lead per gallon, and in the sediment and water together, upwards of a grain per gallon.

I also collected a bottle of water with the sedimentary matter suspended, from one of the new cisterns in connection with the new iron pipes. In this sediment I found oxide of iron and an appreciable quantity of lead.

It is quite easy to understand, that if a specimen of the water had been drawn off without disturbing the sedimentary matter at the bottom of the cisterns, the presence of lead in the water might not have been detected. But I feel confident, from the extent of corrosion exhibited on the surface of the metal, that the amount of lead deposit would increase day by day, and that it would be diffused through the water every time the cistern was refilled.

The importance of examining the sediments at the bottom of lead cisterns is strikingly shown in a case referred to by Dr. Alderson, in his lectures on the effects of lead upon the system. "Every individual in the house had been previously attacked by colic, and one had already died paralytic, (the exciting cause not having been suspected.) I found the head of the family paralyzed and epileptic, and it was then ascertained that the water used for domestic purposes was rain water, and was received into a leaden cistern. On examination of the water by a clever chemist, Mr. Pearsall, lead was found in large quantity." It is also mentioned that there was a considerable sediment in the cistern, and that, on agitating the water, and then testing it after the sediment had subsided, not a trace of lead was exhibited. "The sediment contained the metal in large quantity."

I have been much surprised to find no mention in the Promoters' Evidence of any analysis of the lead pipes and cisterns erected at the Trosachs. If this was not done before the specimens of water so elaborately described in the reports were collected, I consider the omission completely fatal to the conclusions drawn from the negative results obtained on testing the various samples. It is extremely difficult, otherwise than by supposing such an omission, to account for the circumstances reported in the evidence, that Loch Katrine water, after remaining in lead pipes for several hours, and even days, should exhibit no further traces of lead than "one millionth part of the weight of the water," or about 1-14th of a grain per gallon.

I shall now give the analysis, &c., of the other waters I have examined in connection with the present inquiry.

TROSACHS HOTEL WATER.

The water used in the Trosachs Hotel is not taken from Loch Katrine, or from any stream issuing therefrom. It is supplied from a small mountain stream at the back of the hotel. It is first conveyed into a stone cistern, lined with cement, and thence passes through upwards of 100 yards of lead pipe into a lead cistern in one of the attics of the hotel. On two occasions, I collected specimens of the water from the stream before it enters the stone cistern, and I also took a specimen from a cran on the second floor of the hotel.

This water acts very slightly upon lead, and the action is not continuous. By contact with common sheet lead for one day, it gave about 1-50th of a grain of lead per gallon, and after the lapse of 7 days only 1-20th of a grain.

In the sample of water taken after passing through the lead pipe, I found about 1-80th of a grain of lead per gallon.

A general analysis of the water from the stream gave the following results :—

	Grains per Gallon.
Organic matter	1.20
Mineral matter	1.33
	2.53
Degree of hardness	.9°

It contained a small quantity of carbonate of lime.

GASSES.

	Cubic Inches Per Gallon.	Per cent.
Carbonic acid	.4	4.94
Oxygen	2.3	28.40
Nitrogen	5.4	66.66
	8.1	100.

These results show that, as compared with Loch Katrine water, the Trosachs Inn water contains a much less quantity of oxygen, and nearly five times the amount of carbonic acid. Both specimens were taken from the stream after a continuance of dry weather. What the qualities of this water may be after heavy rains, I am not prepared to state.

BROCKBURN WATER.

This water was minutely analyzed and examined in 1845 by Dr. Thomas Thomson and Dr. Robert Dundas Thomson conjointly, by Dr. Gregory, and by myself.

The following extracts from the chemical reports, rendered at the time to the Gorbals Water Company, sufficiently exhibit the excellent qualities of the water, and its suitableness for the supply of a large community :—

"The waters are excellent, being soft and pure, and they are well calculated to serve the purposes for which they are intended."—*Drs. Thomson.*

"On the whole, I cannot easily use terms too strong in speaking of the great purity and softness of the water. It has no signs of mossy origin, and I have never examined water so free from organic matter. So pure a stream of water is exceedingly rare, and I doubt if another such can be pointed out in Scotland. I am most decidedly of opinion that if water of the average quality of these samples be supplied to the city of Glasgow filtered, no city that I ever heard of will possess a supply of water so pure and so especially adapted to washing. It only contains a 10,000th of its weight of solid matter. There is not the slightest doubt, therefore, that the water is in every respect extremely suitable for the purposes of the company."—*Dr. Gregory.*

"From a careful consideration of my experiments and analyses, I can unhesitatingly and confidently state that the Brockburn water is remarkably pure and soft, and perfectly free from all metallic and injurious mineral impregnation. It is agreeable to drink, excellent for washing, and in every respect admirably adapted for domestic and manufacturing purposes. It is very seldom that so exellent a water presents itself in the neighborhood of a large town, and I must add, that the inhabitants using so pure and wholesome a water will possess great and peculiar advantages."—*Dr. Penny.*

In February and March of the present year, I again made a most careful examination of this water, and the results obtained have fully confirmed my opinion of its qualities, and of its superior excellence for the supply of a large community.

I may mention, however, that the results of the analyses of this water in 1845 differ slightly from those obtained with the specimens collected in February last. The water on the latter occasion was found to be purer than in 1845; but the difference is easily explained by the circumstances that in 1845 the samples were taken after a long continuance of dry weather, and when there was very little water in the burn, whereas in February last the specimens were collected when the burn was very full.

The following statement shows the results obtained in 1845, from specimens taken at the same part of the stream, below Balgray House:—

	Drs. Thomson. Grains per gallon.	Dr. Gregory. Grains per gallon.	Dr. Penny. Grains per gallon.
Organic matter, ...	1.26	7.33	1.15
Mineral matter, ...	5.93		6.00
	7.19	7.33	7.15

In 1854 I found it to contain:—

	Grains per gallon.
Organic matter, ...	1.531
Mineral matter, ...	3.666
	5.197

Another sample collected on the 19th April last gave:—

	Grains per gallon.
Organic matter, ...	1.74
Mineral matter, ...	5.15
	6.89

It is, therefore manifest that the amount of foreign matter in this water varies slightly at different seasons, but that even in its worst state, the water is very soft and of excellent quality. Its degree of hardness is, on an average, 3.2°. A minute analysis of the water in the present year gave the following results:

Organic matter, ...	1.531
Carbonate of lime, ...	1.152
Sulphate of lime, ...	.946
Sulphate of magnesia, ...	.284
Muriate of magnesia, ...	.344
Alkaline chlorides, ...	.720
Oxide of iron, ...	.043
Silica, ...	.177
	5.197

GASES.

	Cubic inches. Per gallon.	Per cent.
Carbonic acid,	.55	7.33
Oxygen,	2.25	30.00
Nitrogen,	4.70	62.67
	7.50	100.

ACTION ON LEAD.

I made a careful examination, in 1845, of the Brockburn water in regard to its action upon lead, and I have recently subjected it to additional investigations. The degree of action, even under the most favorable circumstances is extremely slight. With common milled lead in open vessels it has never given, in any one of the many and varied experiments I have made, a sedimentary deposit, nor has the water ever become turbid or opalescent. The quantity of lead in solution, after prolonged contact, was found to be exceedingly small, and when the water was renewed, the presence of the metal was not afterwards appreciable. The metal soon became coated with a protecting film. The following statement contains the most important results of the trials in which action was observed :—

Common Milled Lead, exposing a large extent of surface.

In open vessels for....	1 hour	...1-80th grain per gall.
" "	4 hours	..1-30th " "
" "	3 days	...1-20th " "
" "	10 days	...1-15th " "
In closed vessels......	10 days	...1-20th " "

Lead Piping.

In new pipe.........	3 days	....1-20th grain per gall.
" "	10 days	....1-15th " "
In very soft new pipes,	3 days	....1-10th " "

A careful comparison of these extremely minute results with those obtained by the action of Loch Katrine water, will give a correct idea of the extraordinary powers of the latter water in corroding and dissolving lead.

THE EARN WATER.

The Earn River is one of the new sources from which, as I am informed, the Gorbals Water Company propose to take, when required, an additional supply. In its physical qualities, the Earn water is similar to the water of the Brockburn, and it is equally suitable, in my opinion, for domestic and manufacuring purposes. It contains a less proportion of mineral matter than the Brock water, and a little more organic matter. Its degree of hardness, also, is lower, being about 2 degrees.

An imperial gallon gave:—

Organic matter, ...	1.665	grains.
Mineral matter, ...	3.275	"
	4.940	"

It is fully and purely aërated, and it is quite free from ferruginous and other objectionable impregnation.

In its action upon lead, the Earn water corresponds very closely with the Brock water.

LOCH LOMOND WATER.

Specimens of this water were collected, on two occasions, from the middle of the Loch opposite Inversnaid, and from the Leven, at the outflow of the Loch.

In appearance, taste, and general properties, this water is similar to Katrine water, but the specimens from the upp er end of the Loch were rather more colored. All the specimens contained a minute quantity of carbonate of lime. The mean of two analyses, gave the following results:—

	Specimen from Loch opposite Inversnaid.	Specimen from outflow.
	Grains per Gallon.	Grains per Gallon.
Organic matter..............	1.175	1.145
Mineral matter..............	1.650	1.875
	2.825	3.020
Degree of hardness..........	.85°	1.°

GASES.

	Middle of Loch.		Outflow of Loch.	
	Cubic in. Per gall.	Per cent.	Cubic in. Per gall.	Per cent.
Carbonic acid.........	.28	4.04	.34	5.10
Oxygen	2.14	30.84	2.08	31.18
Nitrogen	4.52	65.12	4.25	63.72
	6.94	100.	6.67	100.

An analysis of the Leven water, taken in 1848, from the stream at Balloch Bridge after a long continuance of dry weather, gave as follows:

Organic matter........	.50	grains per gallon.
Mineral matter........	3.25	" "
	3.75	" "

This specimen contained .5 of a grain of carbonate of lime in the gallon, and a trace of carbonate of magnesia.

Action on Lead.—The action of the water of Loch Lomond on lead is similar in every respect to that of Katrine water. It is, however, less powerful. With sheet lead, in open vessels, the same visible corrosion occurs, and after a few days an abundant sediment of the pearly oxide and carbonate of lead is produced. The Leven water is harder than the water at the upper end of the Loch, and its action upon lead is decidedly less energetic.* I have thrown the results of several experiments with these waters into the following table:

* I have been indirectly informed that at a gentleman's residence adjoining the Leven, a ead cistern had been eaten through by the corrosive action of the Leven water, and that it had been replaced by one of gutta percha.

	Specimen from upper part of Loch Lomond.	Specimen from outflow of Loch Lomond.
	Grains per Gallon.	Grains per Gallon.
Common Milled Lead in open vessels.		
1 hour	3-4th.	½.
3 hours	2.	3-4th.
24 hours	6.	1½.
3 days	Abundant deposit.	Deposit.
Milled Lead in closed vessels.		
24 hours	2.	
New Lead Pipe.		
24 hours	1-3d.	1-10th.
3 days	1 gr.	1-3d.

* * * * *

TAY WATER AT PERTH.

The water for the supply of Perth is taken from the Tay River, below the town. It filters into an artificial well or tunnel, and is thence pumped up into the reservoir on the top of the tower at the water works. Specimens of water from the river, a little above where the supply is taken, and from the reservoir, were collected in my presence on the 15th April last.

This is, unquestionably, a beautiful water. It is brilliant and colorless, cool and pleasant to the taste, and well suited in every respect for the use of a large community. A purer water for the supply of a town could scarcely be desired. It is harder than the Aberdeen water, and contains a little more dissolved organic matter, but the proportion of this latter ingredient will be subject to marked variations at different seasons of the year.

An analysis of this water gave as follows:

General Analysis.

Organic matter	1.240 grains.
Mineral matter	3.787
	5.027

Particular Analysis.

Organic matter	1.240
Carbonate of lime	1.508
Carbonate of magnesia	trace
Sulphate of lime	.874
Sulphate of magnesia	.278
Alkaline chlorides	.955
Phosphates	.102
Silica	.070
	5.027
Degree of hardness	2.4°

GASES.

	Cubic Inches Per Gallon.	Per Cent.
Carbonic acid	1.0	12.5
Oxygen	2.0	25.0
Nitrogen	5.0	62.5
	8.	100.

Action on Lead.

In open vessels, sheet lead:

	Lead dissolved.
1 hour	1-80th grain per gallon.
3 hours	1-50th " "
24 hours	1-30th " "
11 days	1-10th " "

No visible deposit was formed even after three months' immersion in the water. The metal was covered with a firmly adhering bluish crust. With this, as with other similar waters, I have occasionally found a less quantity of lead in solution after three hours, than at the expiration of one hour, and when the lead was transferred to a new quantity of water the action was barely appreciable.

With milled lead, in closed vessels, it gave in three days 1-15th of a grain of dissolved lead per gallon of water. In new pipe, for ten days, it gave 1-10th of a grain per gallon.

In a specimen of water drawn from a lead pipe in a house in Princes Street, Perth, there was not the least trace of lead.

From the above results, it appears monstrously absurd to rank, as some have done, Loch Katrine water with the water supplied to Perth, in regard to its action on lead.

DEE WATER AT ABERDEEN.

Specimens of the water supplied to Aberdeen were taken by Dr. Miller and myself on the 15th of April last, from the reservoir or iron tank in Union Place, into which the water is pumped through an iron main about a mile and a half in length, from the River Dee above the bridge. It is a clear, soft and colorless water, well aërated, and perfectly agreeable to the taste.

A minute and careful analysis of the Dee water was made about three years ago, by Dr. John Smith, Fordyce Lecturer on Agriculture, in the Marischal College, Aberdeen, and a very valuable series of experiments were conducted by him in reference to its action upon lead.

He gives the following statement of the quantities of its several ingredients per gallon:

	Grains.
Carbonate of lime	.850
Sulphate of lime	.121
Sulphate of magnesia	.323
Chloride of sodium and potassium	.670
Phosphate of lime and iron	.080
Silica	.140
Organic matter and loss	1.816
Total solid matter	4.

Degrees of hardness from 1.2° to 1.75°.

A general analysis of the specimen, collected on the occasion before referred to, gave in a gallon:

	Grains.
Organic matter	.81
Mineral matter	2.87
	3.68
Degree of hardness	1.3

The action of this water upon lead is rather more powerful than the Perth water, but very trifling as compared with Loch Katrine water. Dr. Smith found that the quantity dissolved in lead pipes varied from 1-100th of a grain to about 1-20th of a grain of lead in a gallon of water. His trials with bars of bright lead gave nearly the same results, and in one or two experiments about 1-10th of a grain per gallon.

My own experiments fully corroborate his results.

Sheet lead, in open vessels, gave of dissolved lead :

In 1 hour ....1-50th grain per gallon.
In 3 hours................1-30th " "
In 24 hours...............1-20th " "
In 10 days ....1-15th " "

No sedimentary matter was deposited, as with Loch Katrine water.

In a closed vessel, for six days, 1-20th of a grain was dissolved. A new pipe, in six days, gave 1-10th of a grain per gallon.

In the Report by the Government Commission on the supply of water to the Metropolis, we find the following remark in reference to the water supplied to Aberdeen: "Here, then, is a population, it might be supposed, constantly on the verge of danger from lead poison." If we may suppose this of the water used at Aberdeen, what shall we say to the Katrine water, which corrodes sheet lead to the extent of 20 or 30 grains, and dissolves from a lead pipe as much as two grains, in the time that the Dee water dissolves 1-15th or 1-10th of a grain?

* * * * *

WATER FROM STANLEY RESERVOIR AT PAISLEY.

I had occasion a few months ago to analyze this water, in connection with an examination of the Rivockburn and Muirburn waters, from which it is proposed to take an additional water supply for Paisley. It merits special attention on account of its comparative purity and peculiar suitableness for the general use of a large community. Very few waters supplied to towns, unless very hard, can be compared to it as regards its freedom from color. It is bright, transparent, and very pleasant to the taste. It is comparatively a very soft water, and contains only a small amount of foreign matters, all of which are perfectly unobjectionable, in reference to its use either for dietetic or for manufacturing purposes.

An imperial gallon contains—

	Grains.
Organic matter	1.20
Mineral matter	4.24
	5.44
Degree of hardness	$2\frac{1}{2}°$

Gases.

	Cubic inches. Gallon.	Per cent.
Carbonic acid	.50	7.31
Oxygen	2.08	30.41
Nitrogen	4.26	62.28
	6.84	100.

It acts very slightly upon lead, ranking in this respect with Perth water and Brockburn water. It gives no sediment with sheet lead in open vessels, even after lengthened contact. In three days, with an extensive surface of lead, I found only one-tenth of grain dissolved, and the action was not appreciably increased after six days' immersion. The metal becomes covered with a coating which protects it from further appreciable action.

LANARK WATER.

This is an extremely interesting water. The specimen submitted to me for examination was certified to be a fair sample of the water supplied to Lanark, taken, I am informed, "from a shaft sunk into the channel bed in the center of the Burgh Common, whence it is pumped up by an engine, and forced into the town."

This water possesses several striking peculiarities. Considering its great purity and softness, it is in regard to color one of the finest waters that have come under my notice. It remains almost perfectly colorless, even when concentrated to an extremely small volume. It contains a notable qnantity of phosphates and silica, and it is particularly characterized by the presence of a large proportion of dissolved carbonic acid gas, as compared with the quantities of the other gases.

An imperial gallon gave :—

Organic matter, ...	.80	grains.
Mineral matter, ...	3.13	"
Total solid matter, ...	3.93	"
Degree of hardness, ...	1.5°	

GASES.

	Cub. in. per gall.	Per cent.
Carbonic acid, ...	3.13	33.76
Oxygen, ...	1.79	19.35
Nitrogen, ...	4.33	46.89
	9.25	100.

Its action upon lead was carefully tested. With a large surface of the metal in open vessels it gave only 1-20th of a grain of dissolved lead in 24 hours, and no visible deposit even after three weeks' contact. Its action in lead pipes was also very trifling and merely temporary. This, therefore, is another instance of a very fine and soft water, without the objectionable property of corroding and dissolving lead.

CONCLUSIONS.

From the results of the investigations detailed in this report I have drawn the following conclusions :—

1. The water of Loch Katrine is the purest and softest water I have yet examined.
2. It is particularly characterized by the small amount of carbonic acid gas, and the large proportion of oxygen gas it contains.
3. It acts powerfully and to a dangerous extent on commercial lead in all its forms, both corroding and dissolving the metal.
4. Upon sheet or milled lead, in open vessels, its action is energetic and continuous, whether the metal be scraped or unscraped, whether in the dark or exposed to light.

5. In closed vessels its action, as regards the same portion of water, is not continuous, but the water in a short time becomes impregnated with an injurious quantity of dissolved lead. In the case, however, of successive quantities of fresh water, as in pipes, its action is continuous.
6. It acts decidedly and strongly on lead cisterns and on lead piping, both old and new.
7. It acts upon sheet lead and lead piping that have been in contact with other waters, and, in a marked degree, on pipes that have been employed for the conveying of Clyde water, as used in Glasgow.
8. It acts upon lead after it has been in contact with iron.
9. It corroded and dissolved the lead of the Promoters' apparatus at Loch Katrine, which was intended as an imitation of the mode in which the water would ultimately be supplied to the city.
10. Its power of acting upon lead is not destroyed, though considerably diminished, by alloying the lead by 5, 10, or 20 per cent of tin.
11. There are many soft and excellent waters that do not possess the objectionable property of acting continuously on lead.
12. And finally, from the well-known fact that lead is an insidious, active, and cumulative poison, and that very many instances of poisoning have been clearly traced to the contamination of water by lead, I have arrived at the general conclusion that it would be extremely dangerous to use Loch Katrine water as a beverage, or for dietetic purposes, after being supplied through lead pipes and retained in lead cisterns.

My opinion has also been asked on several collateral points involved in the present inquiry, and more particularly with reference to the two following :—

1st. What is the smallest proportion of lead in water likely to prove prejudicial to health ?

2d. Is it likely that the qualities of Loch Katrine water will be changed to so great a degree, when delivered in Glasgow, that it will no longer corrode and dissolve lead ?

I unhesitatingly acknowledge my inability to give specific answers to these inquiries. The first is purely a medical question, on which there is unfortunately a great paucity of recorded facts, and which can be satisfactorily answered only by a medical man of large experience, comprehensive views, and original research.

In the Promoters' Evidence it is stated "that one grain and a third of carbonate of lead" (equal to about one grain of metallic lead) "in an imperial gallon of water, is the smallest proportion which has been known to produce injury to health." This statement does not accord with the facts given by other authorities. We have on record a case related by a distinguished chemist at Bristol, in which 1-9th of a grain of lead per gallon deranged the health of a whole community; and Dr. John Smith of Aberdeen concludes, from his investigations, that the limit of manifestly deleterious action would seem to be somewhere between 1-10th and 1-20th of a grain. It would certainly be easy to adduce the evidence of many eminent practitioners who condemn the continued use of water, having a much smaller degree of contamination than one grain of lead in a gallon of water.

In the case of the Ex-Royal Family at Claremont, referred to by the Promoters, Dr. H. Gueneau de Mussey tells us that the habitual use, *for seven months*, of water containing about one grain of lead per gallon, gave rise to alarming and unequivocal symptoms of lead poisoning in thirteen persons, and, indeed, that four of these patients manifested some symptoms of poisoning after *five months'* use of the water. In the consideration of the Loch Katrine scheme, however, our attention must not be limited to the comparatively short period of five or seven months, but regard must be had to as many years, or even to a lifetime. When thus associated with a lengthened period of time, the question becomes exceedingly difficult of solution.

From all that is actually known on the subject, I think there can be no reason to doubt that highly injurious effects may be produced by the introduction of extremely minute quantities of lead into the system, continuously for many years, and especially in the case of invalids, and those of tender age.

Few, I believe, who have considered the importance of this question would willingly partake, year after year, of water containing even 1-10th of a grain of lead per gallon. It is, indeed, the opinion of many, that all lead contamination is objectionable, and that no degree of it is safe.

To the second question, it scarcely falls within the province of the chemist to attempt an answer.

For my own part, I believe it quite possible to bring Loch Katrine water to Glasgow as pure and soft as it is in the Loch; and, on the other hand, I think it would be quite easy, by *doctoring* it on its journey, as proposed in the Promoters' Evidence, to change its qualities completely, and, by increasing its degree of hardness, to deprive it of its present vexatious power of corroding and dissolving lead.

FREDERICK PENNY, *Professor of Chemistry.*

Andersonian University, Glasgow, July 1854.

Glasgow Corporation Water Works.—Chemical and Medical Reports and Evidence on the Quality of the Loch Katrine Water.—May, 1854.

In the course of the Parliamentary Investigation as to the propriety of supplying the City of Glasgow with water from Loch Katrine, a doubt was raised as to the safety to the health of the inhabitants which would attend such supply, by the assertion that the water from its excessive purity acted very violently upon lead. The Committee of the House of Commons, therefore, to whom the Bill had been referred, adjourned on the 28th March for some weeks to allow time and opportunity for full and proper investigation.

The doubt alluded to was raised by the evidence of Dr. Penny, Professor of Chemistry in the Andersonian University at Glasgow.

* * * * * *

In conformity with the wish of the Committee, they determined upon calling in the advice of the most eminent Chemists, whose avocations would enable them to attend to the question. Amongst those who were suggested or applied to, they ultimately succeeded in obtaining the coöperation of Mr. Dugald Campbell, Analytic Chemist of London; Dr. Anderson, Professor of Chemistry in the University of Glasgow; Dr. A. S. Taylor, Professor of Chemistry, Guy's Hospital, London; Dr. R. D. Thomson of St. Thomas' Hospital, London; Dr. Hofmann of the Royal College of Chemistry, and Professor Graham of University College London. Dr. Lyon Playfair and other gentlemen applied to, were unable to give their assistance.

These gentlemen were all requested to examine the Loch Katrine water, to analyse its quality, and to ascertain its effect upon lead; and that they would each follow out their examination in the way best calculated for enabling them to advise the Corporation upon the propriety of proceeding in, or abandoning their attempt to introduce Loch Katrine water.

Mr. Campbell, Dr. Anderson and Dr. Thomson, have each visited Loch Katrine, and to all the gentlemen employed, samples of that water, as well as of many others, have been delivered.

As it appeared to the Deputation that the more important part of the inquiry would be as to the action of the water upon the lead cisterns and lead pipes already laid down in the city, and thinking it probable that the passage of the water through iron pipes might have some effect in diminishing its action upon the lead with which it would subsequently come in contact, they thought it desirable to try this experiment upon a tolerably large scale, as nearly similar as possible to the mode in which the water is actually delivered to the inhabitants. For this purpose, they gave instructions that a quantity of old and new iron pipes, and of old and new lead cisterns, and old and new lead pipes, (the old pipes and cisterns being those which were then in use in Glasgow) should be taken to the outlet of Loch Katrine, and there laid down in the manner of a small water-work for the purposes of experiment. This work was placed under the charge of Mr. Mackin, the Engineer of the Glasgow Water-works, with instructions to do every thing exactly in the same manner as if he were supplying water in Glasgow in the ordinary way. When the pipes and cisterns were laid and fixed, the experiments were placed under the charge of Mr. Campbell, with whom was subsequently associated Dr. Anderson, as Chemists, and of Mr. G. H. Hill, Mr. Bateman's Assistant, as Engineer.

The results of these experiments, which are of the most satisfactory character as proving conclusively the safety with which the water would be delivered to the inhabitants, will appear in the Reports of the several gentlemen.

* * * * * *

Another important point to which the Deputation directed attention, was the effect which had been produced in towns or places supplied with water of similar quality. Towns situated in similar geological districts, or supplied with water of very pure quality, were accordingly selected for examination, and gentlemen were sent to various parts of England, Scotland, and Wales, to make inquiries. For this purpose, the places visited in Scotland have been Dumfries, Edinburgh, the present and projected sources of the Gorbals Company, the Gare Loch, Loch Goilhead, Inverary, Tarbet, Inversnaid, Loch Lomond, and the River Leven, Perth, Aberdeen, Inverness, Dunkeld, Taymouth, Loch Tay, Loch Rannoch, Loch Ness, Loch Lubnaig, and other places in that district. In England, the Lake district of Cumberland and Westmorland, including Ulleswater, Penrith, Windermere, Ambleside, Grassmere, Derwentwater, Keswick, Cockermouth, Ennerdale Lake, and Whitehaven; and in Wales, Bala, and Bala Lake, the River Dee, Bangor, Beaumaris, and other places. Besides these places, inquiries have been instituted at Manchester, Sheffield, Macclesfield, Bolton, Rochdale, Chorley, Heywood, Blackburn, Accrington, Darwen, and Bury, and water has been procured from Londonderry in Ireland, and from New York in America. The water of some of these places had no effect upon lead—of upwards of two-thirds there is a very sensible action—in most equal, and in some cases greater than that of Loch Katrine. In all cases, the towns or places supplied are served through lead pipes and cisterns, and in no single instance has a trace of lead been discovered in the water which has passed through the pipes.

* * * * * *

Many of the rivers, after flowing out of lakes, the water of which has violent action on lead, and which pass over sandstone or other neutralizing geological formations, have been traced down, to ascertain how soon and from what apparent cause the water is deprived of its power to act on lead. Among these are the Eamont, flowing out of Ulleswater; the Derwent, out of Bassenthwaite Water; the Dee in Wales, out of Bala Lake; the Tay, out of Loch Tay; and the Teith, from Loch Katrine. The Eamont loses its action very soon after leaving the lake, upon entering a limestone district. The Derwent, which flows over the slate rocks of the Cumbrian formation. retains its action to near Cockermouth, where it enters limestone. The Dee, from Bala Lake, retains its action to a considerable extent till mixed with water from the Caradoc sandstone; and the Tay, till after running for some distance over old red sandstone. The Teith, which passes over this formation when it leaves Loch Vennechar, loses much of its power before it joins the Forth, though, in consequence, probably, of the large body of water, and the gravel which prevents any close contact with the softer beds of sandstone, the action is not as much diminished as in other cases.

* * * * * *

At Bolton-le-Moors, in Lancashire, a town having a population of 80,000 persons, the water which has supplied the town for nearly thirty years is extremely soft, and acts very powerfully upon bright lead. It is distributed to the inhabitants through lead cisterns and lead pipes in the ordinary manner, Dr. Black, a physician who has resided there for upwards of twenty years, and has during that period been uniformly supplied with the Water-works water, through lead pipes, and has himself ascertained its power of rapidly corroding bright lead, declares that he has never known a case of injury arising from the supply of the water.

At Blackburn, where the action of the water is less powerful though still considerable, Mr. Dugdale, an eminent surgeon in the town, now Mayor of the Borough, and who has been Chairman of the Water Company since its formation in 1844, expresses the strongest opinion of the perfect safety with which the water has been supplied to the inhabitants through lead pipes, and of the great advantage which has resulted from its use.

At Sheffield the water which has been supplied to the inhabitants for nearly thirty years, acts upon lead nearly as energetically as that of Loch Katrine. It is almost uniformly delivered into leaden cisterns, being conveyed to the cisterns, and from thence to the taps for domestic use, in leaden pipes. Mr. Gunson, the manager of the works, and who has held that situation since their establishment, receives the water he uses in the way above described, and states it to be the universal system of the town. He was perfectly astonished when he saw the effect upon the water by similar experiment to that of Dr.

Penny, never having heard of the slightest injury or inconvenience arising from its use. Mr. Wright, the medical gentleman who has attended his family, receives his own supply of water in the same way, and is a surgeon in extensive practice, connected with all the medical institutions of the town. He has never heard of a case of lead-poisoning connected with the supply of the water through lead, nor of any injurious effect whatever.

* * * * * *

Memorandum of MR. MACKAIN, *Engineer to the Glasgow Water Company, as to arrangements made to test the effect of the Water of Loch Katrine on Leaden Pipes and Cisterns.*

A point the nearest to Loch Katrine, in the course of the stream issuing from it, from whence a sufficient extent of level ground could be had for laying the iron pipes, and where there was a sufficient fall in the course of the river, was selected for the experiment.

The length of iron pipes which it was proposed to use in the experiments was 300 yards.

The fall of the river was required—

1st. To give motion to water in the iron pipes.

2d. To give motion to water in the lead pipes.

3d. To admit of cisterns being so placed as to be filled from the leaden pipes.

4th. To permit water to be drawn off from the lower part of the cisterns.

The total fall obtained, between the extreme points of the line of pipes, from river surface to river surface, was about 9 feet.

Where the pipes were laid into the river, there exists the remains of an old dam, which keeps up the surface of the river above it.

The iron pipes used, consisted of one line formed by about 130 yards of pipes of six inches inside diameter, connected to about 160 yards of pipes of five inches in diameter, which made about 290 yards in one curved line.

These had been formerly used in distributing water by the Glasgow Water Company.

A second line of pipes, of three inches inside diameter, about 306 or 309 yards long, was laid alongside the other line.

These were new pipes just procured from an iron foundry.

To the first-mentioned line of pipes, which may be called the 5-inch line, there were attached two lines of leaden pipes of three quarters of an inch in diameter, which had been used for conveying water to the houses of people in Glasgow.

Two lines of new leaden pipes of the same diameter, and

One line of new leaden pipe tinned inside.

Below the old leaden pipes were placed two leaden cisterns which had been used in Glasgow.

Below the new leaden pipes were placed two new leaden cisterns.

Below the tinned pipe was placed a new cistern, lined with tin.

To the second line of pipes, which may be called the 3 inch line, there were attached two lines of used leaden pipes, beneath which were cisterns which had been used, and two lines of new lead pipes with new cisterns.

To all the cisterns, stop-cocks were attached at about two inches from the bottom.

A street-well or fountain, was attached to each line of iron pipes, by means of lead and iron pipes which had been used for that purpose in Glasgow. By means of these fountains the poorer classes in Glasgow are supplied with water.

Report by DR. THOMAS ANDERSON, *Professor of Chemistry in the University of Glasgow, and* DUGALD CAMPBELL, ESQ., *Analytical Chemist to the Brompton Hospital in London, on the Examination of the " Water of Loch Katrine," in connection with the Glasgow Corporation Water-works Bill.*

We have minutely examined the water of Loch Katrine, and have personally superintended an extensive series of experiments made at the Trossachs, the results of which are embodied in the following Report:—

Our object being to examine the action of the water on lead, and the extent to which its value, as a source, for the supply of the City of Glasgow, may be thereby affected, we have confined our attention mainly to that point. As regards its general physical and chemical characters, we shall content ourselves with stating that it is a very clear and colorless water, and of unusual purity, the total quantity of solid matters contained in a gallon amounting to only 2.20 grains, of which 1.35 is mineral, and 0.85 organic matter. The mineral matter is composed chiefly of salts of soda and lime, the exact proportions of which we think it unnecessary to detail. It contains, in solution, 7.25 cubic inches of air per gallon, 4.75 of which were nitrogen, and 2.50 oxygen, along with a trace of carbonic acid. Its hardness was 0.9.

When exposed in open vessels, along with bright lead, that is to say, lead which has been recently scraped, so as to expose a fresh metallic surface, a strong action manifested itself in the course of a very few hours, the lead being covered with a white film, and a deposit of oxide falling to the bottom of the glass.

The conditions under which this experiment was made are, however, materially different from those under which the water would be supplied to the town, and a few further trials convinced us that very trifling modifications were sufficient to affect to a very great extent the nature of the results.

We particularly found that free exposure to the air, and likewise to the sun's rays increased both the rapidity and intensity of the action, while on the other hand exclusion from light and air had a precisely opposite effect. Experiments were made by enclosing the water in leaden pipes perfectly full, and carefully corked, and though allowed to stand for many days, the action was so small as to be barely appreciable. A similar result was also observed even in open vessels, with lead in the state in which it is usually obtained from the plumber's shop, and though in some instances a slight action was apparent at first, the metal became covered in the course of a few days with a thin coating which prevented all further corrosion.

From these facts, it became manifest that the first experiments, showing a strong action on lead, could not be taken as fairly representing the nature or amount of the action likely to be exerted on the pipes or cisterns of a large town, and that absolute conclusions could only be drawn from experiments in which the actual conditions of the water supply were more closely imitated. It was, therefore, with much satisfaction that we availed ourselves of the apparatus which Mr. Bateman had caused to be laid down at the Trossachs, and which was as close an imitation as circumstances would permit of the mode in which the water will be ultimately supplied to the city.

The apparatus consisted of two lines of iron pipes, one new, the other old, each of which was connected with new and old lead pipes and cisterns, so as to vary the conditions of the experiment as much as possible. As soon as the work was completed, water was passed through the iron pipes in order to wash out the dirt which had got into them during the operation of laying, and when the water began to flow perfectly clear, it was allowed to run through the lead pipes and cisterns until they were clean, which occupied only a few minutes. The experiments were then commenced by filling the pipes and cisterns. After 24 hours, specimens were drawn from all the pipes and cisterns, and others were taken after the water had remained for three and for six days in contact with the lead. All these specimens were examined for lead with the utmost care, and the results were as follows :—

No. 5. Water after passing through old iron pipes, and lying in old lead pipes for one day : no action upon the lead could be observed.

No. 6. After passing through old iron pipes, and lying in old lead pipes for 3 days : action not appreciable.

No. 7. After passing through old iron pipes, and lying in old lead pipes for 6 days : action less than one-tenth of a grain of lead in a gallon of water.

No. 8. After passing through old iron pipes, and lying in new lead pipes for 1 day : a very slight trace of action.

No. 9. After passing through old iron pipes, and lying in new lead pipes for 3 days : action less than one-tenth of a grain of lead in a gallon.

No. 10. After passing through old iron pipes, and lying in new lead pipes for 6 days : action less than one-tenth of a grain of lead in a gallon.

No. 11. After passing through old iron pipes, and lying in old lead cistern for 1 day : no action.

No. 12. After passing through old iron pipes, and lying in old lead cistern for 3 days : no action.

No. 13. After passing through old iron pipes, and lying in old lead cistern for 6 days : action barely appreciable.

No. 14. After passing through old iron pipes, and passing very slowly through old lead cisterns : no action.

No. 15. After passing through old iron pipes, and lying in new lead cistern for one day: no action.

No. 16. After passing through old iron pipes, and lying in new lead cistern for 3 days: action barely appreciable.

No. 17. After passing through old iron pipes, and lying in new lead cistern for 6 days: action barely appreciable.

No. 18. After passing through old iron pipes, and flowing very gently through new lead cistern: no action.

No. 19. After passing through new iron pipes, old lead pipes, and lying in old lead cistern for 1 day: no action upon the lead.

No. 20. After passing through new iron pipes, old lead pipes, and lying in old lead cisterns 3 days: no action.

No. 21. After passing through new iron pipes, old lead pipes, and lying in old lead cisterns for 6 days: action scarcely appreciable.

No. 22. After passing through new iron pipes, old lead pipes, and flowing gently through old lead cistern: no action.

No. 23. After passing through new iron pipes, new lead pipes, and lying in new lead cisterns for 1 day: action barely appreciable.

No. 24. After passing through new iron pipes, new lead pipes, and lying in new lead cisterns for 3 days: no action.

No. 25. After passing through new iron pipes, new lead pipes, and lying in new lead cisterns for 6 days: action barely appreciable.

No. 26. After passing through new iron pipes, new lead pipes, and flowing gently through new lead cisterns: no action.

No. 27. After passing through new iron pipes, and lying in old lead pipes for 1 day: no action.

No. 28. After passing through new iron pipes, and lying in old lead pipes for 3 days: no action.

No. 29. After passing through new iron pipes, and lying in old lead pipes for 6 days: no action.

No. 30. After passing through new iron pipes, and lying in new lead pipes for 1 day: action appreciable less than one-tenth of a grain of lead per gallon.

No. 31. After passing through new iron pipes, and lying in new lead pipes 3 days: action appreciable, but less than one-tenth of a grain of lead per gallon.

No. 32. After passing through new iron pipes, and lying in new lead pipes for 6 days: action appreciable, but less than one-tenth of a grain of lead per gallon.

No. 33. Water from stand-pipe, attached to new iron pipe, after 8 hours: no action of lead.

No. 34. Water from stand-pipe, attached to old iron pipe, after 8 hours: no action of lead.

The conclusions to be drawn from these experiments are: 1st, that the water, after lying for a considerable time in old lead pipes and cisterns, exerts no action upon lead, and that it is only after they have been 6 days in contact, that a barely appreciable action becomes apparent, and that only in some instances; 2d, with new lead pipes and cisterns, an exceedingly minute trace of action was generally, though not always apparent, within the first 24 hours; but even after 6 days, the lead present in the water amounted to less than 1-10th of a grain per gallon, a quantity too small to produce any injurious effects; 3d, when the water was allowed to flow slowly through the cisterns so as to imitate the frequent renewal of their contents which takes place when a cistern is in actual use, not the slightest trace of action on the lead could, in any case, be detected by the most delicate tests.

It is worthy of observation that *the old lead* cisterns employed were patched with *new lead*, and hence may in some degree be said to represent *new* rather than *old lead cisterns* as they are stated to be in the above experiments.

Had they been entirely old, we have no doubt that not the slightest trace of action would have been observed; and even with the new cisterns we believe that, had the experiments been continued for a sufficient length of time to produce a proper coating on the surface of the metal, no further action would have been apparent, and water might have been preserved in them for any length of time without acquiring the least trace of lead. The necessity for being prepared to give evidence before the Committee of the House of Commons by a given time, prevented our continuing the experiments of the Trossachs sufficiently long to establish this point on the cisterns themselves; but we have kept pieces of lead which had been previously immersed in other waters in the Loch Katrine water, for several weeks, without the slightest trace of action being apparent, and even common plumbers' lead, when kept in the water for a sufficient time, ceased to act upon a new quantity.

But the experiments at the Trossachs do not completely fulfill the conditions under which the Loch Katrine water will be carried to Glasgow. In addition to iron and leaden pipes, it will be conveyed through many miles of a conduit built principally of the old red sandstone of the district, and in one place crosses a thin bed of limestone. Being aware that it frequently happens that though the water of a lake may act strongly on bright lead, the stream which flows from it, if examined some miles below its point of exit, is without action—a change manifestly due to the rocks and pebbles of which its bed is composed—we have examined the action of the old red sandstone and limestone on Loch Katrine water. By repeated experiments we have ascertained that when the Loch Katrine water is allowed to stand for 10 or 12 hours over fragments of the old red sandstone, of which the conduit will be made, that the action upon bright lead is so greatly diminished, as to be barely appreciable, and upon lead in its ordinary state, no action whatever could be detected, on applying the most delicate tests.

The limestone produces a similar effect, but its influence is of much less importance as it forms only a thin bed with which the water is in contact for a very short time. With the sandstone, however, the water will be in contact for a considerable period, as we are given to understand that it is the material of which the greater part of the conduit will be built, and the time of flow through it will be about 10 or 12 hours. It cannot, therefore, be doubted that during its passage through it, the water will necessarily be deprived of all power of acting upon lead as exemplified in our experiments. In other respects it will be little changed, and will still be a water of remarkable purity for all purposes. We find the solid contents, per gallon, after standing for 12 hours in contact with the sandstone, to be 3.02 grains, and the hardness 1.9 degrees.

So far we confined ourselves entirely to the water of Loch Katrine, but conceiving that information of an important character might be obtained by the examination of the water of other lakes, we have collected as many as possible for that purpose. The following table contains the result of our experiments:

	Degree of hardness.
Loch Ness, very powerful action......................	0.95
Ennerdale Lake " "	0.85
Ulleswater Lake, " "	1.72
Loch Lomond, " "	0.90
Streams flowing into Loch Lomond, very powerful action	0.90
River Leven, very powerful action	0.90
Loch Lubnaig, " "	0.94
Loch Doine, " "	0.93
Loch Voil, " "	0.97
Loch Tay, " "	0.90
Loch Rannoch, " "	0.88
Loch Achray, " "	0.92
Streams flowing into Loch Achray, very powerful action	0.92
Loch Vennacher, very powerful action................	0.93
Brothers'Loch, (Gorbals proposed Extension Water Works), very powerful action...........................	1.08
Binnend Loch, (Gorbals proposed Extension Water Works), very powerful action...........................	1.36
Black Loch, (Gorbals proposed Extension Water Works), less powerful action.......................	1.24

Among these waters, the three first are, at the present moment, employed for the supply of towns; Loch Ness affording the entire supply of Inverness, Ennerdale Lake of Whitehaven, and Ulleswater of Penrith; and as they are in all respects similar to that of Loch Katrine, and act quite as powerfully upon lead, we have personally examined the whole conditions of the water supply of these towns.

The water supply of Inverness is pumped from the River Ness at a short distance from the town. The water of Loch Ness, of the River Ness, at the point where it enters the pumps, and that drawn from the taps in the town, all act very powerfully on lead. But though leaden service pipes and cisterns are universally employed, no appearance of corrosion could be observed on a minute examination of a great number, both of pipes and cisterns, which had been in use for periods varying from three months to twenty years, nor could the slightest trace of lead be detected in the water drawn from them, although, when exposed in contact with bright lead, it acts with surprising intensity.

No injurious effects on the health of the inhabitants have ever been observed, nor are the cisterns or pipes found to require more frequent renewal than in other places. Indeed, the fact that the water acts on lead was entirely unknown to the inhabitants until it was pointed out to them.

The composition of the Inverness water is remarkably similar to that of Loch Katrine. It contains 2.5 grains of solid matter per gallon, of which 1.55 is mineral matter, and 0.95 organic matter. Its degree of hardness was 0.95.

The Ennerdale water is taken for the supply of Whitehaven from the stream about one and a half miles below the Lake, conveyed in iron pipes a distance of about six miles, and after passing through a gravel filter, is collected in a service reservoir from which it is carried through the streets of Whitehaven in iron, and into the houses in leaden service pipes.

The water of the reservoir as well as that drawn from the service pipes act strongly upon bright lead when the experiment is made in open vessels; but it does not corrode the lead pipes, and the water drawn from them did not contain the slightest trace of lead. As a striking illustration of this, we may mention that a specimen of water was given us for examination which we were told had been lying in a lead pipe for six months in an empty house in the town. Not a trace of lead could be detected in it, although when exposed to bright lead, in open vessels, it acted with great vigor.

Notwithstanding the powerful action of the Whitehaven water on bright lead, we have ascertained by inquiries instituted among the medical practitioners of the town, that no cases of lead poisoning have occurred, and so far from any injurious effects on the health of the inhabitants having been observed, the very reverse is the case, a marked diminution in the mortality having taken place since the water works were completed.

The water supply of Whitehaven has been particularly reported upon by the Government Commission, consisting of Professors Graham, Miller and Hofmann, appointed in 1851 to report upon the chemical quality of the supply of water to the metropolis. They say in their Report, (page 35), "From Whitehaven also, where water of the same extreme softness has been in use for the last six months, we learn that no case of lead poisoning had been seen or heard of by the medical practitioners of the town which could be attributed to the use of the water." Three years have since elapsed, and the statements made in the Report have been fully confirmed by our own inquiries.

The chemical composition of the Ennerdale Lake water corresponds closely with that of the Loch Katrine. Its degree of hardness is rather lower, being 0.85°.

The Penrith Water Works are scarcely yet in operation, and galvanized iron service pipes have been employed with the intention of avoiding any injurious effects, although our experiments lead us to the conclusion that this precaution is unnecessary, and have afforded us an interesting illustration of the change produced on water by flowing over the bed of a river. The works are situated in the River Eamont, about 4½ miles below the outlet of Ulleswater, at which point it has flowed for about 2 miles through a limestone district. The water taken from the bed of the river, immediately above the Water Works, has lost to a great extent the power of acting on lead, and that taken from the pumping reservoir, after passing through the filter beds, and about ½ a mile of pipes, exerts only a barely appreciable action.

The hardness of Ulleswater Lake is 1.72°, that of the River Eamont before entering Water Works 4.10°.

In addition to these cases, which have been especially inquired into by ourselves, we have also examined the water supplied to the following towns, all of which we find to act upon lead, although to very different extents:

	Degree of hardness.
Sheffield, acts very strongly on lead..........	1.52
Heywood " " "	1.24
Bury, acts very sensibly on lead.............	3.68
Blackburn, " " "	2.73
Accrington, acts slightly on lead	3.63
Rochdale, acts strongly on lead	1.76
Chorley, acts very strongly on lead	1.20
Bolton, " " "	1.14

In all these towns, leaden service pipes are employed, and no bad effects have been observed. In every case, we have tested the water drawn from the leaden service pipes, and have not found the slightest trace of lead.

Although the waters mentioned in the previous part of this Report, with the exception of those specially noticed, do not supply any towns, that of the River Leven which flows out of Loch Lomond is made use of at several manufactories and houses upon its banks into which it is carried by leaden pipes of considerable length. We have collected specimens of the water after passing through the leaden pipes, selecting those which we were told were least in use, so as to have water which had lain a considerable time in them, and have invariably found that they contained no lead, although when exposed with bright lead in open vessels, they acted with great rapidity upon it. We specially examined, in this way, water from lead pipes at Messrs. Ewing's, and at Messrs. Alexander and Clarke's works. We have likewise examined the water used in the Inversnaid Inn, which is obtained from a stream flowing out of Loch Arklet; as also that of Tarbet Hotel, and the Trossachs Hotel; the first from a stream flowing into Loch Lomond; the last from a very small stream at the back of the hotel. In each case, the water passes through from 150 to 200 yards of lead pipe. But in none of them was a trace of lead found, although they all acted with great rapidity when placed in open vessels with bright lead.

We have made numerous experiments with these waters, the results of which it is unnecessary to detail. But we have particularly tried the action of Loch Katrine, Loch Ness, and Ennerdale Lake waters upon lead, and leaden pipes which had been previously in contact with other water, and which may be conveniently termed *old*. The experiments were conducted in open vessels which have been fully exposed to air and light, and in some instances with the leads partially, and in others entirely immersed in the water, in order to try them in every way. Already the leads have been in the water for weeks, yet they are not in the slightest degree acted upon, nor do the waters contain the faintest traces of lead, but they have not lost their action upon bright lead, for if a well scraped piece be dropped into any of the jars, the action becomes apparent in a very short time.

Our attention has also been directed to ascertaining whether any mode could be devised of protecting new and bright lead from the action of the water. We have experimented with alloys of lead, and small quantities of zinc and tin, and have found that a small addition of either of these metals, but especially the latter, caused the lead to resist the action of Loch Katrine, Loch Ness, and Ennerdale waters in a very remarkable degree. An alloy containing 5 per cent of tin is scarcely acted on when bright, and not at all in the state in which it comes from the manufacturer.

As the results of the inquiries and experiment detailed on the preceding pages, we have arrived at the following conclusions:

1st. The Loch Katrine water acts strongly upon bright lead, freely exposed to light and air.

2nd. The Loch Katrine water does not act upon old leaden pipes and cisterns arranged so as to imitate as closely as possible the actual conditions of the water supply of a town.

3rd. When the Loch Katrine water is allowed to stand for some time in *new* leaden pipes and cisterns, a slight action takes place, but even after six days the quantity of lead is too small to exert any injurious effects.

4th. When the water is allowed to flow slowly through *new and old* cisterns, so as to imitate the frequent renewal of the water, which actually occurs when they are in use, not the slightest trace of action could be observed, even by the most delicate tests.

5th. By standing in contact with the old red sandstone, of which the conduit will be made, the Loch Katrine water almost entirely loses its action on bright lead.

6th. The Loch Katrine water scarcely acts on lead alloyed with 5 per cent of tin.

7th. The waters of Inverness, Whitehaven, Sheffield, Bolton, Chorley, Heywood, &c., all act powerfully on bright lead, but in practice they do not corrode the pipes and cisterns, and no injurious effects have been observed from their use.

As the general conclusions, we are decidedly of opinion that *as it will be delivered in Glasgow*, the Loch Katrine water may, with the utmost safety, be preserved in the pipes and cisterns now in use. Even on new cisterns, we do not believe it would have the slightest effect, but should any apprehensions be entertained on this point, the most absolute protection would be obtained by the use of an alloy of lead with 5 per cent of tin, although we are of opinion that this would be a very unnecessary precaution.

THOMAS ANDERSON.
DUGALD CAMPBELL.

Report by Dr. Alfred S. Taylor, M.D. F.R.S. *Professor of Chemistry in Guy's Hospital, London, on "Water from Loch Katrine."*

The sample for analysis was received at the Chemical Laboratory of Guy's Hospital, on the 27th of April, 1854.

The quantity received amounted to four gallons.

PHYSICAL PROPERTIES.

The water was clear, bright and colorless. It had a fresh taste and was without odor. It contained a full proportion of air. Oxygen was abundant in it. Carbonic acid was rather deficient. The only gases in it were oxygen, nitrogen, and carbonic acid. It was much more aerated than ordinary river or superficial spring water. There was a small proportion of mechanical impurity in it, *i. e.*, undissolved matter which was rapidly deposited by subsidence, too small in a gallon to render it necessary to determine the quantity by weight.

SOLID CONTENTS.

A qualitative analysis showed a remarkable absence of the usual saline constituents of water. In the entire water only a trace of chlorine (indicative of common salt) was detected. There was no bicarbonate of lime, hence when boiled or cooled there was no deposit or incrustation of any kind. When the water was concentrated to one half of its volume, sulphuric acid and lime were detected in it in small proportions, but there was no magnesia.

An imperial gallon unfiltered (70,000 grains), left by slow evaporation a brownish-colored residue, weighing only two grains, being in the fractional proportion of one 35,000th part of the water by weight.

This residue, when heated to redness, became darkened, evolving a slight odor of burnt *vegetable* matter. The incinerated residue submitted to chemical examination was found to be thus constituted:

Chloride of sodium (common salt)	0.7
Organic matter (combustible, vegetable)	0.3
Sulphate of lime, silica, and oxide of iron, including mechanical impurity	1.0
Total contents in an imperial gallon	2.0

HARDNESS.

There was no difference in the water whether unboiled, or boiled and cooled. The hardness was the same. It was remarked that during boiling no unpleasant effluvia were evolved: the water did not become cloudy or turbid, and its physical properties were not in any way affected or altered. The gases evolved were common air and carbonic acid. The latter was collected.

The hardness of the water on Dr. Clark's scale, and determined by his own soap test was 1¼ degrees.

The hardness calculated on distilled or absolutely pure water being taken as the standard of comparison, and by a stronger solution of soap than that used by Dr. Clark was 1 degree.

So far as the use of soap is concerned, this water possesses all the qualities of distilled, of the purest rain, or the purest ice water. There need be no waste of soap. The water immediately acquires detergent properties without any perceptible loss.

For all domestic purposes such as baking, brewing, and washing it is quite equal to distilled water.

ACTION OF LOCH KATRINE WATER ON LEAD.

Like all waters, chemically pure or comparatively free from saline matter, the water of Loch Katrine, as colected at the Lake, acts very powerfully upon lead when brought into contact with that metal under *certain circumstances.* (No. 1. Sample illustrating this). The circumstances are these: 1st, if the lead be *bright* and *highly polished*, and 2nd if the lead and water be freely exposed to the access of air.

If the surface of the lead be dull, *i. e.* covered with its usual blueish grey coat of sub-oxide, which is seen on the manufactured sheet or pipe-metal, there is no perceptible action on lead.

No. 2. Sample illustrating this (old lead immersed for sixteen days). Common sheet lead as supplied by the plumber for cisterns, the surface being only partly scraped or cleaned, and not polished, has a smaller amount of action than that which is bright and polished.

If the lead has been already in contact with water which has acted upon it, then the Loch Katrine water produces no noxious compound of lead with it, even when exposed to a large surface of lead, and under a free access of air.

Two plates with discs of lead to illustrate this.

No. 3. A.—Loch Katrine water and polished lead from May 2 to May 18, the maximum effect had taken place in 48 hours.

No. 4. B.—The disc of lead in this sample had been exposed 48 hours to the Trafalgar Square (Artesian) water of London, which had given to it a slight coating (this water acts upon lead). The disc was then transferred on the 4th of May to a plate containing the Loch Katrine water. When examined on the 18th of May, it was found that the thin coating previously formed had prevented the lead from exerting any noxious action on the Loch Katrine water.

Two samples illustrating this:

If the lead be alloyed with 5 per cent of tin in its ordinary state as supplied by the plumber, there is no action. If scraped so as to be rendered quite bright, then a slight white coating forms on the lead, but there is no production of carbonate to render the water noxious to health. In an experiment subsequently performed, the above alloy was exposed to Loch Katrine water and air from the 11th to the 18th of May, and there was no change whatever.

If the Loch Katrine water be concentrated by boiling, there is no chemical action on lead in any state. This shows that the conditions for allowing and preventing the action of the water on pure and bright lead, are of a very slight kind. (No. 6. Sample illustrating this:) The action of the water on lead is suspended to a great extent when the access of air is cut off, even supposing all the circumstances to be otherwise favorable. This illustrates the condition of the water in closed leaden pipes or tubes on constant service. (Sample No. 7. Vessel tied over with caoutchouc and tin-foil.) When the water has been placed in contact with the old red sandstone, and with the limestone of the district through which the aqueduct will pass, it loses its property of acting on lead. Samples illustrating this: Nos. 8 and 9.—The water after contact with these minerals was found not to have acquired, by the immersion of bright lead, any injurious impregnation whatever.

The influence of the free access of air is seen in the different action of this water on lead in samples No. 1 and No. 7. This may have an important bearing on the constant service and the intermittent system. In cisterns with an intermittent supply, there is great exposure to air. The water is not always at one level, hydro-carbonate of lead may be formed in the cistern above the margin of the water, which is liable to be washed off, and to expose a fresh surface. Owing to the evaporation continually going on in cisterns, some white incrustation is formed in nearly all cisterns above the water-level whether supplied *with hard or soft water;* the water evaporated being always of the nature of pure or distilled water. Hence before any water, whether hard or soft, can be safely used from a leaden cistern or pipe, it should be specially tested in order to determine whether there has been any action on lead, and if so whether this has gone on to an injurious extent.

The rapidity and the degree to which any protecting coating is formed on lead, whether in pipes or cisterns, can be determined only by a number of experiments on the particular water,—selected and varied according to the circumstances under which it is intended that the water should be supplied. The results of the experiments on the Loch Katrine water after having been placed in pipes and cisterns for different periods, showed an entire absence of lead in twenty-three samples out of twenty-nine; and in the six in which lead was detected, the quantity was less than that which was often found in the Thames water supplied to London, taken from leaden cisterns. The quantity was insufficient to produce any injurious effect by the use of such water.

Waters which have a powerful action on bright or polished lead, have been for some years supplied to towns in England and the United States without producing any effects injurious to health.

CONCLUSIONS.

1. The result of this inquiry is that the Loch Katrine water acts strongly on lead when the metal is bright and highly polished, and there is free access of air to the water and lead.

2. That this water does not exert any noxious action on lead when the metal is in its ordinarily dull state.

3. That the Loch Katrine water, which has been placed in contact with old red sandstone and limestone, obtained from the district which it was proposed that the water should traverse, has no action on lead. The water dissolves a small quantity of salt and carbonate of lime;—these substances protect the surface of the metal from further chemical action.

4. The Loch Katrine water has no action on an alloy of lead and tin, in the proportion of five parts of tin to ninety-five parts of lead.

REPORT ON SAMPLES OF WATER, MARKED IN MR. BATEMAN'S PAPER NOS. 5 TO 34.

Inquiry as to the presence of lead in certain waters numbered respectively from No. 5 to No 34 on Mr. Bateman's paper.

It was first ascertained by experiment that 1-17th part of a grain of carbonate of lead in a gallon of water, or a quantity equal to only the 1-1,225,000th part of the weight of the water, admitted of very easy detection by chemical analysis. This is equal to a grain of carbonate in 17 gallons of water.

The smallest proportion of carbonate of lead in water, which has been known to produce injury to health, was in the Claremont case (the ex-royal family of France) in 1849. It amounted to about one grain and a third in an imperial gallon of water.

The samples as above numbered were for the most part clear, bright and colorless. They presented very little mechanical impurity. There was not in any one, a crystaline opacity or an *insoluble white sediment of lead.* When exposed to air, they acquired no film of carbonate of lead, such as waters containing oxide of lead dissolved, are known to acquire.

Numbers 33 and 34 had a brownish color. This obviously arose from the presence of some impurity. In No. 34 this was found to be oxide of iron.

The waters marked Nos. 8, 9, 10, 30, 31, 32, were the only waters of the series which were found to contain lead. The quantity in all these cases was minute.

No. 30 contained the largest proportion, but here the lead did not amount to more than 1-500,000th part of the weight of the water, *i. e.*, strictly to 1-490,000th part; this is equivalent to 1-7th of a grain in the gallon, or one grain in seven gallons. This proportion of lead in water is, in my opinion, too small to affect the public health. I have found a quantity equal to, and greater, than this in the Thames water supplied to the inhabitants of London.

Nos. 9, 30, and 32 were as nearly as possible equal in the proportion of lead contained in them; it was rather less than in 31, and was estimated at 1-700,000th part of the weight of the water, or 1-10th of a grain in a gallon, or 1 grain in 10 gallons.

Nos. 8 and 10 contained the smallest proportion of lead—the proportion was equal to 1-1,225,000th part of the weight of the water, or to 1-17th part of a grain in a gallon.

CONCLUSION.

Before stating the conclusion derivable from this branch of the analysis, I may observe, that until after it was made, and the results reported I was not aware that the various samples from No. 5 to No. 34 were samples of Loch Katrine water which had been exposed for various periods, from one day to six days, in contact with leaden pipes and cisterns.

From the statements furnished to me, it appears that new and old lead pipes and cisterns were used in these experiments. In twenty-three out of twenty-nine samples, there was no trace of lead, either in a dissolved or in an undissolved state, although less than a millionth part of lead may be easily discovered by chemical tests. In the six samples in which lead was found, the quantity present, as I have already stated, was such as to be quite uninjurious to health. These samples had been in contact with new lead pipes and cisterns.

I therefore conclude from these experiments, that the Loch Katrine water is not liable to acquire a noxious impregnation from its distribution through leaden pipes and cisterns.

ADDITIONAL EXPERIMENTS.

Four ounces of the Loch Katrine water were placed in about two feet of leaden pipe which had been used during two years for the supply of river water to my house. After *five days* in one experiment, and *sixteen days* in another, the water was tested, and no lead was found in it. There was a slight incrustation or deposit on the interior of the pipe, which had protected the metal from the action of the water.*

REPORT ON SAMPLES OF INVERNESS WATER, MARKED A, B, C. ON MR. BATEMAN'S PAPER.

a. Water from Loch Ness.

There was no immediate action on lead, but a chemical action began in about a quarter of an hour after contact. After forty-eight

* It should be observed that the noxious action of water on lead, if manifested at all, is generally manifested within forty-eight hours.

hours, there was a full impregnation, but the action was less than in Loch Katrine water.

b. Water from the River Ness.

The chemical action of this water upon lead was instantaneous. It was so rapid and violent, that in five minutes the water was quite milky from the production of carbonate of lead. In one hour the deposit of carbonate was very considerable. After forty-eight hours the deposit was greater than in the Loch Katrine water. Such water would be pronounced eminently unfit for domestic use, if distributed through leaden pipes or cisterns.

c. Water from a Tap of the Caledonian Hotel, Inverness.

This water produced no immediate effect on lead. In this respect it somewhat resembled sample *a*. In a quarter of an hour the action began, and went on pretty rapidly for forty-eight hours, when it ceased. The deposit of carbonate of lead was less than in *b*, and about as great as in *a*. The action was such as to render the water unsafe for use in highly polished leaden pipes or utensils; its action on lead being equal to that of the Loch Katrine water.

EXAMINATION OF *C* FOR LEAD.

In two separate experiments, on twelve ounces and eight ounces of this water respectively, trials were made to determine whether there was any lead contained in it. There was no carbonate or undissolved salt, since the water was quite clear, and did not acquire a film on exposure. There was no sediment or deposit of an insoluble salt of lead in the bottle.

On applying the test to the two quantities of water above mentioned, there was not the slightest trace of any salt of lead present. Had the 140th part of a grain of lead been present in the twenty ounces of water, it would have been detected; but there was not even so small a quantity as the one millionth part present. This water was tested side by side with an equal quantity drawn from the tap of a leaden pipe at Guy's Hospital (Thames water), the water coming out of a leaden cistern holding 75,000 gallons. The results were the same. There was no lead present in either water. The Guy's water does not act upon lead. The water *c* does not contain any lead, but it acts upon polished lead so as to produce speedily a noxious impregnation.

The results of this analysis are very important in reference to the water supply of towns. I am informed that the town of Inverness is supplied with the water marked *b*, and that it has been supplied with it for some time. This water, placed under precisely similar circumstances, acts much more rapidly and more powerfully on lead than that of Loch Katrine. It is quite certain that a chemist, judging only by the action on *bright* and *polished* lead, would condemn this water as unfit for use. But the remarkable fact is, that the water *c*, which is nothing more than *b*, drawn from a tap in the Caledonian Hotel, after distribution by intermittent service through *leaden cisterns and pipes*, does not contain a trace of lead either in a dissolved or in an undissolved form. Here, then, is a water *acting powerfully on lead*, and *distributed through lead*, yet it *contains no lead;* and it is and has been for a long period used by the population of Inverness in leaden pipes and cisterns without any injury to health. The exemption of the inhabitants from injurious consequences is explained by the water having ceased to act on lead, and by its being found to contain no lead. The interior of the pipes and cisterns has no doubt been speedily coated with a deposit which has wholly prevented any injurious chemical action.

But the remarkable fact is, that this water *c*, thus supplied to the inhabitants of Inverness has not lost the property of acting on lead. If the metal be scraped or polished, and placed in it, there is a chemical action in a quarter of an hour, and this after forty-eight hours had reached such a degree that a chemist, unacquainted with the facts, might have been induced to pronounce the water as likely to be dangerous to health if distributed through leaden pipes or cisterns.

The waters supplied to Aberdeen and Merthyr Tydvil act upon lead, but for the reasons above stated they cause no injury to public health.

The Loch Katrine water may then, in my opinion, be just as safely used for the supply of a town as the water of the River Ness, quite irrespective of all consideration of the neutralizing effect of the geological character of the district through which the water must pass.

ALFRED S. TAYLOR, M.D.

Report of Robert Dundas Thomson, M.D. F.R.S. L. & E., *Professor of Chemistry in St. Thomas's Hospital College, London, on the "Loch Katrine Water."*

Having been consulted on the subject of the supply of water to Glasgow, Dumfries, Kilmarnock, Stirling, London, Newcastle, Swindon, Liverpool, &c., &c., and very extensively on the sanitary condition of waters; the subject of the action of water on lead has for many years been familiar to me, and I have had considerable opportunities of meeting with cases where paralysis had been produced by the action of lead on the human system. As far as I can ascertain from the experience of hospitals, the occurrence of disease from the corrosion of lead pipes is an exceptional circumstance, if it has ever occurred in these institutions, the general cause of affections from lead being occupation in white lead manufactories.

Waters, from whatever source, appear to act on a freshly polished surface of lead.

* * * * * *

Lead, when allowed to remain in these waters for a few days, ceases to suffer appreciable corrosion, or if the lead be removed from the water, exposed to the air, and afterwards immersed, but an insignificant action, if any, can be detected.

Loch Katrine water I examined several years ago, when it was proposed to be introduced for the supply of Glasgow. I considered it then, as I do now, a water admirably adapted for domestic use, and have not had my opinion in the slightest degree affected by the laboratory experiment exhibited on the Committee's table, as I am convinced from my acquaintance with the subject that, if the Loch Katrine supply had been introduced to Glasgow, nothing would have been heard of its influence on lead. I found it to contain about two grains of solid matter in the gallon, its constituents being organic matter, common salt, sulphate and carbonate of lime.

* * * * *

To set the objections at rest which have been urged against the use of Loch Katrine water, I may detail an experiment on a sufficiently large scale of a parallel nature which has been in action for forty years. About 1814, a plumber of Tunbridge Wells introduced at his own risk a spring of water by means of lead pipes and lead cisterns into the houses of that place. A similar objection was taken to its use as on the present occasion, traces of lead were even detected in that portion of the water in immediate contact with the new lead cisterns, but none in the body of the water or in the water discharged from the cisterns. Specimens of this water were sent to London in 1815, and tested by Dr. Thomas Thomson without his being able to detect a trace of lead. I have a letter in the handwriting of the late Dr. Wollaston, dated December 27, 1815, in which he states that he could detect no lead in water sent to London from Tunbridge Wells. Traces were occasionally detected in the new cisterns, as I was assured by the late Dr. Thomson, only on the margins in contact with the lead, the largest quantity obtained being 1 grain in 20 gallons. Yet from these incidental results, the water supplied to the village was condemned by the opponents of the scheme as *poisonous*. But the water still continues in use; the village has increased to a large town of 10,000 inhabitants; it is a popular place of resort for invalids; and after careful inquiry, I have not been able to discover among its residents, even a suspicion of its contamination by lead. I examined the engineer in charge of the company who worked at the original works, and laid down many of the lead pipes and cisterns in his capacity at that time of plumber, and several persons, residents of twenty years, who assured me that they had never heard the subject of danger to water from lead pipes mooted.

* * * * *

Although in the preceding Report, I have given it as my decided opinion that no more permanent danger is to be apprehended in reference to health from the transmission of Loch Katrine water through lead pipes, and detention in lead cisterns, than there is in the case of other waters supplied to towns, I have always recommended the substitution of iron and other materials for water pipes, as much as possible for lead, and also where lead is employed, that it should be alloyed with tin.

ROBERT DUNDAS THOMSON, M.D.

Report by Professor Graham, *of University College, London, and* Professor Hofmann, *of the Royal College of Chemistry, London.*

Specimens of water taken from Loch Katrine, and properly authenticated, were received by us from Mr. T. T. Mitchell, Mr. Bateman, and Mr. George H. Hill, and made the subject of the experiments and observations to be reported by us.

The water of Loch Katrine was submitted to a careful and minute chemical analysis, of which the detailed results will be subjoined. This water is of the first class in point of softness and purity, its hardness being under one degree, and the whole amount of solid matter not more than 2.21 grains in the gallon of which 1.24 are mineral matter.

Like distilled water, and most soft and pure waters, the Katrine water, when taken directly from the Lake, has a considerable action upon lead. This property of the water appears, however, to be of a temporary and fugitive character, being diminished or disappearing entirely under a variety of influences to which it will be unavoidably exposed during its conveyance in conduits and pipes from the lake to Glasgow. Such is the conclusion which must be drawn from the following facts:

I. The solvent action of Katrine water upon lead was observed by us to be already considerably diminished in a specimen taken from the river, at the point at which the water is diverted for experiments.

II. Thirty specimens of Katrine water numbered from 5 to 34 were received and examined by us, which had previously been exposed to contact with lead, in experiments made near the lake, as described below; the result of our analysis of the specimen of water, made to ascertain whether lead has been taken up by the water and remains in it, is added in each case.

No. 5. Katrine water after passing through *old iron pipes*, and lying in *old lead pipes* for 1 day: no lead found in the water.

No. 6. Ditto, after lying for 3 days: no lead found in the water.

No. 7. Ditto, after lying for 6 days: the lead found in the water amounted to, or slightly exceeded one millionth part of the weight of the water.

No. 8. After passing through *old iron pipes*, and lying in *new lead pipes* for 1 day: the lead found in the water did not amount to one millionth part of the weight of the water.

No. 9. Ditto, after lying for 3 days: the lead found in the water did not amount to one millionth part of the weight of the water.

No. 10. Ditto, after lying for 6 days: the lead found in the water did not amount to one millionth part of the weight of the water.

No. 11. After passing through *old iron pipes*, and lying in *old lead cisterns* for 1 day: no lead found in the water.

No. 12. After lying, as in No. 11, covered for 3 days: no lead found in the water.

No. 13. Ditto, after lying covered for 6 days: no lead found in the water.

No. 14. Ditto, after lying covered for 6 days, with water constantly flowing through: no lead found in the water.

No. 15. After passing through *old iron pipes*, and lying in *new lead cistern* for 1 day: no lead found in the water.

No. 16. Ditto, after lying for 3 days: no lead found in the water.

No. 17. Ditto, after lying for 6 days: no lead found in the water.

No. 18. Ditto, after lying for 6 days, with water constantly flowing through: no lead found in the water.

No. 19. After passing through *new iron pipes*, *old lead pipes*, and lying in *old lead cisterns* for 1 day: no lead found in the water.

No. 20. Ditto, after lying for 3 days, (cistern covered): no lead found in the water.

No. 21. Ditto, after lying for 6 days: the lead found in the water did not amount to one millionth part of the weight of the water.

No. 22. Ditto, after lying for 6 days, with water constantly running through: no lead found in the water.

No. 23. After passing through *new iron pipes*, *new lead pipes*, and lying in *new lead cisterns*, for 1 day: no lead found in the water.

No. 24. Ditto, after lying for 3 days: no lead found in the water.

No. 25. Ditto, after lying for 6 days: no lead found in the water.

No. 26. Ditto, after lying for 6 days, with water constantly flowing through: no lead found in the water.

No. 27. After passing through *new iron pipes*, and lying in *old lead pipes*, taken from the pipes, for 1 day: no lead found in the water.

No. 28. Ditto, after lying for 3 days (cistern covered) : no lead found in the water.

No. 29. Ditto, after lying for 6 days : the lead found in the water did not amount to one-millionth part of the weight of the water.

No. 30. After passing through *new iron pipes*, and lying in *new lead pipes*, taken from the pipes, for one day : the lead found in the water amounted to, or slighly exceeded one-millionth part of its weight.

No. 31. Ditto, after lying for 3 days : the lead found in the water amounted to, or slightly exceeded one millionth part of its weight.

No. 32. Ditto, after lying for six days : the lead found in the water amounted to, or slightly exceeded one millionth part of its weight.

No. 33. From *stand pipe* to *new iron pipe*, for 8 hours : the lead found in the water amounted to, or slightly exceeded one millionth part of its weight.

No. 34. From *stand pipe* to *old iron pipe*, for 8 hours : the lead found in the water amounted to, or slightly exceeded one millionth part of its weight.

It will be observed that a considerable majority of these specimens of Katrine water were found not to contain the minutest trace of lead, although such specimens of water, after passing through an iron pipe, had been left in contact with leaden pipes or cisterns, both old and new, for an entire day, or even for three days, in several of the experiments made on the spot. No lead, therefore, appears to have been taken up, and the water has not suffered from its contact with the metal. These specimens are Nos. 5, 6, 11, 12, 13, 14, 15, 16, 17, 18, 19, 20, 22, 23, 24, 25, 26, 27, 28, 33 and 34.

In the next specimens, the presence of lead could only be discovered by the most delicate tests, and did not amount to so much as one millionth. These are Nos. 8, 9, 10, 21 and 29.

In the remaining specimens, the lead present amounted to one millionth, or slightly exceeded that proportion. These are Nos. 7, 30, 31 and 32.

Such minute traces of lead in water are, in our opinion, quite inoccuous, and may safely be disregarded. They appear only to occur also where either the iron pipes, or the lead pipes were new, and generally where the water had been allowed to stagnate in contact with lead for several days.

The experiments above referred to are of the greatest practical importance, as they show that Loch Katrine water does not act upon lead under the circumstances in which it would be placed when used for the supply of a town.

III. The experiment was made by us of agitating Katrine water in contact with the old red sandstone in a broken state, and afterwards exposing this water to lead. The water retained its great original softness, but lost entirely its action upon lead. We infer, therefore, that the Katrine water would speedily lose its power of acting upon lead, by passing through channels composed of the old red sandstone rock such as it is proposed to construct for the conveyance of the water to Glasgow.

IV. A similar experiment was made by substituting for the red sandstone the mountain limestone of the Loch Katrine district. The hardness of the water was increased from one degree to three degrees, while the power of the water, to act upon lead disappeared entirely as in the previous experiment with the old red sandstone. Hence the employment of this rock in the construction of the conduits, or its presence merely in broken pieces in the bed of the stream, would insure an entire immunity to the water from subsequent contamination with lead.

V. The facility with which the Katrine and other similar soft waters lose the power they originally possessed of acting upon lead appears to have some light thrown upon it by the following experiments.

The power of acting upon lead of both distilled water and of Katrine water for twenty-four hours was destroyed by the addition of 1-50,000th part of carbonate of lime (chalk).

The water was equally prevented from acting upon lead by the addition of 1-20,000th of the following substances:

Bicarbonate of ammonia,
Carbonate of soda,
Bicarbonate of soda,
Phosphate of soda.

With the same small proportion of sulphate and of soda, ammonia, and lime, the metal was considerably corroded by the water, but the proportion of lead actually dissolved within a short period, such as 24 hours, was much less than is dissolved in pure water.

The substances which give the greatest amount of protection to water from the action of lead are of an alkaline character, such as soluble carbonates and phosphates; but free carbonic acid also in a proportion not exceeding 1 per cent. gives a temporary protection, extending to 12 or 24 hours, probably due to the extreme insolubility of the carbonate of lead.

It is to be observed that several of these protecting substances may often be obtained by water from the atmosphere, such as carbonic acid and carbonate of ammonia, or from the soil and rocks over which the water passes, such as carbonate of lime, and occasionally, carbonate of soda.

It is also evident that no soft water intended for a town supply need be allowed to remain with the power to act upon lead, seeing that the utmost degree of safety may be obtained by allowing the water to come in contact with carbonate of lime.

In conclusion, we would press strongly the facts that the water of Loch Katrine is in no respect peculiar or exceptional in its composition and properties, and that the safety for town use of the class of waters to which it belongs has already been decided by the most ample experience. It is stated by the Commissioners who reported to Government in 1851 upon the Metropolitan Water Supply, "that no recent and unauthenticated case can be cited of the health of any of the numerous towns lately supplied with soft water being affected by the use of leaden distributory tubes, although apprehensions were often entertained from the introduction of soft water, as at Boston, in the United States, where the subject has excited much attention; and at New York, since the introduction of the Croton River." New York, with a population of 400,000, and Philadelphia, with 300,000, have been supplied, the former for nearly ten, and the latter for upwards of twenty-five years, with a water as soft as that of Loch Katrine, and the water frequently examined for lead, after passing through the usual service pipes of that metal, without any contamination of the water being discovered. The physicians of both places also testify that no case of lead-disease from this cause has been ever heard of. We have also had occasion to examine the water with which the towns of Inverness and Whitehaven are supplied, both before and after passing through lead pipes and cisterns, and find these waters to have the same high degree of softness as the water of Loch Katrine, and also the same decided action upon lead. Yet the injurious action of the metal upon the water in use in these towns has never been observed nor even suspected, nor can a trace of metal be found in the water which has passed through lead. In fine, the apprehension of danger from the use of Loch Katrine water with leaden service pipes is entirely speculative, and cannot fail to be dissipated the moment that reference is made to the experience of other towns supplied with water of equal softness and purity.

(Signed) THOMAS GRAHAM,
A. W. HOFMANN.

Dr. Angus Smith, of Manchester, on Water Pipes. 1850.

The use of lead pipes is common enough; and although the danger from lead has often been pointed out, there is no diminution in the amount used. It is acknowledged that with soft water, lead is very dangerous, but I am disposed to think that it is dangerous even with hard, except when a crust forms upon it. When a lead pump is used, no matter how hard the water is, there is still lead to be found in it. In one case I found lead where there was 62 grains of lime salts in a gallon; the family filtered the water, but that did not quite remove it, although it was much improved. This shows the lead to have been in complete solution, although the water was hard. The pump was made of lead, so that there was a constant friction preserving the surface clean and assisting comminution.

In another case, where there was a lead pump and well, the water also coming from a badly drained and putrid underground; the water was acid, and an acid salt of lead was found in the water strong enough to have a distinct taste of lead, and otherwise nauseous from the other salts, such as nitrates and chlorides. A few bubbles of sulphuretted hydrogen made the whole of a deep brown instantly, and it was lamentable to find that the persons who used it did not suspect any evil from this source.

The use of zinc in lead pipes has been proposed as a remedy, but it is not desirable to drink even zinc. There is a lead pipe made in Manchester, covered with tin; a very thin film of it protects it considerably from the action of water acidulated with acetic acid. Probably, for water pipes, it may be very useful. It is time that some change should be made in the small water pipes now made of lead, and that the use of lead pumps and cisterns should be done away with, unless they can be protected.

Letter from Dr. Thomas Spencer, of Liverpool, respecting the Action of Water upon Lead. Liverpool, 9th May, 1850.

Being requested to draw up an abstract of my opinions relative to chemical action which ensues between different qualities of water and lead, I beg to lay the following brief paper before you.

I may premise that the views I entertain are derived from the results of numerous experiments, some of which have been made and recorded by others, but which have been subsequently repeated and verified by myself.

Another portion, however, is advanced, as far as I am aware, for the first time. I allude to those which show that the oxide of lead is dissolved by most of the salts contained in hard water.

That perfectly pure water, wholly deprived of air, does not oxidize lead, is admitted by all who have given attention to the subject.

This is, perhaps, better expressed when we say that "lead does possess the power of decomposing water," and it is also more in accordance with the views of science. Water, however, is never found absolutely pure or free from air. On the contrary, it usually contains mineral, organic and gaseous matters in solution. Sometimes one class of bodies predominate, sometimes another, but not unfrequently all three are present. Moreover, when in its purest natural state, as rain, water is always mingled with the atmosphere through which it falls; hence it not unfrequently contains gaseous matters derived from smoke. For the subject under inquiry, all foreign bodies found in water must, strictly speaking, be looked on as impurities, as we know that they influence the chemical action between water, lead and air. Although air is the prime oxidizing agent, yet it is only in connection with water that it is so; as the oxygen of perfectly dry air does not combine with lead at common temperatures.

But air does not exist naturally in a perfectly dry state, but is always more or less combined with water. On the other hand, water in its natural state is never found without air. Even boiling it, does not absolutely deprive it of the air which it contains.

In pursuing the inquiry, we have, therefore, to consider the effect which these bodies have upon lead when they are dissolved in water. Both practice and experiment show that air and moisture, when combined, are alone sufficient to oxidize lead, although they do not possess the power of rendering the resulting oxide soluble; this second action being altogether due to the mineral or organic substances which the water may happen to contain.

The first and only chemical change, then, which takes place in *pure water*, when in connection with lead, is the formation of a hydrated oxide on the moist surface, say of a cistern. This chemical change is effected by the united action of air and water alone; but should the same take place in *hard water*, which, on exposure, it is more than equally liable to do, then the oxide will be taken up and held in chemical solution, and thus it becomes diffused throughout the volume of water. If, therefore, the salts which give to water its hardness were not present, the oxide could not be held in chemical solution. Indeed, when the oxide forms in soft water, its tendency is to remain on the surface of the lead, either in that state, or if much exposed to air, as a carbonate. Should agitation or any other circumstances cause its removal, it has no power of diffusing itself chemically throughout the water, since we find that it may be separated by filtration, so that the most delicate tests are unable to detect it.

We thus arrive at two conclusions; one, that air and water jointly form an oxide which *is insoluble in soft water;* the other, that hard water and air also form this oxide, but that *in the latter it becomes soluble.* We are, therefore, fully justified in stating that hard water, in connection with lead, is more dangerous than that which is soft.

Having thus far stated the general case, we have now to consider the circumstances which arise in practice. Although the abstract fact is generally admitted, that *perfectly pure* distilled water, totally deprived of air, does not oxidize lead, yet the question has been usually discussed as between rain water on the one hand, and hard water derived from springs on the other. Those who have reported on the action of water on lead, as far as I can learn, have used rain water caught within, or not far from a town, for their experiments. Now, rain water not only contains a larger proportion of air than water which is taken from a surface brook, but the rain of a town can never be said to be altogether free from fine particles of soot, as well as gaseous matter, derived from the combustion of coal. Even filtration does not altogether remove these matters, as their particular taste is still perceptible.

There is, therefore, no doubt that, under these circumstances, slips of brightened lead become more rapidly tarnished when immersed in such water, than if in ordinary hard or spring water. In proof of which I may state, that where experiments have been made with rain water caught at a distance from a town, the lead remained comparatively untarnished, as in distilled water.

On the other hand, where similar experiments have been made with hard, spring-water, it has been inferred, because the lead has sustained little diminution of brightness, that no oxidizing action had taken place, and therefore that hard water is less dangerous in connection with this metal than soft water.

But the fact has been altogether overlooked, that some of the earthy salts which give water its hardness, have the power of dissolving this oxide as soon as formed, and therefore operate to prevent an oxide from depositing itself on the surface of the lead; thus keeping it bright, and at the same time leading to the conclusion that it has continued unacted upon, even when the water has remained exposed to the atmosphere. Those who have observed the destructive effects of hard water on cisterns, especially in Liverpool, where the water is preëminently hard, but who have not studied the matter chemically, have been at a loss to account for some of the scientific opinions so much at variance with their daily observation. In a word, the closest experimenter has usually come to the conclusion, that *soft water only* acts upon lead, while the practical observer finds that cisterns are more rapidly corroded by hard water; hence has arisen so much conflicting opinion. A little reflection, however, will render it obvious that the effects of practice can scarcely be observed by the mere immersion of brightened lead into glass vessels containing either hard or soft water, and there suffering them to remain for a few weeks, perhaps only so far covered as to prevent evaporation or the accession of dust. To have made an experiment that would realize the practice, the whole circumstances of an intermittent supply ought to have been taken into account.

It must be recollected also, that as cisterns are constructed, lead is not the only metal which has to be dealt with; there being the solder which is used for the joints. Now this substance, which is an admixture of lead and tin, will, when immersed in water along with lead, act as a distinct metal and give rise to a voltaic action between the lead, the solder, and the water. This will cause a rapid corrosion at the joints, but it will be more or less active *in proportion to the hardness or chemical impurity of the water.*

Those who have given attention to the principles which govern electro-chemical action, can have no difficulty in understanding this, and that, were the water perfectly pure, such an action could not take place.

We have next in the order of practice to take into account that intermittent filling and emptying, which so frequently expose the sides of a leaden cistern to the united action of air and moisture. This also considerably accelerates the formation of the oxide. Indeed, I believe that it tends to its production more than any of the circumstances connected with a cistern. That it is much influenced by evaporation, there can be no reasonable doubt. In proof of which we find, that where the water of a cistern is kept at the same level by constantly adding as much as is taken away, thin lead will soon be cut through *at the water-line*, or, rather, the line of evaporation. Under the same circumstances the effects produced by soft water are comparatively slight.

Were lead upon roofs to be as often sprinkled with hard water as it is with rain, and taking into account the rapidity of evaporation, the duration of this metal under such circumstances would be much more limited than we know it to be.

It is the opinion of some that the earthy salts which are contained in hard water operate to prevent this metal from being diffused or oxidized. On any principles of recorded science, it is difficult to understand how a salt in solution can operate to prevent corrosion of a metal, except where it may be said to neutralize an acid. But in this instance there is no acid present; as carbonic acid, as it exists in air, can scarcely be called so, as it does not act upon lead until after the oxide has been formed.

That a neutral in solution can afford what, for want of a better term, might be called a catalytic protection to a metal is so contrary to analogy, that on strictly chemical grounds it is scarcely reconcilable.

But if sulphates and silicates afford the protection they are said to do, it can only be understood on the principle that when, water contains salt in solution it becomes, for lack of room, less capable of containing another body than when purer, and this is in the direct ratio of its approach to saturation.

In this sense such protection becomes strictly mechanical, and is better expressed when we say that water which contains another body in solution, necessarily possesses *less* interstitial space than when unoccupied.

On this principle we can also conceive how it is that rain-water contains more air than water which is preoccupied by mineral salts.

Altogether independent of this, however, I find by experiment that neither the sulphates nor the silicates which are found in water have the power of dissolving oxide of lead. We are thus far positive, therefore, that the presence of these bodies, as far as lead is concerned, is much less objectionable than most of the other salts which are found in spring water.

We now arrive at the consideration of these salts of hard water which may be proved to be positively objectionable in connection with lead. I had been aware, from observation and experiment, that hard water not only oxidized lead when exposed to air, but that it also dissolved and consequently held such oxide in solution, but which latter property was *not* possessed by soft water. I found likewise that water taken from different wells, and which indicated the same degree of hardness according to the scale, yet their action upon lead differed very materially; the water of one well, for instance, dissolving more oxide of lead in a given time than that taken from another: the fact being inferred from the variable discoloration of the water by sulphuretted hydrogen, which fairly indicates the quantity of oxide dissolved in a given time. I have also found that the formation of the oxide itself takes place more rapidly in some waters than in others, where the degrees of hardness are alike. It seemed, therefore, tolerably clear that this disparity must arise from the different properties of the salts contained in the waters. Nor was there much difficulty in arriving at this conclusion, as the chemical constitution of our Liverpool waters differ so considerably from each other. For example, we find that water taken from two wells, each of which shall indicate, say 18 degrees of hardness, according to the scale laid down by Clarke, yet one of them shall contain 12 grains of magnesia to the gallon, while the other may contain only 4 or 5; but, on the other hand, the first water may contain only 5 or 6 grains of lime, and the other will then contain 12 or 13 of the same substance. Now, although in the usual acceptation of the term these waters are nearly of equal hardness, yet, it being derived from difference of chemical constitution, the action upon lead will differ materially.

It is perhaps not unworthy of remark, that in sandstone districts the spring water varies considerably in chemical constitution; even where the wells are little apart from each other.

General observations of this nature led me to examine the salts of hard spring water separately, to ascertain if possible which of them exerted the most power in dissolving the oxide of lead, seeing that wherever water is exposed in open leaden vessels this substance is always formed.

After making a series of experiments to ascertain this important point with the waters of various wells, the chemical constituents of which I had previously ascertained by analysis, I arrived at the following conclusions:

First. That, as a rule, most of those salts which give to water its hardness are capable of dissolving the hydrated oxide of lead.

Secondly. That their solvent power is unequal.

It would follow, therefore, that those salts which possess the solvent power in the greatest degree must be looked on, when in connection with lead, as the most dangerous.

After making a series of experiments I find that water which derives its hardness chiefly from supercarbonate of magnesia is more dangerous than water which altogether or in greater part derives its hardness from supercarbonate of lime. I find then that the following salts of hard water are capable of dissolving the hydrated oxide of lead. They are placed in the order of their solvent power, and consist of

Supercarbonate of Magnesia.
Supercarbonate of Lime.
Chloride of Sodium.
Chloride of Magnesium.
Chloride of Calcium.

As it may be necessary to verify these results by some readily made experiments requiring little chemical experience, I subjoin the following:—

Make a hydrated oxide of lead, by dropping its ascetate (sugar of lead) into a solution of ammonia. The resulting powder is the oxide, and represents that which is formed by atmospheric action in water. Let it be washed until the water shows no indications of lead by sulphuretted hydrogen.

A few grains of the oxide thus formed are to be put, while moist, into a bottle containing a few ounces of what is termed fluid magnesia (sold in the shop as Sir James Murray's fluid magnesia).

It may be diluted with half or four or five times its bulk of water, its solvent power being in the ratio of its strength.

After agitation for a few minutes let it be filtered, and when the usual tests are applied to the filtrate of magnesian water, it will be evident that the oxide of lead has been dissolved.

This fluid magnesia is chemically identical with the supercarbonate of magnesia found in hard water; the simple carbonate being in both cases held in solution by carbonic acid.

This experiment shows the solvent power of magnesia when found in hard water. Another experiment may be made to prove that the supercarbonate of lime also dissolves this oxide. To do so it is only necessary to repeat the foregoing one, but substituting carbonate of lime water for the magnesian. That sold in the shops as "Carrara Water" (being carbonate of lime held in solution by carbonic acid) precisely represents the carbonate of lime which is found in hard water.

Upon applying the test as before, it will be found that this also dissolves the oxide, but less so than in the preceding instance.

The free carbonic acid which is to be found in these artificial waters, does not contribute to these results, for should it combine with the oxide the resulting carbonate is insolluble.

An experiment may also be made with common salt (chloride of sodium) dissolved in water, or with chloride of calcium or of magnesium, and, when the test is applied, the oxide will be found in chemical solution ; but in these cases sparingly.

The salts which I have enumerated are contained more or less in all potable hard waters. When, therefore it can be satisfactorily proved that their action upon the oxide of lead is such as I have found it to be, the system of storing up water in open leaden vessels ought to be discontinued.

With us, in Liverpool, we have hard waters in public use which contain as much as from 20 to 40 grains of these substances to the gallon, while many private wells contain from 100 to 200 grains in the same quantity of water.

I am fully convinced that the proportion of air which is naturally contained in either hard or soft water contributes little practically to the formation of either the oxide or carbonate of lead. Where I have made the experiments with fresh caught soft water, and therefore containing its full proportion of air, little or no action has been observed on slips of lead when immersed in it. It is important, however, to bear in mind that this has only been so where I have taken the precaution to cover the surface of the water with oil, thus rendering further access of air from the atmosphere impossible. Where I have neglected to adopt this precaution, the oxide formed, be the water hard or soft.

I have not found that others have had recourse to this plan of excluding the air during the experiments, otherwise I think it probable that it would have had some influence in modifying their results.

I find also, upon much inquiry, that, wherever a constant supply of water is given, little or no signs of corrosion are manifested upon the interior of the leaden service pipes, they being kept always full, and necessarily free from air.

It is well known that a highly comminuted powder of metallic lead may be made to become mechanically diffused by agitation throughout either hard or soft water; and while in this state it most readily attracts oxygen.

When I have agitated pieces of lead in water deprived as much as possible of air, the bottles being also perfectly filled with water, this powder has not been formed so copiously. That the atmosphere exercises a main influence in diffusing lead, will be further evident, when we take into consideration that this metal is to some extent volatile, it being known to impart a peculiar odor, which is abundantly evident upon its being handled.

In conclusion, I may state generally that I have not been able to detect lead in ordinarily soft water, which had passed through pipes which have been kept always full and consequently free from atmospheric exposure.

ABSTRACT OF THE FOREGOING.

When lead and soft water act upon each other in perfectly close vessels or pipes, it is due in all ordinary cases to that air which water may be said to contain naturally.

When this action takes place, it never extends beyond a slight formation of a low oxide of lead, *which is insoluble in soft water.*

Where an oxide is extensively formed, it is due to the extraneous absorption of air from the atmosphere, but which can only occur when the surface of the water is exposed, as it is in a cistern.

We thus deduce, as a direct consequence, that leaden pipes, when kept charged with water, are little objectionable, inasmuch as they are then comparatively free from atmospheric action. In practice it is also found that leaden service pipes which are kept full, as in a constant supply they must be, exhibit little or no traces of oxidation after long use.

As it is obviously impracticable to keep cisterns always full, as well as it is to keep them free from the operation of the atmosphere, it would therefore follow that their use is highly objectionable for either hard or soft water.

The following applies more particularly to *hard water.*

When hard water is exposed to the atmosphere in an open leaden cistern, the hydrated oxide of lead and its carbonate are more rapidly formed than in soft water; the evaporative action upon the moist sides of the cistern, much promoting the formation of these substances.

In the vicinity of the soldered parts of a cistern, however, the oxide is still more rapidly produced, in consequence of the voltaic action which takes place where dissimilar metals are present, the superior electrical conductive power of *hard water* promoting the action.

Hence it is that cisterns which contain hard water corrode so rapidly at the joints.

When decayed organic matters accidentally fall into a deep cistern, hard water also acts more injuriously than soft.

It is well known that water holding any substance in solution is more easily decomposed than purer water. In such case water is decomposed, and carburetted hydrogen is given off, whilst the resulting oxygen enters into combination with the lead. Holes are thus frequently found at the bottom of cisterns where such matters have rested.

When oxide of lead is formed in commonly pure or soft water, it *is not soluble, yet hard water is capable of dissolving it.* It becomes thus diffused, chemically, throughout the volume of water. It may therefore be said, as regards lead, that water is dangerous in the ratio of its hardness.

All hard waters, however, are not equally capable of dissolving this oxide, their solvent power depending on the character of the salts which they contain. For instance, water which contains carbonate of magnesia in solution has a higher solvent power than that which contains an equal amount of carbonate of lime. In like manner chloride of sodium (common salt) dissolves this oxide of lead more readily than chlorides of magnesium or calcium.

I have the honor to be, sir, your very obedient servant,

THOMAS SPENCER.

HENRY AUSTIN, Esq.,
Guydyr House, Whitehall.

Report of the General Board of Health on the Supply of Water to the Metropolis. London, 1850.

* * * * *

IN the evidence of witnesses connected with the present hard water supplies, we find strong allegations of the danger of the introduction of pure water from its powerful action on lead. There can be no doubt of the more powerful action of soft water upon lead under given circumstances; which circumstances, however, we find from experience, on a large scale, seldom or never occur under a proper system of distribution. Some fatal accidents have been occasioned by the fall of leaves in leaden gutters and cisterns, the infusion of which appears to have caused powerful decomposition.

The use of lead piping and lead cisterns has long been objected to, and the remedy would be the disuse of that metal. Iron piping is altogether better and cheaper than lead, and may now, it appears, at no great additional expense, be protected from oxidation by an earthenware glaze. But for the obstinate prejudice of professional men and builders in favor of the most expensive materials, earthenware would have been manufactured and used for the distribution of water. It was so used by the Romans. Vitruvius recommends it as far preferable to lead; he shows that it was used for the distribution of water up to one hundred feet of pressure. He states:

"If the water must be conveyed more economically, the following means may be adopted: Thick earthenware tubes are to be provided not less than two inches in thickness, and tongued at one end so that they may fit into one another."

He then describes in detail the methods, having previously provided against leakage from hydraulic concussions. He adds:

"Water conducted through earthen pipes is more wholesome than through lead; indeed, that conveyed in lead must be injurious to the human system. Water should, therefore, on no account be conducted in leaden pipes, if we are desirous that it should be wholesome."

* * * * *

The remains of Roman works display their earthenware distributory apparatus. In France, we are informed that earthenware pipes have been laid down, and have been long in action for the conveyance of water at 160 feet of pressure.

* * * * *

But whilst strong declarations have been made by professional witnesses, in several places, as to what must be the effect of the introduction of supplies of pure soft water into towns, in substitution of hard water, no idea appears to have been entertained of referring to the experience of those towns where supplies of soft water have been introduced, to ascertain whether any such consequences had been experienced there. We have, therefore, directed particular inquiries to be made on the subject.

Mr. James Stirrat, bleacher, Paisley, a very respectable and intelligent witness, and a member of the town council of that borough, who has been led to pay very special attention to the subject of the improvement of the supplies of water in Scotland, was asked:

"In London, it is stated, that inasmuch as pure water corrodes lead more than other water, a supply of soft water might be dangerous, and might poison the population. How have you found the fact to be at Paisley? There is no such effect; such an idea is downright nonsense; corrosion in pipes takes place only under the intermittent supply, by the action of the atmosphere on the pipe in a damp state; and, as I have said before, an iron pipe constantly charged will not corrode at all, whether the water be hard or soft, and will last at least four times as long as a pipe where the air is admitted into it."

Other witnesses corroborate the fact that with some waters, the wear of pipes by the intermittent supplies is frequently very rapid, the rationale being, that oxidation takes place whilst the pipe is empty, and that the oxide is swept away by the return of the water.

In cases where *colica pictonum* and dangerous accidents to health have occurred from the contamination of lead, we believe that it may be ascribed to the intermittent action of water upon the long lines of leaden pipe.

It may be useful here to mention, that what, from several experiments, appears to be a simple mechanical preventive, has been discovered by Professor Clark:

"Some of the Bagshot water alluded to had poisoned some of the Queen's hounds, and brought on *colica pictonum* in one of the huntsmen. Through the kindness of Sir James Clark, I obtained a specimen of this water, and in a few days came to the unexpected result, that filtration would separate the lead. Thus a very simple practical means for separating lead wherever it contaminates water, was discovered. At a marine villa of Lord Aberdeen's, some of the servants suffered in health from lead in water derived from pipes. Sand filters were put up under my direction at this villa, and subsequently at Haddo House. On making inquiry, recently, his lordship's agent, in Aberdeen, I learn that the filters have been in use ever since, and that the waters have been tested from time to time, without any lead having been discovered in them. I have been told, indeed that so satisfied has Lord Aberdeen been with the result, that on hearing of the Count de Neuelly's family at Claremont being troubled with lead in the water, he wrote recommending the same process being tried there; and, from general rumor, I had previously heard that the process had been adopted there.

"I hold it in all cases to be dangerous to allow water to pass through any considerable length of lead pipes, or to allow water to remain for a long time even in short pipes. In the case of the marine villa before alluded to, the water came a considerable distance through lead pipes; I suppose above a quarter of a mile. The water in Aberdeen is brought from the iron mains in the streets, into the houses, by means of lead pipes; and in general without any disadvantage, because the supply from the pipes is constant, and the use of the stop-cock very frequent in a family; but in my class rooms and laboratory I find that whenever a pipe has been out of use for a few days, the water taken from it affords a trace of lead, which disappears when the water has been allowed to run briskly from the stop-cock for a few minutes."

Though we have been informed of no serious accidents from contamination with lead, in any of the towns where new supplies of soft water have been introduced, we believe that minor injuries from such partial contaminations as Professor Clark describes, may occur and pass unnoticed; and that for this reason, the use of lead pipes should be discontinued as early as practicable. As a question of danger, however, a preponderance of testimony establishes the conclusion, that hard water, with an intermittent supply, is actually more dangerous than soft water with a constant supply.

Rose's Treatise of Chemical Analysis. London, 1848.—*Lead.*

Lead has a grey color and much brilliancy; it stains paper, and is very soft. Its specific gravity is 11.445; it is therefore heavier than silver; it begins to fuse at about + 280 degrees cent. (536 degrees Fahr.); heated in contact with the air it begins to volatilize at a low red heat, but in closed vessels a white heat is required to volatilize it. It is not altered by exposure to dry air, but in damp atmosphere it becomes slightly oxydized, its surface becomes dull, grey, and sometimes iridescent.

Plunged in distilled water with the contact of the air, but sheltered from the influence of carbonic acid, white spangles of hydrate of lead only are produced according to Bonsdorf. To obtain this effect, however, it is necessary that the water should be perfectly pure, for the least quantity of salts or of foreign substances prevents the formation of the hydrate.

The nitrates form the only exception, for their presence does not prevent the formation of the hydrate of lead, unless they be in very large quantity; wherefore metallic lead may be resorted to as a test of the purity of water. In effect, when fine recently prepared lead filings are thrown into a tumbler full of water, in two or three minutes a small cloud of hydrate of lead will appear if the water be pure; whilst, in the contrary case, no turbidness is produced.

If metallic lead be put in contact with water and with ordinary atmospheric air containing carbonic acid, a little hydrate of lead is at first formed, but a combination of hydrated carbonate of lead is soon deposited in the form of thin white spangles, having a waxy appearance.

If metallic lead be left in contact with air and water for several months, or for several years, dentoxyde of lead may be formed.

Turner's Chemistry. Philadelphia, 1846.—*Lead.*

In distilled water, previously boiled and preserved in close vessels, it undergoes no change; but in open vessels it is oxidized with considerable rapidity, yielding minute, shining, brilliantly white, crystalline scales of carbonate of the protoxide, the oxygen and carbonic acid being derived from the air. The presence of saline matter in water retards the oxidation of the lead; and some salts even in very minute quantity, prevent it altogether. The protecting influence, exerted by certain substances, was first noticed by Guyton Morveau; but it has been minutely investigated by Christison of Edinburgh, who has discussed the subject in his excellent treatise on poison. He finds that the preservative power of neutral salts is materially connected with the insolubility of the compound which their acid is capable of forming with lead.

Thus, phosphates and sulphates, as well as chlorides and iodides, are highly preservative; so small a quantity as 1-30,000th part of phosphate of soda or iodide of potassium in distilled water preventing the corrosion of lead. In a preservative solution the metal gains weight during some weeks, in consequence of its surface gradually acquiring a superficial coating of carbonate, which is slowly decomposed by the saline matter of the solution. The metallic surface being thus covered with an insoluble film which adheres tenaciously, all further change ceases. Many kinds of spring water owing to the salts they contain, do not corrode lead; and hence, though intended for drinking, it may be safely collected in leaden cisterns. Of this, the water of Edinburgh is a remarkable instance.

* * * * *

With regard to the poisonous property of the salts of lead, a remarkable fact has been observed by my colleague, Dr. A. T. Thomson, who has proved that of all the ordinary preparations of lead, the carbonate is by far the most virulent poison. Any salt of lead which is easily convertible into a carbonate, as for instance the subacetate, is also poisonous; but he has given large doses of the nitrate of the protoxide and chloride of lead to rabbits without producing perceptible inconvenience.

L. Tanquerel des Planches on Lead Diseases. Lowell, 1848. Translated by Dr. Samuel L. Dana.

Dr. Wall has seen all the residents on a farm attacked with lead colic, from drinking water from a pump, the reservoir or cistern of which, and the pipe, were lined with lead. This metal, in the course of three years was known to have been in great part destroyed and mixed with the water. By the advice of Wall, the farmers used other water not in contact with lead; from that time they were not attacked with colic.

It is easy to account for the development of colic in these circumstances. Lead, exposed to moisture, is easily transformed into oxide, then into carbonate of lead, by the oxygen and carbonic acid of the air.

The sub-carbonate, thus formed, is wholly or partially dissolved in water, by means of the carbonic acid that it generally contains in excess. Thus in cases where water remains some months in lead cisterns, a white line may be perceived at the top of the water, which remains distinct when the latter diminishes; this white line is carbonate of lead.

* * * * *

Is it then surprising that the inhabitants of Amsterdam and Haarlem suffered from lead colic, in consequence of using water containing carbonate of lead?

But water not in contact with air generally effects no change on the lead in which it is contained. It is partly through pipes of this metal that water is distributed in different public and also private establishments in Paris, and Tanquerel has never learned that water thus conveyed has caused *lead colic*. Water circulating in these lead pipes is not in contact with atmospheric air, therefore, carbonate of lead, can, with difficulty, be formed. He repeats, "with difficulty," for the water which passes through these lead pipes most frequently comes from springs, which are generally very much charged with carbonic acid and carbonate of lime, and until this last salt covers the inside of the conduit, carbonate of lead is formed and dissolved by the excess of carbonic acid which the water contains. So the inhabitants of some cities, establishing fountains, have suffered with colic from using the water which first passed through the new pipes.

* * * * *

The inhabitants of Amsterdam, while using water preserved in lead reservoirs, were often affected with paralysis as well as colic. Lead paralysis has often been produced by the use of wine, or beer adulterated with litharge. Two cases of colic occasioned by acetate of lead were accompanied by paralysis. It has been produced also by the use of butter adulterated with white lead, and by acetate of lead given as medicine. A family, according to Van Swieten, which had been in the habit of using water contained in a leaden vessel, were attacked with paralysis; another family were also attacked with paralysis from using water charged with sulphate of lime, drawn from the well with a leaden vessel.

* * * * *

Christison on Poisons. Edinburgh, 1845.

OF THE ACTION OF AIR AND PURE WATER ON LEAD.

When lead is exposed to the air it becomes tarnished. This arises from a thin crust of carbonate of lead being formed. For the crust dissolves with brisk effervescence in acetic acid. The formation of carbonate is accelerated by moisture and probably by the presence of an unusual proportion of carbonic acid in the air.

The action of water on lead, which is of much greater consequence, has been made the subject of observation by the curious for many ages. The Roman architect, *Vitruvius*, who it is believed flourished in the time of Cæsar and Augustus, forbids the use of this metal for conducting water, because cerusse, he says, is formed on it, which is hurtful to the human body. *Galen* also condemns the use of lead pipes, because he was aware, that water transmitted through them contracted a muddiness from the lead, and that those who drank such water were subject to dysentery.

If we trace the sciences of architecture, chemistry, and medicine downwards from these periods, nothing more will be found than a repetition of the statements of Vitruvius and Galen, with but a few particular facts in support of them till we arrive at the close of the last and beginning of the present century.

The first person that examined the subject minutely was *Dr. Lambe* of Warwick; who inferred from his researches, that most, if not all, spring waters possess the power of corroding and dissolving lead to such an extent as to be rendered unfit for the use of man, and that this solvent power is imparted to them by some of their saline ingredients. The inquiry was afterwards undertaken more scientifically by *Guyton Morveau;* who, in opposition to Dr. Lambe, arrived at the conclusion that distilled water, the purest of all waters, acts rapidly on lead by converting it into a hydrated oxide, and that some natural waters, which hardly attack lead at all, are prevented doing so by the salts they hold in solution.

A few years later *Dr. Thomson* of Glasgow also examined the subject, and, assenting to Dr. Lambe's proposition, that most spring waters attack lead, maintains nevertheless that the lead is only held in suspension, not in solution; and that the quantity suspended in such waters, after they have passed through lead pipes, pumps, and cisterns, is too minute to prove injurious to those who make habitual use of them. In the first edition of this work an extended account was given of an investigation I made into the whole subject of the action of different waters on lead. Additional observations were afterwards published on the same point by *Captain Yorke*, and by Mr. Taylor. And I have added some new facts in a late paper.

The inquiry is of so great practical consequence, that I need not offer any apology for reproducing it here in detail, with such additions as ulterior experience and the researches of others enables me to make. *Professor Orfila* takes no notice of this important subject, except in a few lines containing several inaccurate statements.

Distilled water, deprived of its gases by ebullition, and excluded from contact with the air, has no action whatever on lead. If the water contains the customary gases in solution, the surface of the metal, freshly polished becomes quickly dull and white. But if the water be not at the same time exposed to the air, the action soon comes to a close. When the air, on the other hand, is allowed free access to the water, a white powder appears in a few minutes on and around the lead; and this goes on increasing till in the course of a few days there is formed a large quantity of white matter, which partly floats in the water or adheres to the lead, but is chiefly deposited on the bottom of the vessel. If this be made with atmospheric air deprived of carbonic acid, the white substance puts on the form of a white powder, which I find to be a hydrated oxide; for when dried at 180 degrees F. it gives off water on being heated to redness, and dissolves without effervescence in weak nitric acid.

But if the surface of the water be exposed to the open air, the substance formed consists of minute brilliant pearly scales, which with the aid of a powerful microscope are seen to be thin equilateral triangular tables, often grouped into hexaedral tables, or worn at the edges into the form of rosettes. This substance, which has a pale grayish hue when dried, I have ascertained to be carbonate of lead, consisting of two equivalents of neutral carbonate and one of hydrated protoxide. The formation of carbonate takes place with considerable rapidity. In twelve ounces of distilled water, contained in a shallow glass basin, loosely covered to exclude the dust, twelve brightly polished lead rods weighing 340 grains, will lose two grains and a half in eight days; and the lead will then show evident marks of corrosion.

The process of corrosion goes on so long as atmospheric air is allowed to play freely on the surface of the water. In twenty months I have obtained 120 grains from an ounce of lead rods kept in 24 ounces of distilled water.

During these changes, a minute quantity of lead is dissolved.

This is best proved by carefully filtering the water, then acidulating with a drop or two of nitric acid, and evaporating to dryness. I have never failed to detect lead in the residue by expelling the excess of nitric acid by heat, dissolving it in distilled water, and applying hydrosulphuric acid, hydriodate of potass, and chromate of potass to the solution.

The lead is first dissolved in the form of hydrated oxide. For, if the air admitted to water be deprived of carbonic acid, a clear liquid is obtained by filtration and this is turned brown by hydrosulphuric acid. But a great part of the hydrate is speedily separated in the form of carbonate. For the filtered liquid speedily becomes turbid if exposed to the air; and on evaporating it, the residuum dissolves in weak nitric acid with brisk effervescence. Captain Yorke estimates the quantity dissolved when the water is saturated at a 10,000th part.

By far the greatest part of the lead, however, which disappears, will be found in the white pearly crystals. This crystalline powder is not, as alleged by Guyton Morveau, and after him by some systematic writers, a hydrated oxide of lead, but, as stated above, a particular variety of carbonate, containing more hydrated oxide than exists in common white lead. At first I thought it was neutral carbonate. Captain Yorke was led to suppose it the hydrated oxide. In 1842, I found that if it be exposed for some time to the action of aerated water, after the lead has been removed, it invariably consists of two equivalents of neutral carbonate and one of hydrated oxide.

It will be inferred from the preceding facts, that distilled water for economical use should never be preserved in leaden vessels, or otherwise in contact with lead. Even the distilled waters of aromatic plants should not be so preserved, because the essential oil, which communicates to them their fragrance, does not take away the power which pure distilled water possesses of acting on lead. This fact was first announced in the second edition of the present work. A druggist in Edinburgh requested me to examine a reddish gray, crystalline. pearly sediment, formed copiously in a sample of orange flower water, I found this to be carbonate of lead, colored by the coloring matter of the water, and obviously produced by the action of the water on lead solder used instead of tin solder, and coarsely and liberally applied to the seams of the copper vessel in which the water had been imported from France. The filtered fluid did not contain a particle of lead.

* * * * *

OF THE ACTION OF SOLUTIONS OF NEUTRAL SALTS ON LEAD.

The property which pure aerated water possesses of corroding lead is variously affected by foreign ingredients which it may hold in solution.

Of these modifying substances none are more remarkable in their action than the neutral salts, which all impair the corrosive power of the water. Important practical consequences flow from that action; for it involves no less than the possibility of employing lead for most of the economical purposes to which the ingenuity of man has applied that useful metal. The first experimentalist who made it an object of attention was *Guyton Morveau;* whose experiments are imperfect and in some respects erroneous. Having found that distilled water corrodes lead, he proceeded to inquire why no change of the kind takes place in some natural waters; and being aware that most spring and river waters differ from that which has been distilled, chiefly in containing sulphate of lime and muriate of soda, he tried a solution of each of these salts, and discovered that a certain quantity of either to distilled water takes away from it the power of attacking lead; that this preservative power is possessed by so small a proportion as a 500th part of sulphate of lime in the water; and that the nitrates are also probably endowed with the same singular property. Here his researches terminated.

Extending Guyton Morveau's inquiries to other proportions of the same salts, I was led to the conclusion that all of them, without exception, possess the power of impairing the action of distilled water on lead. At least I found this power to exist in the case of sulphates, muriates, carbonates, hydriodates, phosphates, nitrates, acetates, tartrates and arseniates.

The degree of this preservative power differs much in different salts. The acetate of soda is but an imperfect preventive when dissolved in the proportion of a hundredth part of the water; while crystals are formed, and the lead loses about a fourth of what is lost in distilled water in the same time. On the contrary, arseniate of soda is a complete preservative when dissolved in the proportion of a 12,000th; and phosphate of soda and hydriodate of potass are almost effectual preservatives in the proportion of a 30,000th part only of the water. Muriate of soda and sulphate of lime hold a middle place between these extremes, and are both of them much more powerful than Guyton Morveau imagined; the former preserves in the proportion of a 2,000th to the water, the latter in the proportion of nearly a 4,000th. Nitrate of potass is little superior to the acetate of soda. In the proportion of a hundredth it prevents the action of the water almost entirely; but if the proportion be diminished to a 160th, the loss sustained by the lead is fully a third of the loss in distilled water.

When lead has been exposed for a few weeks to a solution of a protecting salt, and has acquired a thin film over its surface, it not only is not acted on by the solution, but is even also rendered incapable of being acted on by distilled water.

The preservative power depends on the acid and not on the base of the salt. The acetate, muriate, arseniate, and phosphate of soda, differ exceedingly in power. On the other hand, the sulphates of soda, magnesia and lime, as well as the triple sulphate of alumina and potass, preserve as nearly as can be determined in the same proportion.

When we attempt to ascertain the relative preserving power of the neutral salts it will appear that those whose acid forms with the lead a soluble salt of lead are the least energetic; while those whose acid forms an insoluble salt of lead are most energetic. The protecting powers of acetate of soda, nitrate of potass, muriate of soda, sulphate of lime, arseniate of soda, and phosphate of soda, are inversely as the solubility of the acetate, nitrate, muriate, sulphate, arseniate, and phosphate of lead. The existence of this ratio might naturally lead to the inference that the protecting power depends simply on the salt in the solution being decomposed, so that there is formed on the surface of the lead a thin crust consisting of the oxide of the metal in union with the acid of the decomposed salt, and constituting an insoluble film which is impermeable to aërated water: For example, that phosphate of soda acts in the small proportion of a 30,000th part by forming on the surface of the metal an impermeable film of phosphate of lead, which is known to be one of the most insoluble of all the neutral salts. But this is not altogether a correct statement of the fact.

When the protection afforded is complete, as for example, by a 27,000th of phosphate of soda, a 12,000th of the arseniate of soda, or a 4000th of sulphate of soda, the lead undergoes not a change in appearance or in weight for several hours, or even days. At length the surface becomes dull, then white, and gradually a uniform film is formed over it. This film, examined at an early period, is found to consist of carbonate of lead, being entirely soluble in diluted acetic acid, although the salt in solution is a sulphate. But after a few weeks the carbonate is mixed with a salt of lead, containing the acid of a part of the natural salt dissolved in water: If, after five or six weeks immersion in a preservative solution of phosphate or sulphate of soda, the film on the lead be scraped off and immersed in diluted acetic acid, effervescence and solution takes place, but a part of the powder remains undissolved; and if the protecting salt has been the muriate of soda, the whole powder is dissolved, but muriatic acid will be found in solution by its proper test, the nitrate of silver. In all such protecting solutions the lead gains weight for some time, but at length it ceases to undergo further change, and is not acted on even if removed into distilled water. The crust when formed thus slowly adheres with great firmness. The most careful analysis cannot detect any lead, either dissolved in the water or floating in it, or united with the insoluble matter left on the side of the glass by evaporation. In short, the preservation of the lead from corrosion, and of the water from impregnation with lead, is complete.

When the protection afforded is not quite complete,—for example in distilled water containing a 4,000th of muriate of soda, a 6,000th of sulphate of soda, a 15,000th of arseniate of soda, or a 35,000th of phosphate of soda,—besides a powdery crust, small crystals, with several facettes, are sometimes formed on the lead, while at the same time, a minute white film will very slowly appear on the bottom of the glass, on its side where it is left dry by the evaporation of the water, and likewise on the surface of the water itself. These detached films are composed of carbonate of lead, with a little of the muriate, sulphate, arseniate, or phosphate of lead, according to the nature of the acid in the alkaline salt which is dissolved in the water. In the course of the changes now described, the lead in general no longer gains, but loses in weight. The loss, however is exceedingly small. No lead can be discovered in solution, if the water before evaporation is carefully filtered.

On progressively trying solutions of weaker and weaker preservative power, it will be remarked, that the quantity of the detached powder, and the proportion of carbonate in it, progressively increase; and likewise, that what is formed on the lead adheres more and more loosely. In distilled water and weak solutions of acetate of soda, or nitrate of potass, the lead never becomes so firmly encrusted, but that gentle agitation of the water will shake off the powder.

It is worthy of notice that, although a small quantity of lead is dissolved by distilled water after it has remained sometime in contact with the metal, yet not a trace is found in solutions where a protecting salt is present. In solutions even weakly preservative, I never could detect any lead dissolved. Thus, in distilled water containing a 4,000th of muriate of soda, or a 160th of nitre, the lead lost weight, and loose crystals of carbonate were formed; yet even after thirty days no lead could be found in solution by the process with which I have always detected it in pure distilled water. Free exposure to the air is probably in part the cause of this. For it will be seen afterwards that some natural waters in passing through a long course of lead pipes, within which the action goes on without direct access of the atmosphere, contract an impregnation, which is invisible when the water is newly drawn, but after a few hours exposure to the air shows itself in the form of a white film and milkiness.

The general results of these experiments appears to be, that neutral salts in various, and for the most part minute, proportions retard or prevent the corrosive action of water on lead,—allowing the carbonate to deposit itself slowly, and to adhere with such firmness to the lead as not to be afterwards removed by moderate agitation,—adding subsequently to this crust other insolluble salts of lead, the acids of which are derived from the neutral salts in solution, and thus at length forming a permanent impermeable screen, through which the action of the water cannot any longer be carried on.

An important subject of inquiry regards the natural causes by which the preservative power of the neutral salts is impaired. This topic I have not hitherto been able to examine with all the care which is desirable.

From the effect of the water of Edinburgh when highly charged with carbonic acid, I was led to infer in former editions of this work that an unusual quantity of carbonic acid is a counteracting agent. For if Edinburgh water charged with it be corked up with some lead rods in a phial half filled with water, and half with atmospheric air, the lead, which in common Edinburgh water, as will presently be mentioned, hardly loses any of its brilliancy for six or seven days, becomes white in twelve or sixteen hours. Subsequent experiments by Captain Yorke seemed to him to render this conclusion doubtful; nor do I attach much consequence to the observation just quoted. On the other hand, it is said, *Professor Daniell* has found all waters dissolve lead, if they contain an excess of carbonic acid. The point would be best settled by the effect of a natural carbonated water passing through a long lead pipe.

ON THE ACTION OF NATURAL WATERS ON LEAD.

The preceding observations on the action of water on lead may be resorted to for explaining many interesting facts, and correcting some erroneous statements, which have been published by authors as to the corrosion of lead by natural processes.

RAIN AND SNOW WATER.

It has been stated by *Dr. Lambe* that rain water does not corrode lead, that "its effect is so slight as not to be discernible within a moderate compass of time." But this observation is far from being correct. Rain or snow-water, collected in the country at a distance from houses, and before it touches the earth, being nearly as pure as distilled water, ought to act with almost equal rapidity on lead. I have accordingly found by a comparative experiment with that mentioned in p. 517, that in 12 ounces of snow-water collected ten miles west from Edinburgh, and at some distance from any house, twelve lead rods weighing 340 grains lost two grains in eight days; and the usual crystals began to form in less than an hour. But when collected in a great city, rain or snow-water is much impaired in activity. Thus in an experiment made with eaves'-droppings collected from the roof of my house in Edinburgh, after half an hour of gentle rain from the south-east—the first rain which had fallen for several weeks—there was no action at all. Yet even when collected in a great city, and in circumstances which at first sight would appear not very favorable to its action—for example, from eaves'-droppings, a few hours after the beginning of a shower—it retains a little of its corroding property; and when collected in like manner after twelve or twenty-four hour's rain, it corrodes almost as rapidly as distilled water. . . . .

We must obviously be prepared to look for an explanation of these differences in the relative purity of the different waters.

Accordingly, in the eaves'-droppings at the beginning of the shower the nitrates of baryta and silver caused, the former a distinct, the latter a faint precipitation, which, as oxalate of ammonia had no effect, arose from the presence of alkaline sulphates and muriates. But after a few hours' shower nitrate of baryta alone acted, and caused merely a faint haze; and after a twenty-four hours' shower, as well as in snow-water from the country, none of the three tests had any effect whatever.

Hence, perhaps even in a town, but at all events certainly in the country, it would be wrong to use for culinary purposes rain or snow water which has run from lead roofs or spouts recently erected. When the roof or spout has been exposed for some time to the weather the danger is of course much lessened, if not entirely removed; because exposure to the weather encrusts it with a firmly adhering coat of carbonate, through which, as already observed, even distilled water will not act. But I believe it would be right to condemn the turning even old leaden roofs to the purpose of collecting water for the kitchen. Although the purest rain water cannot act on them when it is once fairly at repose, we do not know what may be the effect of the impetus of the falling rain on the crust of carbonate; and if the crust should happen to be thus worn considerably, or detached by more obvious accidents, the corrosion would then go on with rapidity as long as the shower lasted. Acid emanations too disengaged in the neighborhood, and other more obscure causes may enable rain water actually to dissolve even the crust of carbonate.

These remarks on the effect of rain water on lead are pointedly illustrated by what *Tronchin* has recorded of the circumstances connected with the spreading of the lead colic at Amsterdam, about the time he wrote his valuable essay on that disease. Till that period lead colic was seldom met with in the Dutch capital. But soon after the citizens began to substitute lead for tiles on the roofs of their dwelling houses, the disease broke out with great violence and committed great ravages. Tronchin very properly ascribed its increase to lead entering the body insidiously along with the water, which for culinary purposes was chiefly collected from the roofs during rain. He further attempts to account for the rain water having acquired the power of corroding the lead, by supposing that it was rendered acid in consequence of the roofs having been covered with decaying leaves from trees which abounded in the city; and without a doubt this explanation accords with the season at which the lead colic was observed to be most frequent, namely, the autumn. But he does not seem to have been aware that rain water itself possesses the corroding property, independently of any extrinsic ingredient except the gases it receives in its passage through the atmosphere. Merat has referred to a Dutch author, Wanstroostuyk, for an account of a similar incident which happened at Haarlem.

The coöperating effect of acid emanations in the atmosphere is well exemplified by an interesting incident which occurred this year in Manchester, as in some documents put into my hands by *Dr. Hibbert Ware.* A gentleman being seized with symptoms, which in the opinion of his medical adviser were owing to the insidious introduction of lead into the body, it was found by *Mr. Davies* that the rain water from a leaden roof, which had been used in the family for nine years, contained a considerable impregnation of lead.

* * * * *

SPRING WATER.

Most spring waters, unlike snow or rain water, have little or no action on lead, because they generally contain a considerable proportion of muriates and sulphates.

As an example of a spring water which does not act on lead at all, the mineral water of Airthrey, near Stirling, may be mentioned. In four ounces of water from the strongest spring at Airthrey I kept for thirty-five days three bright rods of lead weighing 47.007 grains; and at the end of that period the rods were very nearly as brilliant as when they were first put in, and weighed 47.004 grains. This result is easily explained on considering the nature of the water. It contains no less than a seventy-seventh part of its weight of saline matters, which are chiefly muriates, and partly sulphates.

Another good illustration occurred to me lately, which contrasts well with some instances of an opposite description to be mentioned presently. The house of Phantassie in East Lothian was supplied with water by a lead pipe from a distance of a mile. About a year afterwards, when I had an opportunity of examining into the circumstances, I found the cistern singularly clean and free of incrustation, and the water quite free of lead. The composition of the water explained these facts, it contains a 4-900th of salts, a large proportion of which consists of carbonates of lime and magnesia.

The water of Edinburgh is another example of spring water nearly destitute of action on lead. But it is not so completely inactive as the water of Airthrey.

* * * * *

Dr. Thomson, of Glasgow, in an interesting inquiry made in 1815, into the purity of the water which supplies Tunbridge, has stated that, when he lived in Edinburgh, some years before, he could always detect a minute trace of lead suspended in the water, which at that time was brought six miles in leaden pipes. I presume it is owing to the main pipes being now made of iron, that this impregnation no longer exists. For I have found that the residue of two gallons of water, very carefully collected by gentle evaporation of successive portions in a small vessel, did not furnish the slightest trace of lead, when strongly heated with black flux and then acted upon by nitric acid.

The feeble action of the Edinburgh water on lead arises from the salts it holds in solution. It contains about a 12,000th part of its weight of solid matter, of which about two thirds are carbonate of lime and one third consists of the sulphates and muriates of soda, lime and magnesia. Many instances might be quoted of spring waters which act with inconvenient or dangerous rapidity on lead. But it is hardly worth while mentioning more than one or two of these, because the nature of the waters has been seldom described.

A striking example was related by *Dr. Wall*, of Worcester. A family in that town, consisting of the parents and twenty-one children, were constantly liable to stomach and bowel complaint, and eight of the children and both parents died in consequence. Their house being sold after their death, the purchaser found it necessary to repair the pump, because the cylinder and cistern were riddled with holes and as thin as a sieve. The plumber who renewed it informed Dr. Wall that he had repaired it several times before, and in particular had done so not four years before the former occupant died. The nature of the water was not determined. Most of the water around Worcester is very hard; but this will not account for its operation in the instance now described. Another incident of the same kind, but hardly so equivocal in its circumstances, was related in 1823, by *Dr. Yeats*, of Tunbridge. A plumber undertook to supply the town with water for domestic purposes, and in 1814 laid a course of leaden pipes for a quarter of a mile. In the subsequent year many cases of lead colic occurred among the inhabitants who were supplied by those pipes; and one lady particularly, who was a great water drinker, lost the use of her limbs for some months. The inhabitants naturally became alarmed; iron pipes were substituted, and no case of colic appeared afterwards. *Mr. Brande* analyzed the water which had passed through the pipes and detected lead in it, while at the same time none could be detected at the source. Some uncertainty was supposed to have been thrown over these statements by the analytic researches of Drs. Thompson, Scudamore, and Prout, and Mr. Children. But water like that in question can scarce fail to act powerfully on lead in favorable circumstances; for according to the analysis of Dr. Thomson it is extremely pure, as it contains only a 38,000th part of saline matter, three fourths of which are a feebly protecting salt, the muriate of soda. I am satisfied, therefore, from my experiments, and the facts which follow, that no such water could be safely conveyed through new lead pipes, and that it would be dangerous even to keep it long in a lead cistern. It is difficult to account for the failure of the gentlemen above mentioned to find lead in the water, except by supposing that they had analyzed what had been exposed for some time to the air, and deposited its oxide of lead in the form of carbonate. Since my attention was first turned to this subject, the three following incidents have occurred to me, which show the danger of conveying very pure water in long lead pipes. 1. A gentleman in Dumfriesshire resolved to bring to his house, in leaden pipes, the water of a fine spring on his estate, from a distance of three quarters of a mile. As I happened to visit him at the time, I took the opportunity of examining the action of a tumbler of the water on fresh cut lead, and could not remark any perceptible effect in fourteen days. It appeared to me, therefore, that the water might be safely conveyed in lead pipes; and they were laid accordingly. No sooner, however, did the water come into use in the family, than it was observed to present a general white haze, and the glass decanters in daily use acquired a manifest white, pearly incrustation. On examining the cistern, the surface of the water, as well as that of the cistern itself, where in contact with it, was found completely white, as if coated with paint; and the water taken directly from the pipe, though transparent at first, became hazy and white when heated or left some hours exposed to the air. On afterwards analyzing the water direct from the spring, I found it of very unusual purity; as it contained scarcely a 22,000th of solid ingredients, which were sulphates, muriates and carbonates.

The reader can be at no loss to perceive why the experiments with a few sticks of lead in a tumbler was not a correct representation of what was subsequently to go on in the pipes; in fact, as the pipes were 4,000 feet long, and three fourths of an inch in diameter, each portion of water may be considered as passing successively over no less than 784 square feet of lead before being discharged. The remedy employed in this case will be mentioned presently (p. 535.) 2. A gentleman in Banfshire introduced a fine spring into his house from a distance of three quarters of a mile, by means of a lead pipe. Two years and a half afterwards he was attacked with stomach complaints, obstinate constipation and severe colic, for which he was under medical treatment for three months, with only partial and temporary relief. At last on leaving home and repairing to Edinburgh, he soon got quite well. Two other members of his family were similarly, but more slightly affected. On returning home some time afterwards, the same symptoms began to show themselves; but he had not been many weeks there, when his attention was accidentally drawn to a notice of my experiments, and the last case, in Chamber's Journal. He then saw that a white film lined the inside of the water bottle in his dressing room; and the water was declared by a chemist to contain lead. I lately had an opportunity of analyzing the water, and found it to contain only a 16,500th of solid matter, the principal salt being chloride of sodium, and the others being sulphate of magnesia and lime, with very little carbonate. This, therefore, was exactly a case in which action upon lead might have been anticipated, as the principal proportion of the very small quantity of saline matter present was a feebly protecting salt. 3. The third instance occurred at a country residence of Lord Aberdeen.

Mr. Johnston, surgeon at Peterhead, being called to visit the housekeeper, found her affected with vomiting, constipation, acute pain at the pit of the stomach, retraction of the navel, and great feebleness. Little improvement was effected in three days, when Mr. Johnston, astonished at this, and reflecting on the cause, suddenly was attracted by the appearance of a silvery film on the inside of his patient's water bottle, and recollected at the same time my narrative of the Dumfriesshire case. He then perceived that the disease was lead colic, treated it accordingly, and slowly accomplished a cure. The housekeeper's niece, a young girl who had resided only a few weeks with her, and who was the only other individual that had lived in the house above a few days together for more than a year before, had begun also to suffer from the premonitory symptoms. About twelve months before this incident happened, a spring of water, which had been analyzed and pronounced extremely pure, was brought to the house in a lead pipe; and the housekeeper had used this water for eight months before she took ill. Mr. Johnston found that the water issued from the pipe quite clear, but that a white silvery film formed on its surface under exposure to the air; and he ascertained that the first drawn water contained lead in solution, and that the film was carbonate of lead. I had an opportunity of analyzing the water, which proved to be by no means very pure, as it contained a 4460th of solids. But as the solid matter consisted almost entirely of chlorides, namely, in a great measure of chloride of sodium and a very little of the chlorides of magnesium and calcium, as there was no carbonate present, and the sulphates constituted only a 32-000th of the water, it is plain from the principles formerly laid down that the action which took place was to be anticipated from the nature of the spring.

For other instances of the corrosive action of spring water on lead the reader may refer to Dr. Lambe's treatise. Dr. Lambe was led by his researches to imagine that no spring water whatever was destitute of this property in a dangerous degree. This wide conclusion is not supported by valid facts. Yet his work contains several accurate and instructive examples of the action in question. Thus among other instances he mentions that he had found the water of Warwick to act on lead with great rapidity, and once saw holes and furrows in a cistern there, which was the second that had been used in the course of ten years. *Sir G. Baker*, in a letter to Dr. Heberden, has related another striking instance of the same kind. Lord Ashburnam's house in Sussex was supplied from some distance with water which was conveyed in leaden pipes. The servants being often affected with colic, which had even proved fatal to some of them, the water was carefully examined, and found to contain lead. The solvent power of the water was ascribed to its containing an unusual quantity of carbonic acid gas. This may be doubted.

*　　*　　*　　*　　*

Water retained long in lead cisterns has proved eminently poisonous. Thus the crew of an East India packet having been put on short allowance of water, in consequence of being delayed by contrary winds, the men got their share each in a bottle; but the officers united their shares and kept it all in a lead cistern. In three weeks all the officers began to suffer from stomach and bowel complaints, and had the lead colic for six weeks; while the men continued to enjoy good health. The surgeon detected lead in a tumbler of water without the process of concentration, by adding to it the sulphuret of potass.

A similar accident has been briefly alluded to by *Van Swieten.* He mentions, that he was acquainted with a family who were all attacked with colica pictonum in consequence of using for culinary purposes water collected in a large leaden cistern and kept there for a long time. The composition of the water has not been mentioned in any of these instances.

* * * * *

Another fact of some practical consequence, which flows from the experimental conclusions stated above is, that although it may be perfectly safe to keep some waters in leaden cisterns, it may be very unsafe to use covers of this metal, because the water which condenses on the covers must be considered as pure as distilled water. It has been found that white lead forms in much larger quantity on the inside of the covers of cisterns than on the cisterns themselves, where both are constructed of lead. A remarkable illustration of this is mentioned in a paper read before the Academy of Science at Paris in 1788, by the *Comte de Milly.* About a year after getting two leaden cisterns erected in his house, to keep the water of the Seine for general domestic purposes, he was attacked with severe and obstinate colic; which led him to examine his cisterns. He found that the sides, where they were occasionally left exposed by the subsidence of the water, and more especially the leaden cover, were lined with a white liquid, which was constantly dropping from the lid into the cistern, like the drops in caverns where stalactites are formed. The water was in consequence so strongly impregnated with lead as to give a dark precipitate with liver of sulphur. The reason of this occurrence is, that the water in the cistern is a solution of preventive salts; but what reaches the lid is in a manner distilled.

* * * * * *

It may be well to conclude these remarks on the action of spring-waters on lead with a general summary of the chief circumstances to be adverted to in using lead for keeping or conveying water; to which may be added a few hints for preventing action where it is found to have taken place.

The general results of the preceding inquiries are, that rain or snow-water for culinary use should not be collected from leaden roofs, nor preserved nor conveyed in lead; that the same rule applies to spring-waters of unusually purity. Where, for example, the saline impregnation does not exceed a 15,000th of the water; that spring which contains a 10,000th or 12,000th of salts may be safely conveyed in lead pipes, if the salts in the water be chiefly carbonates and sulphates; that lead pipes cannot be safely used, even where the water contains a 4,000th of saline matter, if this consists chiefly of muriates; that spring-water, even though it contain a large proportion of salts, should not be kept for a long period in contact with lead; and that cisterns should not be covered with lids of this metal.

Where action is observed to take place in the instance of particular waters, it may in some cases be impossible to prevent it by any attainable means.

But the inquiries detailed above suggest two modes by which a remedy may be generally found. It appears that, where a crust of carbonate is allowed to form slowly and quietly on the surface of lead, even distilled water ceases to have any material action; and that the action is reduced almost to nothing if a crust be thus formed in a solution containing a minute quantity of some powerfully protecting salt, such as phosphate of soda. It appears to me then that a remedy may be often found in the instance of unusually pure spring-waters—either by leaving the new pipes filled with the water for a few months, care being taken not to draw any water from them in the interval—or perhaps even more effectually by filling the pipes for a similar period with a solution containing about a 25,000th of phosphate of soda.

* * * * *

In the remarks now made on the action of water on lead no account has been taken of the effect of the galvanic fluid in promoting it. This, however, is a most important coöperating agent, or rather perhaps it ought to be considered a distinct power; for it acts with energy where water alone acts least, namely, where there is saline matter in solution, because then a galvanic current of greater force is excited. In general it is necessary that two different metals be present in the water before galvanic action be excited; but a very slight difference may be sufficient.

For example, it seems enough that the lead contain here and there impurities, constituting alloys slightly different from the general mass of the pipe or cistern.

It is probable that galvanic action may be thus excited by the joinings being soldered with the usual mixture of lead and the more fusible metals.

At least I have seen pipes deeply corroded externally, when made of sheets of lead rolled and soldered; and the action was deepest on each side of the solder, which had itself entirely escaped corrosion. Even inequalities in the composition of the lead may have the same effect. Sheet lead long exposed to air or water is sometimes observed to be corroded in particular spots; and these will always be found in the neighborhood of parts of the metal differing in color, hardness or texture from the general mass. I have not analyzed such spots; but I conceive the supposition now made is exceedingly probable, and supplies a ready explanation of the corrosion. Similar effects may arise simply from fragments of other metals lying long in contact with the lead.

They may also arise from portions of mortar being allowed to lie on the lead; but the action here is not galvanic.

I have no doubt that many of the instances of unusually rapid corrosion of lead by water, are really owing, not to the simple action of the water, but to an action excited obscurely in one or other of the ways now mentioned.

On the Action of Hard Water on Lead.—By Dr. Nevins, of Liverpool.—1851.

THE question of the supply of water to large cities, has within the last two years occupied a considerable share of public attention; and in connection with this subject, the nature of the channels through which the water is conducted, and of the vessels or reservoirs in which it is kept stored for use.

* * * * *

It was supposed that soft waters, containing but a very small portion of earthy or saline ingredients, were alone capable of acting on lead, and that hard water exerted no such action. Recent investigations have, however, shown that whilst certain kinds of hard water exercise a protecting influence on lead, there are others which produce action upon that metal, and which, therefore, ought not to be kept for use in leaden reservoirs. The following experiments carefully made by Dr. Nevins, will, therefore, be read with much interest.

Sheet lead and common lead piping were exposed to the action of water containing the following solutions, with the results now to be described. In every case the lead remained in the water for a week.

Description of Experiments.—In the first set of experiments, sheet and pipe lead were exposed to the action of a strong solution of sulphate of magnesia (gr. 4, and also gr. 10 to the ounce) in distilled water.

2nd Set.—The same solutions of sulphate of magnesia, combined with bicarbonate of soda (gr. 4 in the ounce.)

3d Set.—Carbonate of magnesia, partially re-dissolved by carbonic acid in distilled water.

4th Set.—Carbonate of lime, partially re-dissolved by carbonic acid gas in the same way.

5th Set.—Solution of common salt (gr. ½ in the ounce) in distilled water, and the same strength in the common spring water of Liverpool, which contains a moderate quantity of sulphate of lime.

6th Set.—Solutions of common salt as above, only stronger (gr. 2 in the ounce.)

7th Set.—Solutions of common salt (gr. ½ and gr. 2 in the ounce) in combination with gr. 1 and gr. 4 of sulphate of magnesia respectively (i. e., gr. ½ with gr. 1, and gr. 2 with gr. 4.)

8th Set.—The same experiment, only substituting chloride of calcium for chloride of sodium.

Object of the Experiments.—It will be seen on examining the above experiments, that nearly every point in dispute was brought under investigation; viz: the action of *hard* water, which does not contain sulphates, in experiments 3 and 4; the action of *strong* solutions of sulphates in experiment 1; the modifying effect of the presence of excess of carbonic acid along with the sulphates in experiment 2; the effect of chlorides of various strength in distilled water, and in water containing small and large amounts of sulphates, of both lime and magnesia; in experiments 5, 6, and 7, the difference in the effect of chlorides of equal strength, dependent upon difference in the base which the chloride is combined; and lastly the difference in the effect produced upon sheet lead and common pipe lead.

Results.—Different kinds of Lead.—The difference between the effect of the sheet lead and the pipe lead was so slight in every case, as scarcely to merit notice. If any thing, the pipe lead was the least affected, as shown by the visible effect of sulphuretted hydrogen, for quantitative analysis was not resorted to in any instance. When, however, tea lead was operated upon, the difference was very great; which corresponds with the results I obtained many years since, in which I found, that whilst the deposit from pure lead in a certain time, weighed 5.5 grains, that from an equal surface of tea lead placed under precisely similar circumstances weighed 11.5 grains.

This result might almost be anticipated, as impurity in common pipe lead is more likely to be zinc than any other metal, and this would retard rather than hasten the action of the water upon the lead, by forming a galvanic arrangement; whilst the tin, which is stated to be present in the tea lead, would hasten the action upon the lead, as it is less easily acted upon by chemical agents than lead itself. The difference in effect of the different strengths of the same solution, was by no means strongly marked, the result being so nearly the same at the end of the week's trial, that it is unnecessary to make any distinction in speaking of them, between the solution of four grains of sulphate of magnesia and that of ten grains; between the half grain and the two grains solution of chloride of calcium, &c.

Sulphates.—The solution of sulphate of magnesia produced a very decided effect. The bottom of the jar in which the experiment was made, became covered with a thick white layer, and a coating, similar in appearance, covered the surface of the lead, but was removed without difficulty by gently scraping with the nail. On transmitting sulphuretted hydrogen, white sediment became black powder, and the water assumed a brown hue. Thus it was that the strong solution of the sulphate did not form a protecting layer upon the lead, though repeated experiments, year by year, shown to my class of chemical students, have confirmed beyond dispute that the Liverpool water, which contains a small quantity of sulphate of lime, does protect it. It appears to me, that the difference in the effect of a strong and a weak solution of sulphate, is owing to the rapidity with which the precipitate is formed by the first, which prevents its adhering firmly; while in the second it is formed so slowly, that its adhesion is uniform and perfect.

CARBONATES.

All the carbonates acted upon the lead, so far as to cause the water to become decidedly colored by the sulphuretted hydrogen, and a dark colored deposit was formed amongst the superfluous carbonate of lime and magnesia. The effect from the bicarbonate of soda was the most decided, and this, notwithstanding the presence of a small quantity of lime in the common spring water, and of a large quantity of sulphate of magnesia in the distilled water, whence it is evident that neither a large nor a small quantity of a sulphate acts as a protection, in the presence of a soluble carbonate.

CHLORIDES.

In every case the water became brown on the transmission of the sulphuretted hydrogen, but the solution of chloride of calcium was far the most affected, and a decided coating was formed upon the lead in it, which was not the case in any of the solutions of common salt, in which the lead retained its ordinary appearance, and no precipitate was formed upon the bottom of the jars. The effect of the chlorides was, therefore, less marked than that of the other solutions employed.

CONCLUSIONS.

From the above experiments it is clear that *hard* waters do not protect lead, simply from the fact of their being hard, but that the protection, when effected, is dependent, not only upon the nature of the salt causing the hardness, but also upon the proportion present; for whilst all experience proves that a small amount of a sulphate, at any rate of sulphate of lime, does protect the lead, a large quantity of sulphate of magnesia acted considerably upon it. It appears also to be proved, that chlorides act upon lead, whether with or without the presence of a sulphate, but that their action is not so great as that of soluble carbonates, which produce a rapidly injurious effect upon the metal.

At the same time, these results do not practically affect the question of the safety of using lead for common water, so far as sulphates, at any rate, are concerned, inasmuch as the solutions here employed, were out of all proportion stronger than any ordinary spring water, and the experience of years has proved, that there are no bad consequences practically occasioned by the employment of the metal for water containing sulphates. [As a precautionary measure, we would recommend the employment of gutta percha as a lining for water cisterns and reservoirs, by which means the danger arising from the use of lead will be avoided.—*Eds. Patent Journal.* A suggestion which has our entire concurrence.—*Eds. Chem.*]

When lead is exposed to the action of air and pure water, it is partly corroded, and hence lead pipes and lead vessels for conveying or containing water for culinary purposes, may act as sources of poison. By such exposure the lead becomes converted at the surface into an oxide, which the water dissolves; the solution absorbs carbonic acid, and a film of hydrated oxy-carbonate of lead is deposited in silky scales; a fresh portion of oxide is then formed and dissolved by the water, and so on. This action is greatly modified by the presence of different salts in the water, although the quantity may not exceed three or four grains to the gallon: the corrosive action being increased by the chlorides and nitrates, and diminished by the sulphates, phosphates and carbonates, so much so, that oxide of lead is scarcely soluble in water containing these salts. Bicarbonate of lime exerts a remarkable preservative influence, and as it is a very common impurity in water, few spring waters exert much action on lead. In such cases a film of insoluble carbonate of lead is formed upon the surface which serves as a protection to the metal. Rain water which pours into cisterns from roofs of houses, is usually sufficiently impure, especially in towns, to reduce its action on the metal. The hydrated oxy-carbonate of lead is the least soluble among the salts of lead; pure water not taking up more than about 1-60th of a grain per gallon. By exposure to the air, a solution of oxide of lead, by absorption of carbonic acid, forms silky crystals of the hydrated oxy-carbonate, and in a few hours, only a very minute portion of the metal will remain in solution; but water highly charged with carbonic acid may dissolve lead to a dangerous extent, from the insolubility of carbonate of lead in excess of carbonic acid; but, by boiling, the gas is expelled and the carbonate subsides. Traces of lead may generally be found in water that has been stored in leaden cisterns, so that slate ones are to be preferred.

Lead is corroded in the presence of moisture by contact with sulphate of lime; hence, in using it for building purposes, the contact of stucco or plaster should be avoided. (*Britannica Encyclopœdia*, vol. xiii. p. 301.)

Dr. Ure's Dictionary of Arts, Manufactures and Mines; vol. 2d.—London, 1853:

LEAD ACTED ON BY PURE WATER SO AS TO MAKE IT POISONOUS.

Dr. H. Guenaude Mussy was summoned to Claremont in the beginning of October, 1848; and, on his arrival was shown into the room of one of the members of the ex-royal family of France, who had been residing there since the preceding March. He found him lying down, with an anxious countenance, the conjunctiva of a yellowish color, and the flesh flabby, evidently proving a loss of substance. He told him he had been suffering for several days from violent colics which had been relieved after a constipation of two days by abundant alvine evacuations produced by a purgative draught. This was the third attack of the same nature during the space of five weeks. Some time before, towards the end of July, he had been suffering from colic, with nausea, frequent eructations and irregularity of the bowels.

"I learnt that a brother of my patient had experienced the same symptoms; but no one was astonished at it, as it was supposed he was suffering under a liver complaint contracted on the western coast of Africa.

"A third patient, of forty-eight years of age, who was also subject to constipation, had violent colic a few days before, attended with nausea and even vomiting.

"A few days elapsed and no bad symptoms disturbed our security. My patients had resumed their usual occupations, and good appetites and pretty fair digestion, but were still very weak; and pale sallow complexions had replaced the icteric color.

"My delusions did not last long. About ten days after, a new access of symptoms began, with a painful sensation of constriction about the epigastric region, anxiety, nausea, and eructations."

After describing the symptoms and the treatment resorted to before the real cause of the disorder was suspected, the doctor mentions the circumstances which led to the discovery, which induced him to administer sulphur in combination with iron internally, and to order sulphurious and soapy baths. He proceeds:—

"The chemical action showed itself almost immediately by the black discoloration of the nails of the feet and hands, and by the appearance of similar spots on different parts of the skin.

"One of the patients came out of the second bath with the abdomen entirely black. The soapy frictions and baths usually washed away the spots from the skin, but not those of the nails. The appearance of this reaction, which is very common with men working in lead manufactories when using sulphurious baths, is explained by the combination of sulphur with the saturnine molecules adhering to the skin.

"In these cases it was evident that the lead was brought to the surface of the body by means either of sudaminal or follicular exhalations, and perhaps by both.

"The metal is eliminated and transformed into sulphuret of lead by the sulphurous baths, and then taken off by the soapy frictions and baths.

"These were not useless, for without them the lead deposited on the surface might have been carried again by absorption into the economy.

"But the skin was not the only means of giving exit to the poison. I discovered it in the urine by a solution of hydrosulphate of ammonia. Some physicians and chemists look on sulphur as the only efficacious remedy; others, on the contrary, assert that it is without any effect.

"What I can tell you is, that the success was beyond my hopes. After two or three weeks I had the satisfaction of seeing my patients progressing rapidly and surely towards recovery. This happy result induced me to try the same means with another person, older and of a weaker constitution, and consequently for whom I was most uneasy, and the result was as satisfactory.

"One of my patients was accustomed to drink Vichy water at table. This was a very unfortunate predisposing circumstance; it is probable that the salt of Vichy water, *i. e.* bicarbonate of soda, united to the bed of Claremont water, had much to do with the violence of the attack under which he suffered.

"At the time of my arrival at Claremont, there were thirty-eight inhabitants.

"Thirteen of these had been attacked, eleven men and two women. Four of them had some symptoms two months previously to my arrival, the other cases occurred under my own eyes. Some even after the pipes had been cut off were effected, and one when on the continent a week after leaving England.

"Six children in the household, aged from three to seven years, have been exempt from it. Only half of the patients have had the gums marked with the slate colored line and spots of the same color on the mucous membrane of the mouth, and these spots and the bluish line of the gums were observed on several others who did not experience or exhibit any thing else, and those signs of the poison having been taken into the economy have not yet disappeared. The morbid cause has acted in these cases, as it often does, with caprice, and according to individual dispositions which defy every reasoning.

"The malady has shown no respect for condition, and attacked indiscriminately servants, aides-de-camps and princes.

"The spring that furnishes the palace of Claremont with water issues from a sand bed at about two miles distance. It was chosen for its uncommon purity from among a great many others in its vicinity, and the water was thirty years ago conducted to the palace through leaden pipes. In the present day some other metal would perhaps have been selected, for experience has taught us that pure water, and especially distilled water, acts rapidly on lead when it comes in contact with it.

"Thus Tronchin proved that the inhabitants of Amsterdam were indebted to the rain water, kept in leaden cisterns, for the colic they were so much subject to in his time.

"The purity of the Claremont water becomes a most dangerous property, and not only to it but to other springs. Whilst I was combating its pernicious effects, I heard that there had been several similar cases in different parts of England; they are not uncommon in the county of Surrey, and especially in the neighborhood of Claremont. Besides the cases published by Dr. Thompson, I know of several others at Weybridge, Windsor, and in different other places.

"I should inform you that Professor Hoffman has ascertained the quantity of metallic lead contained in the water examined by him. He has found that it amounted to a grain per gallon, an enormous quantity when we consider that the poisoned water was used in all culinary and table purposes; and, previously to the discovery of its deleterious character, even in the preparation of ptisans and lavements."

Cases of Poisoning from Lead Service Pipe at Norwich, Connecticut.

We visited Norwich in April, 1858, to understand the arrangement of pipes there, and the circumstances which led to the cases of lead poisoning, of the previous season.

In the absence of any general system of water supply at Norwich, certain of the citizens taking advantage of numerous small springs in the upper part of the city, have collected these into cement cisterns, whence lead pipes have been laid into certain of the streets supplying the houses of a limited number of the inhabitants. There are five such cisterns, or independent heads of water. The one connected with the cases of sickness referred to, is situated 40 to 50 feet above the level of the street which it supplied. It is a brick cistern of 8 feet diameter, lined with cement. The cistern is covered. There are four springs within 50 feet of this cistern; the waters from these springs are carried to the cistern by five leaden pipes of half inch diameter each. From the cistern, this collected water is carried to the street below by a $1\frac{1}{4}$ inch lead pipe which was tapped again by small lead pipes delivering the water into the different houses. This pipe main after proceeding as far along the road or street as the limited capacity of the springs made it desirable to carry it, terminated in a dead end, about 100 feet, in this case, beyond the house of Mr. Kingsley, whose family appear to have been the greatest sufferers.

The five springs referred to run out of crevices in the gneiss rock of the ridge where they are found; the water is very clear and soft. These springs get low in summer, and then the water which, in midsummer, is not sufficient in quantity to maintain a constant supply, is allowed to gather in the cistern aforesaid, and passed off into the lead main every alternate day only. On the idle day the $1\frac{1}{4}$ inch lead main becomes more or less emptied of water and filled with air. At times, the lowness of the springs and the very slow filling of the cistern, obliges the proprietor to hold the water off for several days, and occasionally in great droughts, it is said for several weeks.

At the time that the water became suspected of causing the sickness in the street, Dr. Osgood (Druggist) took a portion of it to Dr. Chilton of New York, who found it to contain four grains of lead to the gallon. Afterwards, when the water was flowing regularly, the proprietor, as we were informed, took some of it to New York to Professor Doremus for examination, who found it to contain five-eighths ($\frac{5}{8}$) of a grain of lead to the gallon.

Dr. Osgood was one of the sufferers as he believed from this cause, though in a much less degree than some of the others. Dr. Tyler (druggist) lived in the third house from the dead end of the pipe, he explained to us that he had been for many years a sufferer from indigestion and pain which he could not understand or control. A general lethargy followed, ending in paralysis of the hands entirely and of the arms partially. He was led to suspect the water, and immediately gave it up and removed the lead pipes from his house. Improvement of his health followed immediately, and now he is entirely recovered. In the house nearest the dead end of the lead main there were four deaths. Mr. Kingsley, who was entirely paralyzed, being one of them. In the next house to Mr. Kingsley, there was one death. All the cases are stated by Dr. Tyler to have presented distinct characteristics of lead poisoning. Abandonment of the lead pipe, by the different parties, led to the restoration to health of the survivors.

It is unfortunate that no minute reports of these cases have been made by the attending physician. The above statement was gathered from conversation with some of the sufferers. The general circumstances had previously been made public through the newspapers.

Muspratt's Chemistry. 1858.

CHEMICAL PROPERTIES OF LEAD.

THE affinity of lead for oxygen is very great, even at ordinary temperatures; but this is increased when its temperature is elevated. Under the latter condition, it burns in the air with a bluish white light, and affords oxide of lead or litharge. Faraday has shown, that when finely divided, this metal is more inflammable than gunpowder. Nitric acid acts energetically upon lead, converting it into an oxysalt of this acid; acetic acid likewise dissolves it, but sulphuric and hydrochloric acids have only a feeble action upon it, especially in the cold. With the aid of heat, however, concentrated sulphuric acid dissolves it with the evolution of hydrogen.

At a red heat, hydrochloric acid vapor acts upon lead, producing a chloride of the metal and liberating hydrogen. This metal is capable of uniting with all the non-metallic elements, with the exception of hydrogen, borium, silicium and carbon; with all the metals, except iron, it enters readily into combination, giving alloys which are of considerable importance in the arts, and some of which have been described under the heads, ANTIMONY, BISMUTH, etc. Its oxides, which are numerous, are employed for various useful purposes, and one of them, the protoxide, commonly known as litharge, readily combines with all the oxygen acids, forming salts, some of which are used in the arts to a very large extent. In the form of sheet lead and lead piping, this metal is applied to a great variety of purposes. To the metallurgist it offers a ready and advantageous means of obtaining silver and gold in their purity, by alloying them with it, and subsequently removing the lead from the compound metal by cupellation.

PHYSIOLOGICAL EFFECTS OF LEAD AND ITS COMPOUNDS.

With the exception of one or two of the most insoluble compounds of lead, all the others are known to have very active poisonous properties. The sulphide of lead, the sulphate, and sulphite, if possessed of such, are not, however, so virulent as those salts of the metal which are soluble in water, or in dilute acids. It is to be remarked, that miners of galena are seldom, if ever, incapacitated by any derangement to their health arising from saturnine poisoning; when, however, they chance to be removed to the smelting establishments, after a while occasional indications of the physiological effects of lead on the system are observed. Dr. Scoffern, when, a few years ago, advocating the use of acetate of lead for the purification of saccharine juices, affirmed the innocuousness of sulphite of lead, owing to its insolubility; but no well confirmed proofs exist of the truth of the assertion.

Lead, *per se*, is supposed to have no effects on animals; nevertheless its ready solution by the fluids and juices in the stomach, brings it into a state in which it is rapidly absorbed into the system, and thus becomes poisonous. Therapeutically considered, the preparations of lead have sedative and astringent properties, since they diminish the volume and frequency of the pulse, and reduce the secretive functions. Thus, when it is employed for some time, the arteries become reduced in size and activity, as indicated by the smallness and slowness of the pulse; hence its use in checking hæmorrhage, whether natural or artificial, and in reducing the temperature of the body. These characteristic effects extend to the secreting and exhaling vessels, as may be known from the dryness of the mouth and throat, the thirst, etc., which succeed its absorption. If present in quantities, other very decided indications are observed, such as the well known leaden discoloration of the gums, of the buccal mucous membrane and of the teeth; the peculiar taste and odor of the breath; the lead jaundice, and, ultimately, general emaciation. The coloration of the gums, membrane and teeth, is recognized by a leaden or slate blue line from one twentieth to one sixth of an inch in breadth, which forms on the margin of the gums, nearest to the incisors in either jaw, whilst the rest of the gums appear of a bluish red tint; the membrane lining, the gums and cheeks, are also of a bluish color, and the lower part or neck of the teeth are stained brownish. It would appear that these various shades of color are occasioned by sulphide of lead, produced doubtless by the traces of sulphocyanogen which is known to exist in the saliva flowing from the glands of the mouth. Saturnine breath is known only to those who are affected by lead through the respiratory organs, such as persons engaged in the manufacture of the compound of this metal already referred to. Emaciation, which is another of the most marked of the primary effects of lead, shows itself more evidently in the face of the patient, giving to it a carē-worn, wrinkled and aged appearance. When the lead accumulates in larger proportions, whether by accident or long continued use of small quantities of plumbous compounds, it gives rise to various diseases known as *lead colic*, *anthralgia*, *paralysis*, and that which is characterized as *encephalopathy*, and which manifests itself by different morbid phenomena, such as delirium, coma and convulsions, with or without loss of one or more of the senses. Physicians have observed, that patients are liable to several of these at once, although the most frequent of them is the lead colic.

Acute lead poisonings are rarely observed, excepting they arise from inadvertence or accident, either purely so or malicious; but the first stages of slow poisonings are very frequent, and well known to most of the general medical practitioners in every large town, as well as in the rural districts. The source is almost invariably found to be the water employed for domestic purposes, the lengthened use of which causes a depression of spirits, emaciation, and, finally, colic and paralysis. Several cases of this description have come under the notice of the Editor, wherein whole families were affected, and though the leaden indications in the gums were undiscerned, as their medical attendant in many of them appeared baffled by the continued and frequent complaints, still, carefully conducted analyses proved that lead was the undermining agent. Iron glazed pipes and pumps, with slate or cemented cisterns, were recommended for adoption, and with a very marked effect, the health of the individuals being completely restored. Many waters containing lead are preserved as by an antidote from effecting any injury to the consumer, and are consequently quite safe for consumption. The substances that reäct thus are the sulphates, phosphates and carbonates of the alkalies, and also the sulphates, carbonates, etc., of the alkaline earths; in fact any neutral salt, the acid of which is capable of combining with lead or its oxide, and of constituting an insoluble compound, has this effect. It is owing to the presence of one or more of these, that mineral or spring water, though passed through lead pipes and retained in cisterns of that metal, remains for the most part unimpregnated with lead. So small a quantity as three or four grains of a sulphate or a phosphate in a water, prevents after some time the corrosion of the metal; carbonates have a similarly marked effect, more especially the soluble bicarbonate of the alkaline earths, since an oxycarbonate of lead is formed, which is one of the most insoluble combinations of lead, only one part being taken up by four million parts of water. It must, however, be remarked that these salts do not protect the lead from the solvent action of waters which contain *nitric* or *nitrous* acids in solution. These two acids are products of the decomposition of animal matter, and any water containing them will infallibly act upon lead; and consequently, it would be highly dangerous to pass such a water through leaden pipes, or to store it in leaden cisterns. All of these insoluble precipitates, after accumulating for some time on the sides of the cistern and on the interior of the pipe, form a solid coating, which in a measure isolates the metal from contact with the water, and, consequently it is protected, and the water remains good and wholesome. Chloride of sodium acts also as an anticorrosive substance to the water, but its effects are less certain than those of the compounds above referred to, since the chloride of lead is much more soluble than either the sulphate, phosphate, carbonate, or similar salts. As it frequently occurs, however, that in spring waters there are appreciable quantities of nitrates, and even free nitrous and nitric acid, as in a water from the private well in the neighborhood of Birkenhead examined by the Editor; the action of such waters upon lead becomes exceedingly marked, and not unfrequently do they give notable indications of lead being in solution after some time, even though they contain sulphates. In these cases the active solvent agent is still left in the water, and continues to act upon the metal, even after the entire suphuric acid present has combined with the oxide of lead dissolved. Water, therefore, which retains nitric acid either in the free state or combined, whether it be mineral or catchment water, is not so safe for storage in lead cisterns.

In like manner, the water which retains decomposing, organic, nitrogenous matters in solution or suspension, is unsafe so far as regards the action on lead; for as stated above, the transformation of the elements of such by the eremacausis which they undergo, tends to produce, first ammonia, and by a further process of oxidation, nitrous or nitric acid, and at the completion of this change their corrosive action becomes very remarkable, so much so, indeed, as to cause the solution of several grains of lead per gallon. Besides the fact, that waters containing organic decomposing matters are in themselves unhealthy, their subsequent effect upon lead renders them doubly so.

Medlock has latterly patented a method, whereby the nitrates which exert such a powerful action upon lead are removed, together with the organic matter, if the latter be not present in great excess. It consists in suspending coils of iron wire or pieces of sheet iron in the water, and after a stated period filtering off the deposit which forms. By this means the nitric acid is decomposed by the iron, which is transformed into sesquioxide and falls to the bottom, whilst nitrous gas is set free and oxidizes the carbonaceous matters, which remain still in the fluid so as to yield carbonic acid and a lower oxide of nitrogen.

From experiments made upon some of the water lately supplied to Liverpool, and which proved itself to be a most eligible subject for examination, from the quantity of organic matter, both animal, and vegetal, and nitrates, which it contained, the Editor arrived at very satisfactory conclusions, that the object proposed by the patentee may be completely fulfilled.

ACTION OF WATER ON LEAD.

When water which has been purified by distillation from pure caustic potassa, and kept out of contact with the atmosphere, is poured over clean sheets of lead, and so retained for a considerable period, no solution of the metal will be observed to have taken place, nor will the examination of the water indicate that any of the metal has been taken up. This will not be the case if a comparative experiment be made with rain water, however carefully collected, even in the open country; for with this the metallic luster is soon dulled, and a film of carbonate and of oxide of lead forms on the plates, showing that a chemical action must have occurred; and besides, if the liquid is chemically treated, distinct evidence of the presence of lead in solution is found. The same observation will be made with regard to distilled water and lead, when the vessel containing them is exposed to the air, though not to the extent of the former. In these instances, there is a compound of oxide and carbonic acid corresponding to *white* lead, formed through the intervention of the carbonic acid with which the water, in case of rain water, is charged, or it absorbs this gas in the experiment with distilled water. If the vessel be freely exposed, portions of this carbonate are dissolved; but independently of this, the carbonic acid which is always imbibed from the air, proves much more effectual for its solution, and, therefore, a considerable part will manifest itself to chemical tests, after some lapse of time. Another agent in rain and other waters, that acts with great rapidity on lead, is *nitrous acid;* and latterly Dr. Medlock has shown, that ammonia, by its transformation into this, is capable of ultimately causing the water in which it is present, if retained in contact with lead, to become poisoned. The annexed equation exhibits the interesting transformation:

$$\underbrace{NH_3}_{\text{Ammonia.}} \quad + \quad \underbrace{6\,O}_{\text{Oxygen.}} \quad = \quad \underbrace{NO_3}_{\text{Nitrous acid.}} \quad + \quad \underbrace{3\,HO}_{\text{Water.}}$$

Of course, some of the nitrous acid will be constantly metamorphosed into nitric acid, oxidation continually going on. This chemist affirms that the nitrate of lead produced in contact with the metal, is speedily transformed into the quadribasic *nitrite*, with evolution of binoxide of nitrogen, which, by combining with another equivalent of oxygen, re-forms nitrous acid. The production of the lead salt is thus explained:

$$\underbrace{5\,(Pb\,O,\,NO_5)}_{\text{Nitrate of Lead.}} \quad + \quad \underbrace{11\,Pb}_{\text{Lead.}} \quad =$$

$$\underbrace{4\,(4\,Pb\,O,\,NO_3}_{\text{Quadribasic nitrate of lead.}} \quad + \quad \underbrace{NO_2}_{\text{Binoxide of nitrogen.}}$$

Medlock, *contrary to all preceding rules, with regard to the action of certain waters on lead*, thus correctly sums up:

Firstly. The action of any water on lead is entirely due to the presence of *nitrous* and *nitric acid*, resulting primarily from the decomposition of organic matters, and of ammonia contained in the water.

Secondly. Waters deprived of these acids, and of substances capable of producing them, *have no action on lead*, and may be conveyed with perfect safety through leaden pipes, or stored in leaden cisterns. To store or collect water containing a nitrogen acid in cisterns or tanks lined with lead, as is usually done for domestic use, is highly pernicious, since the injuries arising from taking lead into the system, and stated above, may follow. And as no other more convenient means for the storage of water and its conveyance are known, especially in small quantities, the first question relative to the sanitary value of a water which ought to present itself to municipal or corporate bodies, as well as to private individuals, is, does it exert a solvent action upon lead, or does it contain a nitrogenous acid, or any compound likely to produce one? It is true that water which would dissolve this metal in abundance, and, therefore, be rendered unfit for use, is by the presence of certain mineral ingredients rendered less liable to do mischief.

The following is an *analysis* of the *Lake Cochituate Water*, made by *B. Silliman, Junr.*, in 1845. It was omitted in its proper place in the preface:—

	Grains in one gallon.
Chloride of Sodium	.2540
Sulphate of Soda	.0843
" " Alumina	.0146
" " Lime and Silica	.5700
Phosphate of Alumina	.1700
Carbonate of Magnesia	.2560
" " Lime	.3860
" " Soda, equivalent to Crenate and Nitrate of do. by loss	.4757
	2.2106
Carbonic acid gas in one gallon (cubic inches),	4.5490

The comparative hardness of the undermentioned waters is found by *Clark's Soap Test*, to be as follows:—

	Degrees.
Cochituate water, (from the pipes)	2.25
Croton water, (do.)	3.15
Nassau water, (from percolations into the Conduit and Canal, drawn from the pipes)	2.30
Well water, Brooklyn, corner of Pierrepont and Hicks Streets	10.10

The following taken from the *reports* of *Chemists*, are added for comparison:—

Thames water	14.5
Loch Katrine water, Glasgow	0.8
Brockburn water	3.2
Loch Lomond (Leven River)	1.
Tay River, Perth	2.4
Dee water, Aberdeen	1.75

INDEX AND CONTENTS.

www.ingramcontent.com/pod-product-compliance
Lightning Source LLC
LaVergne TN
LVHW010209110826
845151LV00002B/643
* 9 7 8 1 4 2 5 5 3 5 0 5 6 *